TYRANNY OF THE SPIRIT

TYRANNY OF THE SPIRIT

Domination and Submission in Adolescent Relationships

DAVID K. CURRAN, PH.D.

JASON ARONSON INC.
Northvale, New Jersey
London

Production Editor: Elaine Lindenblatt

This book was set in 11 pt. New Aster by Alpha Graphics of Pittsfield, New Hampshire, and printed and bound by Book-mart Press of North Bergen, New Jersey.

Library of Congress Cataloging-in-Publication Data

Curran, David K., 1951–
    Tyranny of the spirit : domination and submission in adolescent
relationships / by David Curran.
        p.   cm
    Includes bibliographical references and index.
    ISBN 1-56821-833-8 (hardcover : alk. paper)
    1. Interpersonal relations in adolescence. 2. Dominance
(Psychology) I. Title.
BF724.3.I56c87   1996
306.7'0835—dc20   96-11820

Manufactured in the United States of America. Jason Aronson Inc. offers books and cassettes. For information and catalog write to Jason Aronson Inc., 230 Livingston Street, Northvale, New Jersey 07647.

CONTENTS

Preface   ix

1. Introduction   1

   Caroline and John I   19

2. "Like a Bird on the Wire":
   Culture, Masculinity, and the Problem
   of Love   29
   Male Identity and the Problem of Love   29
   The "Tension" and "Risk" of Love and
      the Origins of Domination   40
   Domination and the Intolerance
      of Uncertainty   47
   Male Status, Self-esteem and the Problem
      of Abuse   56

   Caroline and John II   67

3. "Paper Tiger": Characteristics of the
   Dominating Male   75
   Family Background   81

Demographics 89
Race 90
Religion 91
Socioeconomic Factors 91
Age 97
Personality Characteristics 101

4. Characteristics of the Dominated Female 113
The Onset of Adolescence: Vulnerability
   to Submission 123

5. Early Warning Signs 137
Neediness 139
Possessiveness 142
Jealousy 148

**6. The Onset of Domination: Sex, Love,
and the "Serious" Relationship 161**
Therapeutic Implications 175

7. Out of the Blue and Into the Black 185
Physical Abuse 201
Alcohol 204
Mutual Aggression 205
Therapeutic Implications 213
Confidentiality 220

8. Changing the Relationship 231
Therapeutic Implications 238

9. Breaking Up: Danger and Opportunity 257
The Danger and Difficulty of Separation 258
Multiple Separations and the Reasons
   for Returning 261

The Impact upon the Male 263
The Impact upon the Female 266
Therapeutic Implications 269

Caroline and John III 299

References 305

Credits 319

Index 321

PREFACE

Apparently I can write only out of love and anger. Powers of a different sort may motivate others, but this is how it is for me. Looking back I know these emotions were responsible for my first book, which was about adolescent suicidal behavior. It was a kind of love for the victims and anger toward those who would trivialize them that carried me rapidly toward the subject.

I must admit that my feelings for the subject of this book were much slower to accumulate and finally to overflow into their present written form. This effluence is also a product of love and anger. I think the anger came first in this case. I grew increasingly annoyed and finally outraged by the unrelenting news stories of men who couldn't handle love relationships, who couldn't bear separation and loss, and of the women who paid for it. As a man, these men offended me.

Meanwhile, every week in my office I spoke to the girls and young women who were well on their way to making the news or disappearing altogether. I learned about the desperate little dictatorships in which they lived. And I slowly realized that the land of adolescence is where it often all begins, where the bonds of domination are quickly wrapped very tight, and that for the therapist there may be no greater challenge, no higher stakes. What emerged in the form of this book is not quite the complete gathered findings of all who have studied the subject (though there is, I hope, quite enough of it).

Instead, I have tried to present a story. I have laid background, set the stage from which the deep rumblings of ominous danger sometimes rise. I have described the beginning stages and the signs of warning—the first rumblings become audible and the drama begins.

For adolescents, male and female, the course of their still-sensitive development may hang in the balance as the contending forces of domination and resistance, the life or death of the spirit, struggle toward an uncertain conclusion. This is the story I tell.

Despite the rise of feminism, there continues to be much in our culture that drives young couples into this dangerous, even deadly struggle. Even the dissipation of confining sex roles within an open society with increasingly hazy institutional norms has seemed to contribute to the problem, leaving young individuals and couples uncertain how to be. Some seek to resolve the resulting anxiety with control.

This book is intended to inform and guide therapists in particular, and those who work with and care about young people in general. I have written it with that larger audience in mind. I have woven the narrative of a couple, Caroline and John, through the larger story of dominating relationships. Through their tale and those of others

I have sought to breathe some life into these otherwise lifeless words. I thank Jason Aronson and Catherine Monk for supporting, even demanding, this perspective.

I must also thank my wife, Eileen Patricia (O'Keefe) Curran. You see, I am incapable of using or even wanting to learn to use a computer, even a word processor; I write in longhand instead. Publishers have long since stopped accepting handwritten manuscripts, I believe, and so there would be no material to be submitted without her. I thank her for having the interest and enthusiasm in me and the subject matter to type, read, and critique every word of every page at every stage.

Finally, I must thank those who have taught me everything of any value contained herein. There are, of course, the actual Caroline and other Carolines who have allowed me to know them. They have shown me what it is like to live what I have only written about. They have taught me what helps and what certainly doesn't. This has been their gift to me. This book is offered as a most unequal gift to them.

1

INTRODUCTION

Today, driving to work, I heard on the radio the story of a young man who drove to his ex-girlfriend's house and doused himself and his car with gasoline before ringing her doorbell. He taunted and berated her, concluding by haranguing her with "Watch this, bitch. You just watch this!" He got into his car, lit a match, and exploded into flames before her eyes. The only thing spectacular about the event was its method; otherwise it is an everyday occurrence nationwide. Newspapers regularly report the deaths of individuals and murders by individuals who, in the end, could not bear the viscissitudes of love, whose excessive need to possess in order to exist overwhelmed their capacity to cope and survive, whose overpowering jealousy, rage, hurt, and fear, unleashed by love and the threat of loss, led them to a bitter end. Acts such as this one are the culmination of a process. They are the exclamation point at the end of a special but ubiquitous kind of story. Love had consumed him; it was too much for him. And while he had to go out alone, he made sure that he left his mark on his girl forever, branding her mind with a roaring image of himself that might obscure all else for all time.

Wife beaters and battered wives have come increasingly into the spotlight. However, as is the case in most stories presented for general consumption, only the most vivid aspects seem to be conveyed. While physical abuse, with its danger, terror, and the physical and emotional scarring it can cause, is more than worthy of attention, it is not the whole story. Physical abuse of a lover never exists outside a context of verbal and psychological abuse and a pathological need for domination and control within the relationship. While battering may occur infrequently within a relationship, domination lives everyday, all day, all night. Furthermore, many pathologically dominating relationships exist that have not and may not burst into physical violence, and therefore are not counted among the battering relationships in research studies or surveys. For the most part, they are not studied at all. As with media attention, psychological and sociological research has largely focused on the incidence, circumstances, and demographics of battering while virtually ignoring the similarly noxious and potentially dangerous relationships which share so many of the same features, minus the battering.

Surveys of women who have been battered report that these women considered the verbal, emotional, and psychological abuse they suffered to be more damaging, more long-lasting in their effects and harder to forget. These forms of abuse are always present within the pathologically dominating relationship as they are in battering relationships.

Constructing studies of domination and non-physical abuse presents numerous methodological problems, however. Controlling behavior is far less black-and-white than hitting. It is harder to form comparison groups of pathological controllers/verbal abusers versus non-controllers/verbal abusers, since all couples (to some extent) seek a degree of control or influence upon each other. Most couples have engaged in angry bouts of name-calling and nasty treatment. It is difficult, therefore, to draw a line and call those on one side pathological relationships and those on the other side normal or the control group. How would one quantify the amount of dominating/abusive behavior necessary for discriminating between the groups? What would be the criterion for selection? What specific behaviors or attitudes must be present that would then be measured, counted, or otherwise quantified?

If the judgments of the subjects in the study were to be considered, how would the researcher deal with the problem of differing attitudes toward control and being controlled, differing definitions of what constitutes domination and psychological abuse? How much jealousy and possessiveness is considered pathological and harmful rather than simply a positive sign of intense love and need? As may be generally known, many victimized women keep their plight a secret. They may defend, cover up, and minimize the unhealthy or dangerous nature of their relationship if they are not ready to give it up. They may exonerate their mates and put all blame on themselves. They may be confused and very poor judges of their situations.

Males who batter have been shown to be unreliable reporters of their battering behaviors. They tend to under-report, minimize, and deny their acts. My clinical experience leads me to believe that, almost by definition, the dominating man will be largely unable to acknowledge, and is therefore a poor reporter of, the pathological aspects of his way of loving in a serious relationship with a woman. Furthermore, deep-seated, culturally supported, traditional sex roles and beliefs will in some cases support an acceptance of excessively dominating relationships.

Observations from other persons or other independent sources of information likewise prove problematic and limited. The opinions of others would be just as variable on the issues as those of the subjects and may be prejudiced by other factors as well. Besides, few outside observers could have adequate access to another person's love relationship. They can see only bits and pieces, mainly those that the couple in question allows to be seen.

Other sources of independent information will be unavailable for identifying the non-physically abusive dominating man and relationship. Courts, hospitals, and women's shelters, often sources of data on battered women, are far less likely to service or identify non-battered abused women.

For these reasons, then, the males and females focused on in this book have been a little-studied group. However, it is reasonable to extrapolate from the ample research on battering to draw information and inferences that can teach us a good deal about those in dominating relationships where physical violence is not (yet) a part. Consequently, relevant studies dealing with battering in relationships will be reviewed and used to support important ideas, in conjunction with existing research on non-battering domination and its victims. A good deal is known about the very harmful effects of this type of relationship on its female victims. The pathologically dominating relationship stunts a woman's development and erodes her self-esteem, self-confidence, and sense of competence and adequacy. It crushes the personality. It limits and denies avenues of growth. For an adolescent it can disrupt development in ways that she may not be able to go back and redo, create losses that may not be made up, and establish patterns that may steer her toward a deeply flawed adulthood. It creates stresses that can cause serious physiological and psychological health problems. It undermines and opposes every healthy life force the individual woman may possess. It can culminate in death without even lifting a finger. Death of the spirit, however, is the far more common end, the more silent, unnoticed end. The slow withering away of one person by another, noted only by a shrinking number of family and friends, is the often quiet, unspectacular tragedy that this book is about.

The primary victim is certainly female since she is the one operated upon, but the man who dominates her is a victim as well. He does not prevail in this; he does not get off free. His style of love dooms him. He has, with rigid certainty, gone down the wrong road and can never, ever get what he wants. He wants ecstacy, passion, comfort, support, acknowledgment, recognition, respect, honor, care, and everything anyone would want, but he needs it more, because he is unable to provide enough of it for himself from within. Further, he must have it all *absolutely*, without equivocation. He can bear no uncertainty in this regard. He must have all of these needs fulfilled, completely and immediately, whenever any of them rise up within him. He is dependent on her to fulfill him in these ways since he cannot do it sufficiently for himself. Most of all, he cannot bear the possibility, much less the fact, of her ever leaving him. The merest ripple of an idea within his imagination that this could happen can instantly become amplified to an intolerable degree, shaking him to his very foundation. His utter dependence on her, his essential hollowness, which he believes only she can fill, keeps him in a state of great wariness and hypervigilance. If she is his life support he must naturally keep her under close control. Nations do the same, if they can, with essential natural resources, oil supplies, for instance. They are said to guard these possessions jealously and to control them tightly. A morbid jealousy and an insatiable possessiveness are the hallmarks of the pathologically dominating relationship. Despite the bombast and authoritarianism, they signify the extreme dependency, weakness, insecurity, lack of self-esteem, neediness, and fear of abandonment that love has stirred awake and that motivate the dominating male. And none of it works. In diminishing, if not destroying, his lover by demanding too much, he depletes and ruins his main, perhaps his only, source of sustenance. In the end he only frustrates himself. He continues to be ungratified, unfulfilled, unsteady. He never achieves the peace of mind he seeks. He breaks one of the cardinal rules of life—he fouls his own waters.

So the male is a victim as well. The literature, which up to recently blamed mainly the conniving and inconstant female for his pitiful condition, now reviles him and focuses on how to save women from him. Little is done to educate men about this pitfall, this wrong road. Little direction is offered to young men learning about relationships and how to be a man in a relationship with a woman. Young females are increasingly being offered instruction and exposed to information about date rape, physically abusive partners, and assertiveness. Men are being ignored, however, other than to be reminded that boys don't hit girls. Neither boys nor girls, however, are taught the dangers of non-physical abuse and domination. The two-headed monster of jealousy and possessiveness and the literally deadly dangers it can pose are largely ignored, even though most teenagers are experienced with the problem and are willing and ready to learn.

The problem begins early. We don't know for sure, since the research isn't there, but I suspect it begins with the very first serious adolescent relationships. Certainly,

I have seen full-blown pathological domination in many high-school relationships. Males don't necessarily grow into it, nor do they necessarily grow out of it. Apparently, a young man does not first have to undergo a number of painful losses in past relationships, struggle with hard times, educationally, occupationally, and financially, become saddled with a wife and kids he can't reliably provide for, and drink excessively in order to develop an abusive, controlling personality toward his mate. Instead it appears more likely that he may enter adolescence and his first significant relationships with the underlying needs from which the dominating manner quickly emerges already firmly in place. Adolescence activates it—it flicks on the switch. As he separates from childhood, family, and the parental figures from whom he had previously derived whatever self-confidence and self-esteem they were able or willing to bestow, he searches his adolescent world for new sources of sustenance. His desperation in this regard will depend on the health and availability of familial sources, and on his willingness to accept it, plus the strength of his own internal resources. The adolescent male with domination needs is likely to have entered his first serious love relationship with neither source of self-esteem in good shape. Parental sources are either incomprehensible, unavailable, rejecting, ortherwise unhealthy, or they are rejected or misunderstood by the adolescent. In any case, the connection is ruptured too completely too soon, leaving him on his own with inadequate characterological supplies for this challenging journey. A girlfriend, consequently, becomes much more than that. She may represent to him a veritable life preserver to which he may cling with desperation, a vivid fear of losing, and an absolute need to control.

One should not expect increasing years and the boons of motivation to naturally pull him out of it. For one thing, many people don't grow up much, in a psychological maturational sense. Probably very few of us grow up all the way; perhaps none of us does. Many never get much past 12 to 14 years old in their capacity to reason, deal with and understand emotions, balance objectivity and subjectivity, utilize empathy, practice patience, make oneself do what one doesn't want to do but should, give, take, or love maturely. So we shouldn't place too great a hope on the likelihood of a dominating teenager growing out of it any time soon, unless something makes him.

Most research and literature in the field have focused on the abusive relationships of older couples, married couples, and, as I have said, those developing the physically abusive manifestation of control. These are couples bound together not just by emotions but often by children, economics, years spent together, and a life built together. These relationships exist within a context that presents problems different in some respects from those of younger, unmarried, childless couples. The young have special problems, but they also have advantages. It should be easier for a young female to get out of a dominating relationship since she is less encumbered. The earlier she gets out of such a relationship, one that she and her mate have been unable to change, the more she can minimize the damage to herself and her future. She may spare herself the trauma of divorce. She may spare her future children the damaging effects of witnessing such a relationship. (Research has consistently demonstrated that among the strongest correlates with physically abusive behavior in a male is his coming from a family where he witnessed spouse abuse.) She may avoid a completely disrupted life and having her children endure it as well. And if it is true, as research strongly suggests, that physical abuse within the pathologically dominating relationship increases in frequency and severity over time, perhaps she can reduce the damage and danger from that as well.

First, though, she has to see it coming. She must be aware that dominating and abusive relationships do exist in the young and that they are harmful and dangerous even when no battering has developed. She must not presume that it will go away by itself. But she must know that these relationships are progressive—they tend to get worse over time. She should identify and understand the signs of pathological domination and control. She must understand that excessive jealousy and possessiveness are serious warning signs rather than signs of a larger love. Jealousy, possessiveness, and the excessive supervision and monitoring that develop even at the earliest stages of a dominating relationship must be understood as more than just signs of being needed by the man or boy. She should be aware of the darker implications of that need so that she may be less likely to succumb to its apparent flattery. She must, therefore, come to understand her own susceptibility and vulnerability.

Men, on the other hand, seem to receive even less help or education in this regard. It seems as if no one tells them anything. When a pathologically dominating and abusive relationship exists, it seems, in my experience, that people are much more likely to try to intervene on the female side. Friends and family who become aware of its unhealthy nature seem more willing to help, advise, counsel, set limits, or offer warning to the woman or girl. Little seems to be said to the male.

There are many possible reasons for this. First, a dominating male may not attract much attention in a culture that has historically sanctioned such relationships. Second, in our society it has always fallen to women to be the negotiators, regulators, accommodators, the fixers and workers in a relationship with its problems, unfair as that may be. Third, men tend to talk far less about their love relationships and feelings in general than women, consequently little of the true character of their enormous neediness, dependency, fear, insecurity, jealousy, and possessiveness may be known to family and friends. Furthermore, many men, particularly young men and adolescents, work to give the opposite impression. Publicly, in their comments to friends, they will downplay their feelings of attachment. They often deny completely any powerful neediness or insecurity and deny absolutely any dependency. They will minimize the appearance of jealousy and possessiveness that is so strongly suggestive of that dependency. The man will seek to give the impression that it is the girl or woman who clings to, is dependent on, and is so needy of him. In so doing he may effectively shield from the view of those close to him the nature of his feelings, his way of being in love, and the unhealthy, dangerous, and ultimately unfulfilling road he is going down. No one tells him that in squeezing so tightly, he may be causing the relationship to run out between his clenched fingers, or that he is ruining that which he so clearly depends upon for existence. Therapists are in danger of being fooled or misled in this regard as well. Few dominating males will seek treatment for their dominating attitude and behavior. Those in counseling are likely to be there for some other reason. Therapists must be knowledgeable and sharp-eared to detect its presence. While many therapists are trained to passively follow the lead of their client, I would advise them, instead, to direct a dominating client (male or female) to an awareness of the nature of such relationships and the dangers it poses to the client and his or her relationship. It is proper for the therapist to do so, not as a value judgment but simply as responsible health care.

It is said that the physically abusive male, the batterer, is highly resistant to therapy or to change. This is one reason why most books on the subject simply and rather unequivocally advise the dominated woman (or man) to just get away. He is resistant to change in part for internal psychological reasons, including his typical choice of defense mechanisms (denial and projection). His apparent intransigence might also derive from lack of input from others, from his peers or from those close to him whom he respects. It is certainly very unlikely that he received any formal advice or education while young, during the formative adolescent period, on his relationships with girls or women. He is, therefore, unable to recognize the signs of danger in himself and in his manner. We should not presume that abusive and dominating men want to be that way, or that if they were shown, particularly when young, the folly and tragedy of that road that they might not work to choose another. Batterers programs for adult men are now reported to be largely unsuccessful. The recidivism rates are high; the motivation or investment in self-exploration and change on the part of the (often court-ordered) clients are often highly questionable. A useful treatment approach and one that may offer prophylactic benefits would be one directed toward young men of high-school and college age. It should deal also with larger issues such as masculine roles and images in modern society, fatherhood, and the challenges of serious relationships in general. It is often said that no one is taught how to be a mother or a father other than by the incidental observation of parents. It is also true that no one is taught how to cope with serious relationships or how to love maturely other than through the incidental, inconsistent, and often unhealthy models provided by the media, parents, and peers. It is amazing, really, that issues and aspects of living so central to a good and healthy life are so neglected while so many arguably more trivial areas of one's education and development are so energetically catechized.

The challenge in this for therapists is the greatest and thorniest that one can face. It can be frustrating, dangerous, and confusing, calling into play a wide range of dynamic, legal, and ethical issues. The therapist's own attitudes, experiences, and prejudices regarding love, relationships, males, and females must constantly be watched and controlled so that he or she may continue to see clearly, though all around may seem disorder and discord. The only times I have ever felt I could be in physical danger have been when working with cases such as these. Some of the most deadly dangerous situations involving my clients have been those associated with dominating relationships that are coming apart. The stakes can be very high and there is much to learn.

The therapist must be, but cannot *only* be, an empathic listener; he or she must be active as well. Therapy with this clientele, with either the male or female half of the relationship, must at times involve a highly directive style, giving specific advice and information, clear step-by-step directions. The therapist must also be a teacher and a coach. I have on occassion even had to be a policeman. One must know the law, the practices of area courts and police departments, and, hopefully, some of the key personnel. The therapist must be clear on ethical responsibilities, and on "duty to warn" obligations in potentially violent or deadly circumstances, including suicide, and must understand appropriate therapeutic, ethical, and confidentiality issues and practices as they apply to work with adolescents and minors.

Therapists working with female clients should be alert to the presence of unhealthy domination in the love relationships of women who may have sought counseling for overtly different reasons. Many girls or women will seek therapy for "stress" or "depression" and not view it as deriving from a pathologically dominating relationship. Or they may be consciously seeking a band-aid treatment of the symptom rather than the cause if they are not ready to change or leave the relationship. The therapist should never, of course, go searching for what isn't there or in any direction the material does not legitimately lead.

Once the issue of a dangerously unhealthy relationship is mutually established, however, the therapist must help the female client understand what is harmful and wrong with it. She must be helped to decide what needs to change, how, when, and in what order. She must be helped to see when it is time to leave, how and when to do it, and how to stay out once she's gone. There will be a lot of teaching and logistical planning involved and the therapist must be clear, directive, knowledgeable, and confident. There exist several good self-help books and handbooks dealing with this stage in the process (e.g., Levy 1993, NiCarthy and Davidson 1989).

Therapists who find themselves working with dominating males have a very different job, and few books have dealt very much with this topic. Even more than women clients, men or boys who have this problem are far more likely to present other concerns or symptoms rather than that of being troubled by being a pathological dominator who wishes to change. However, once the problem is brought out and established as a serious issue in his life, the male must be helped to see that it is not in his own best interests to remain on his present path. He needs to be helped to understand that he is actively jeopardizing the relationship he clearly depends on. He may drive away or destroy what he seems to need to live. It is a hard thing to understand that one must sometimes loosen up in order to hold on, but this is what the therapist must try to teach to the dominating male client who is in trouble. He carries within him also the potential for suicide and murder. Among teenagers the leading precipitant of suicide attempts is the loss of an important relationship. The therapist must be prepared to deal not only with the male's problems within the relationship but his reactions to its actual or perceived loss. The challenge for the male and for his therapist is enormous. The change required within the male to break away from his controlling style is profound, yet it is so clearly in his interest to do so.

In writing this book I have had young people in mind. It is written as a warning of danger, an explanation of the peril, and as a guide toward health and safety for those professionals who may be able to help them. Adolescence, as a stage in life, keeps expanding. It is stretching itself at both ends. As an indicator, or better still a symptom, of a complex society, adolescence lengthens as the complexity grows. Complexity creates stress, and adolescence has become more stressful. National figures on suicide, attempted suicide, drug and alcohol use, cigarette smoking, pregnancy, and academic achievement will bear this out; better still, ask anyone who works in a public high school.

Democratic, technologically advanced societies offer enormous freedom, choice, and opportunity to their citizens, yet they also require a longer period of preparation and education before the young can effectively enter and manage adulthood. It is harder to decide what and how to be when one can be whatever one wants to be. Societies such as our own produce the longest and most difficult adolescence. Prior to World War II, adolescence was brief or nonexistent worldwide for all but the very rich and most privileged classes. We read of them as the existentialists, among others. The gloomy, insecure, and indecisive artists and intellectuals of the 1920s and '30s drifting around Europe, congregating in Paris or New York, self-absorbed, intoxicated, struggling with love and searching for themselves. They included Hemingway, Fitzgerald, and Wolfe, and though none of them was a teenager, all were still adolescents, their restless lifestyles and preoccupations recognizable as adolescent.

For everyone else, adolescence was a luxury they could not afford. They went from childhood to adulthood with no stop in between. They pursued the occupations their mothers and fathers held, or chose within a very narrow range of choices. Education ended young, as work began young. One simply had to move along briskly to the next stage. Every aspect of life was far more contained and controlled until very recently.

Adolescents of the past two generations have seen restrictions and constraints fall away with accelerating rapidity. There is much to be said in favor of this, of course. Freedom is a pretty good thing. Choice is a pretty good thing. So are tolerance of and acceptance of diversity, individual fullfillment and the many wonderful features of an open society. But they can be very confusing, very scary and very hard. They have changed American family life. Parents are, in general, far less involved with their children than in earlier times. Often, both parents hold full-time jobs. They are unlikely to be working in their homes or on their street. Cars have allowed them to live at a distance from their jobs and most are happy to have it that way. Travel adds to the time away from home and children and subtracts from the knowledge children have of their parents' lives. Most kids cannot describe what their parents do for work. This also subtracts from how well family members can know each other. Television and its offshoots have filled some of the empty space between parents and their kids and are helping to raise them. This has not been an improvement. By the time children become teenagers, the family meal has become a rarity.

Their lives have become largely separate under the same roof. All of this has left teenagers rather alone. Of course, to be left alone is what they constantly demand of adults, parents in particular, but as it is said that one should beware of getting what one wishes for, the adolescent has been severely challenged by having been "left alone."

Nonetheless, they can't wait to get there. Adolescence is portrayed to the latency-aged child as the Emerald City was to Dorothy and her mates. Remember how it appeared to them when they emerged from the sedating poppy fields and saw it gleaming spectacularly in the distance? They ran to it wide-eyed. Everything from cereal boxes to morning cartoons (along with their incessant commercials) and the nightly sitcoms hold out adolescence as a dazzling land of fun and adventure populated by good-looking people doing things incomparably better than what children do. There is a tremendous pull upon elementary-school-aged kids upward toward adolescence, supported by the specious myth that they are "the best years of your life." Adolescence doesn't last longer only because it is prolonged by the increasing difficulty of establishing oneself professionally and financially. It lasts longer because it begins earlier as well.

Physically, puberty is arriving earlier and earlier. On the average, American girls begin menstruating at 13 years and that is earlier than previous generations of American women. For the past one hundred years, the average age at menarche in the United States has been dropping at the rate of three or four months every decade (Larson 1990).

The glorification of adolescence provokes premature entry into its behavioral style of children who are not psychologically prepared to deal with it. Unable to understand the meaning of the stage, they precociously emulate the featured trappings of it. They wear the clothes, talk the talk, listen to the music. They begin to smoke cigarettes. Marijuana and alcohol use are growing among junior-high-school-age kids. They seek out boyfriends and girlfriends; sexual relations begin earlier, and strong attachments are fostered. In high school it is considered bad form for a girl or a boy to date a lot of different people either in succession or simultaneously. Playing the field, as my parents' generation called it, is out. Girls who do this are called sluts, even by other girls, while boys who do so are called players. They are terms of disrespect, censure, and even derision. Single-person, long-term relationships are sought and maintained as a badge of honor and a sign of maturity and good mental health regarding one's ability to relate. Those who have had only short-term relationships, lasting only one to three months, worry that there may be something wrong with them. Long-term relationships are highly valued and maintained with great persistence, in part so that all that time won't have been wasted. Consequently, many young people send a lot of good money after bad, so to speak, in an effort to prolong their relationships.

It isn't just peer influence and the cultured norms of adolescence that promote the desirability of such close, long-term, serious, often sexual relationships. For many it fulfills strong needs for dependency, security, recognition, and affiliation that may no longer be accepted by the teenager from his family or perhaps may no longer be provided. The premature leap that so many young people make from latency to adolescence cuts them off from essential sources of psychological sustenance and support. The dissolving American family seems able to maintain only a very light grip. In this climate of diminished parental succor and influence, many adolescents turn to their peer group. Having made their leap or been cast adrift in such an undeveloped state, and desperate not to be alone, many adolescents will transfer to a love relationship all of the unmet needs for which their still maturing psyche craves satisfaction. These relationships can quickly begin to feel like the source of life itself to their inhabitants. Dependency can become intense, the fear of loss intolerable, the need for security paramount, and, for some, the need for control absolute. All of this can develop before young individuals, male or female, can maturely and safely identify what love is or who might best provide it.

Modern American adolescence has become fertile ground for the growth of pathologically dominating relationships. Other factors, such as the adolescent male's heightened need to fulfill a traditional sex role, early sex, popular support of long-term relationships, diminished parental influence, and the apparent increase in the extent to which physical abuse has been modeled at home, have also contributed to the problem. It seems, therefore, worthwhile to study the existence and nature of these relationships among the young and the pre-married and to consider how they might best be prevented and dealt with from a therapeutic and an educational perspective.

Caroline and John I

Caroline awakens quickly to her alarm at 5:50 A.M. An arm shoots out from beneath the covers and shuts it off before the first ring has finished. Her movement is deft, rapid, and alert without any clumsy fumbling or disorientation. In total darkness and without seeming to look, she has found the small, unlighted button and returned the room to silence. She waits a moment, still buried in her blankets, listening carefully for any sounds of stirring in her father's room on the other side of the wall. All is still. Soundlessly, she sits up, finds her phone, and still in darkness dials it. She waits quite a while, 8, 10 rings, expressionless. Then, in the blackness, her face comes alert. "Time to get up," she whispers in a timid, sing-song voice. She sounds weakly cheery, apologetic. "Get up, John," she whispers. "Come on. . . . Yes, it is. . . . No . . . no. Yes, it's 5:50. Get yourself up then. . . . Then why do you have me call? . . . I have to go. . . . Yes . . . I have to go. Bye." Again without a sound she replaces the phone, listens again to her father's room, and lays back in bed. At 6:00 she gets up, turns on her light and her radio, and begins to bustle about her room, opening and closing drawers, pulling out clothes, getting together what she needs for the day. She finds her books, drops them heavily on her dresser and leans over them to take the first look of the day at herself in the mirror, seeming to wonder if her appearance has emerged from the hours of sleep unscathed.

She is effortlessly pretty. Her straight light-brown hair falls easily into place with a slight shake of her head. Its medium length frames her exquisite, well-formed face.

Her dark eyebrows and lashes are sharp and distinct against her light, smooth, poreless skin and need no coloring. She is perfect and could go off to school exactly as she is, in the sweatpants and sweatshirt she wore to bed, needing only to add socks and sneakers, and she'd still be the envy of nearly every girl at her school.

She stares blankly at herself. Then, absently, collects various makeup items and articles, places them in a small case, and puts the case into her bag. She showers, dresses in jeans, T-shirt, and sweater, adding no jewelry, and gathers her things to leave. She does not eat breakfast. From the moment she snapped off her alarm, she has appeared to be fully awake, alert, and organized. Yet since her brief and muted phone conversation she has not spoken or even changed facial expression. She has not smiled, frowned, muttered, sung to the radio, or offered any sign of life, save her body movements. She grabs her bag and books and heads for the door. The house is dark. The sun is just coming up.

"Caroline. . . . " Her father's voice startles her. He has come out of his bedroom and is at the end of the hall looking down toward the front door. Caroline turns halfway and looks over her shoulder at her father, her face caught in a worried, expectant expression. "You're leaving early. Are you picking him up again?" Her father has remained at his door at the end of the dark hall. His arms are folded and his tone and expression are sullen.

"No. I'm just picking up Gina." She waits for her father's reaction.

He looks at her a moment and says with directness, "Don't be late," and returns to his bedroom.

She has just rounded the corner to John's street. She can see his house from here. "Damn." She pulls the car quickly to the curb and reaches for her bag. She takes out lipstick and eye makeup and begins to make up her face.

She does it quickly, and when she is finished she throws the stuff roughly back in her bag, sits back, takes a deep breath, pauses, and then drives on.

She pulls up in front of John's house and waits. In a moment, John's mother comes to the door. She is smiling broadly. She looks thrilled to see her and waves energetically. She is always frantically happy to see Caroline. She greets her always like a visiting dignitary. Caroline likes Mrs. White and is glad that she likes her, even her exuberance. It's a welcome change from the mood at home, but often it is embarrassing, cumbersome, and sometimes causes trouble with John. "He'll be out in a minute, dear." She waves again, grinning madly, and goes back inside. Minutes go by and Caroline is getting nervous. She changes stations on the radio frequently and impatiently. She takes out one of her books, checks to see if her homework is in it, and puts it back. Takes out another and does the same thing. Then another. She keeps her books and papers in nice neat order. She keeps checking his door. It is now almost certain that they'll be late to school again. She's thinking of how she'd love to lean on her horn and just keep it going until he came out. She'd love to get him to *run* to the car. Put a worried, confused look on *his* face for a change. Make him wonder with concern, even anxiety, what the hell was going on with *her*.

She hears his screen door slam and he starts out. Then he stops and goes back in. She hisses loudly between clenched teeth and grips the wheel tight. Tight. Suddenly, he's hopping into the car next to her with a big smile.

"What's all this shit? God!" He grunts as he lifts her heavy bag off of the seat between them and throws it into the back. Caroline doesn't answer or look at him but grimly, obviously not pleased, pulls out and speeds down the street. He manipulates the radio, absorbed in it. Finally, she speaks, still not looking at him.

"You know I'm going to be late again, right?"

"So?" He's still working on the radio, not looking at her, either.

"So you know they'll call my father this time. So you know he doesn't want me driving you because we're always late. So that's bad for me. Right?"

"Just say you were late without me."

"The other thing is *I* don't like being late. It's a pain in the ass and I hate starting the day like that.

"What are you going to do if I don't drive you? It could happen. It probably will. If I get caught I lose the car for going to school. It's only October. We've got a long way to go."

"I don't know." He seems entirely unconcerned.

"Well, think. Because you can't depend on me."

"Caroline, will you *shut up*? Man, you are such a *baby* about this. Whinin' about your father. Whinin' about school. What a baby. O.K., we're here. Let's hurry in so we can learn many new and interesting things about ourselves and the world around us," says John in a mocking tone. They have indeed arrived and walk in together saying nothing further. She labors with the weight of her bag, leaning to its opposite side as she walks. He stays at her side bouncing along easily. When they arrive at her locker they exchange an expressionless kiss and an "I love you" and then John leaves her. The halls are nearly empty. You can hear faint laughter, a locker being shut, classroom doors closing, a bell, and the low rustle of bodies, chairs and voices as the school day begins to settle in. Caroline takes no notice of any of it. As is increasingly the case, sensations she feels are entirely within herself, enclosed, churning, yet nameless. Above these, at another level, lies and excuses are forming themselves for later use, assembling drearily, proceeding like a dirge.

She walks down the long, empty, now quiet hallway. She searches for a tissue and blows her nose, then pauses a moment, puts the tissue this time to her mouth and rubs roughly at her lips. She stares a moment at the redness, looks both ways up and down the hall and throws the tissue hard against the wall. It bounces lightly and softly to the floor.

John was built narrow and slight. Pink gums were widely exposed when he smiled. He had blond hair, many splotchy freckles, and a light, pink-skinned complexion that could never tan. At age 18 he was far from shaving. If it wasn't for his 5'10" height he might have passed for 12. He'd probably have to show ID until he was 30. He was active, animated, spirited, funny, and popular. He was a below-average athlete, not talented enough for varsity level on any high school team, but he was a huge sports fan and always wore hats, sweatshirts, and T-shirts representing various college or professional powerhouses. He tended to be a front runner in the sense that he favored only the teams who were reigning champions, switching his allegiances with the changing tides of victory rather than loyally sticking with a particular team. His friends were athletes or big sports fans like himself and covered their very short hair with baseball hats at all times as he did.

In school he was a poor student but in no real danger of not graduating on time. He had no intellectual interests; he could not make himself read. In class, he was often bored, slept when he was allowed to, or was restlessly inattentive and talkative. He never got in serious trouble; he generally knew when to stop. Occcassionally, though, he would come to believe that a teacher was being unfair to him in some way or perhaps did not seem to like him. He found these situations extremely difficult to tolerate.

It appeared to him that most people liked him and it disturbed and then angered him quite a bit when it seemed that someone didn't—anyone, even complete strangers. He could bristle, red-faced, at an ambiguous look from someone, especially while he was driving. He was particularly sensitive then, and had been known to yell at and challenge people in other cars who had looked at him at a stoplight. He could get like this toward teachers, too, but with more restraint. In most instances the situations were quelled quickly and John would apologize with genuine sincerity. Most teachers liked John—he was just emotional. However, there had been occassions during his four years in high school when a conflict could not be resolved and a class change had been needed. For these teachers he maintained a living burning hatred.

Though he was a relentless talker he was in no way eloquent or articulate. Mostly it was a matter of simply not being shy. He was equally at ease talking to boys or girls. There were always two or three girls he was friendly with whom he would talk with on the phone several times a week. He talked with them about their boyfriends and gave them advice, or he would talk to them about other boys in whom they were interested. He was a go-between for many established, developing, and potential couples. He liked being involved and he liked being an important and valued connection to as many popular people as possible. He was frequently in trouble, though, because in his zeal to be connected and relied upon he would sometimes say too much about someone to the wrong person. When this happened he usually felt indignant and furious at the petty and ungrateful attitudes of others, and would claim that he was through "helping people." But human brokering was just about his favorite thing in the world and he could never give it up, not even for a day.

His phone use drove his parents crazy, since they

associated it with his resistance to homework and his low grades. They were partly right. John's low grades were mostly due to his nearly complete inability to make himself do what he didn't want to do. In that sense, as in others, John was exceptionally immature. He could have spent a lot of time on the phone *and* done his homework if he used well the time he had, but the regularity of his homework completion never advanced beyond sporadic. He maintained a hazy belief that all schoolwork was pointless and he never could quite stop taking it personally that this work was being assigned to him. It interfered with his life. As such, it seemed mean and unfair, presenting an almost bullying image to him. He couldn't quite get on top of that self-reference and see a bigger picture. So schoolwork was always, for John, a source of persistent annoyance and frustration. Consequently, he usually either copied the work of another or simply didn't do it.

His parents, who were divorced but lived near each other in the same town, railed and fretted in their own distinctive ways over this. Though neither of them had liked school or done well, they were able to completely ignore their own experience and insist that all of their children do well and do so enthusiastically. The idea that one would seek to do anything less than his very best at all times amazed them. The idea that school was the way toward respect and monetary success was like a creed and a blinding light which obscured all other notions, paths, or points of view. The idea that someone could not even see this light was more than preposterous—it was a lie. They thought that John believed as they did and just refused to do as even he thought he should, that it was a fully conscious disobedience. In fact, John didn't believe any of it. It would have been closer to the truth to say that John had no thoughts at all. John did believe in a high school diploma, but he did not believe in learning. He had contempt for dropouts, but did not believe in being a student. He vaguely presumed that since food, shelter, and relative well-being had always been available they would always be forthcoming. His only thoughts of the future consisted of moving out someday soon and owning better cars. He did not think of where the money would come from or how his workday would be spent in years to come.

His parents dealt with this by means of the good cop/bad cop routine. His father, who *was* a cop, lambasted him every which way he could think of. He'd yell, scream, insult, threaten, and storm about in a fury of crude impotent oaths and ludicrous contradictions.

"You're a lazy son of a bitch. For Christ sake, you're always runnin' around, doin' this, callin' that, never sit still through a goddamn meal with us. You always got somethin' better to do. Well, I'll tell you somethin'. I shoulda sent you up to the St. Joseph's High School where they'd make you get your head out of your ass and get some work done. You think you're foolin' us with these D's? You should be gettin' A's and B's, and you know it and we know it."

Punishments and restrictions would be pounded out but never enforced. His father's storm would eventually blow itself out. It seemed that whenever he was yelling at John, he was also dressing and gathering his scattered equipment preparing to go out. His disorganization only increased his futile exasperation. He'd always conclude by calling John a "low-life" and a "loser."

John's mom had a different approach. She would try to talk to him softly, pleading with him to do better. She would build him up, tell him how smart he was, remind him about college. When he was younger she would do a lot of his work for him, but believe she was only "helping" him. Now he brought no work for her to do and it made her feel desperately out of touch. While he'd sit still for his father, he was always on the move when his mother spoke to him. So she'd have to follow him around the house, even trying to whisper to him as he dialed the phone and carried on conversations with friends. While his father's tirades seemed to go right through him and out the other side, his mother's entreaties bounced weakly off. In the end, he could always do whatever he wanted.

And so while John was sometimes the object of clamor and consternation at home and school, he avoided serious trouble, and generally cruised along satisfactorily. He hung out or drove around on weekend nights. He drank whenever he could. He stayed pretty much within his own town and had little interest in expeditions to nearby cities. His life and horizons were limited and entirely provincial.

When John was in the eleventh grade, he began his first and only serious romantic relationship. More specifically, it was the only romantic relationship he'd ever had of any kind. He had liked many girls before, even in elementary school, *really* liked them. He had the need and the nerve to call girls on the phone as a fifth-grader. He would "ask them out," meaning he would ask them to be his girlfriend and often they would say yes, only to shun him entirely the following day in school, whispering and giggling to their friends about him. He would cover up any sign of hurt or humiliation. If word got around that he had called a girl, he would deny it. He would turn to the raucous companionship of his male friends with a zeal that gave him comfort, a distraction that gave the impression that he cared little about anything else.

But it happened again and again through grades six, seven, eight, nine, and ten. He rejected with contempt the timid overtures of the more homely and unpopular girls that had occasionally come his way. He considered and pursued only the most beautiful and desirable, the queens of his school. Yet his "immaturity," his immediate intensity, and his looks worked against him. His toothy, big-gummed, freckle-faced, bristle-haired, pale-skinned, thin-bodied, gooney appearance hurt him. To guys he was okay, fun, and thoroughly one of the boys. To most girls he was decidedly un-cool. They talked to him, were "friends" with him, spoke with him about other boys and girls, but that was it. So it was with wonder and even with private laughter that his relationship with Caroline was first greeted by their peers.

2

"LIKE A BIRD ON THE WIRE": CULTURE, MASCULINITY, AND THE PROBLEM OF LOVE

MALE IDENTITY AND THE PROBLEM OF LOVE

When I was in fifth grade my family moved from one mid-sized eastern Massachusetts town to another, not far away. It was not a move that I or any of my brothers were happy about. We'd had wonderful, fun times in our neighborhood with our many friends and did not relish this change, which had been thrust upon us. Though our new home was only a twenty-minute drive from our old one it was nonetheless an entirely new and different world for us as kids—a new neighborhood, all new and completely unknown kids, and a new school. The fact that moving day was May 1st made it even worse, since it seemed to us that socially, groups and relationships would have been well established this late in the school year and, in our somewhat anxious view, set in concrete and strenuously reject-

ing all intruders. I expected cold scrutiny, silence if I was
lucky. I knew how we in our class treated new kids and I
recalled that we hadn't been very friendly. Apparently my
older brother, Tom, and I felt especially anxious regarding the move and, as was our style, expressed that in
anger—okay, vandalism. On the gray drizzly morning of
the move, my parents and oldest brother, John, were concerned with organizing and loading the moving truck.
Tom and I had been relieved of any specific duties of this
sort so that the others could more efficiently do it all themselves. A good deal for all and one that allowed us to pass
the remaining hour or so in more gratifying ways. We
chose rocks.

A neighbor had recently put up a sort of wooden picket
fence around his adjacent yard. A section of it was visible
through an opening in the hedges across our backyard.
Something about that sweet, white, homey structure, the
day, and the peculiar temper and compatibility of our
minds combined in causing us to view this fence suddenly
as provoking, even taunting, eventually goading. These
weren't the precise words that came to mind at the time;
rather, the idea crystallized in more preverbal, pictorial
images, amounting crudely to the same thing. It happened
that the 20-foot section of offensive fencing was visible
from behind a corner of the rear of our house at the accessible distance of about 100 feet. At this corner was the
lower end of a drain pipe, and on the ground below the
end of this pipe was a natural filter abundant with small
and medium-sized stones.

It began, so it seemed, as casual target practice, the
goal being to merely hit the fence. As the slats began to
crack and snap, however, the goal quickly degenerated
into pure and exhilarating destruction. We threw hard and
fast. We both had good arms, my brother's being near

legendary among our peers. He had been an outstanding Little League pitcher. I wasn't a star, but I had potential.

Dimly, in brief queasy flashes, I was aware that the wreckage being carried out could in no way be hidden. Our aim had been good from the start and quickly improved. Within fifteen minutes the fence looked like an ugly set of broken teeth and was worsening. It was loud and messy. Jagged breaks became yawning gaps. Rocks lay thick among the sharp white strips of shattered wood. No one else could have been suspected. No one else had access to this fence as we had. Yet we couldn't stop. If anything, our drive accelerated. Finally, there was nothing left of the fence.

We had been destructive before but this was odd. In other instances we had always been careful not to get caught and as far as I can remember we never were. So this was odd because it was virtually certain that we would be caught. There could be no story or excuse that would deflect blame and I knew it even as we did it and I suppose Tom did too, though we never said so. Yet we did it anyway. I guess we just didn't want to move. But I will tell you that after we had done what we had done we agreed that, if move we must, it would be best to get out as soon as possible.

We didn't—we got caught. The neighbor came angrily, with stunned wonder, to my father to report and ask reimbursement. My father assured him he would have it. I don't remember him getting terribly angry with us, nor did he even tell our mother. As I said, this whole affair was rather unusual for us. The very next morning we began class at our new school. John went alone to the high school. Tom went alone to the junior high. I went alone to the elementary school. The principal, a large red bear, met me in his office, greeted me kindly, and brought me to my new class.

The day had already begun. The old oak halls were empty and quiet. He stopped, opened the door to a classroom, and walked in with me. The principal brought me in and stood me in front of the class. He said, "This is David Curran. He just moved here from Framingham." Before he could add more, boys in different parts of the room began calling out. "Let him sit over here." "Put him over here." I had never seen this happen in any of my classes. It was great.

I was put in the front row on the teacher's right, in the first seat. It turned out to be an important break since it happened to be right in front of "the toughest kid in the school," 13-year-old Chuckie La Brache, who already had prominent self-made tattoos. I was very impressed and hoped to take the opportunity and impress him, somehow. So when Chuckie had something to say to me that day and I was thrilled that he often did, I was very responsive, regardless of what the female teacher was directing us to do. My priorities, as had been my fears, were exclusively social. The image I sought to project was decidedly disobedient.

A boy at the very end of the row next to mine caught my ear with his deep powerful whisper. He, like Chuckie, was big and looked older than the other kids. When I turned he proudly showed me the largest, most fearsome-looking ruler that I had ever or have ever seen to this day. A flashing copper broadsword of a thing, eighteen inches long, three or four inches wide, made of thick solid metal. He was grinning madly with pride and delight at my wide-eyed reaction. The other boys in the area stirred with awe and excitement at the display of this much-revered, apparently sacred object. He gestured that he would slide it up the aisle to me to hold and inspect more closely. From the reactions of the others it was clear that I was being offered something rare and special. He slid it, I caught it, and held it under my desk in my lap. And it was marvelous. It was also the end of my time in that seat. Mrs. Jaworek had had enough of this and I was moved and seated among girls.

I can remember none of their faces. I can only remember that my chagrin at having to sit with them was outweighed by my pride at having gotten into trouble my first day. I felt that that surely would help with my acceptance by the boys.

Acceptance and inclusion, however, worked more slowly than that. But I wasn't picked on either. Everyone pretty much did have their own friends. At recess I walked around. I didn't initiate. I thought I'd play it cool, not say much, not seem too desperate. Boys said hi to me but went about their business. I took note of who the popular ones were, who the leaders and most respected ones were. They were the big or small athletic, tough, aggressive ones. Two in particular were bullies, clearly mean people. In the boys' room after recess I watched one of them punch a smaller kid in the stomach just for the pleasure of accomplishing it before the kid could see it coming and cover up. He hit him hard, too. He walked out laughing with his entourage in his wake. This kid was without question a jerk, yet he was also very popular and a person whom it would be good, socially, to be close to. The other bully was the most popular boy in the class. He was a great, precocious athlete, one of those kids who reaches physical maturity by about age 12 and just mows 'em down in Little League, striking out about fifteen batters a game, and smiles when he inevitably hits a couple. He was bright, handsome, intensely energetic and the most obvious leader in the school. Even the sixth graders usually deferred to him. But he was unmercifully critical. His brutality was verbal rather than physical; nonetheless, he would destroy people. Recess for the popular boys consisted of sports but nearly every boy tried to play. The ballgames were exclusively

male. He chose the teams. His team always won. Teammates who made errors were publicly humiliated by this
most respected person no matter how far his team was in
the lead or how safe the inevitable victory. He was excessively hard on himself too, but of course suffered no social
scorn over it. Yet poor athletes, certain to perform imper-
fectly, flocked to his games and were happy to be picked
by him for his team, to be near him.

I looked for Chuckie because he had spoken to me but
couldn't find him. The boy with the ruler was in the game.
Their friendliness now seemed more an effort to show off
to me rather than to befriend me.

I have no memory of speaking to any girl that first day
(or any subsequent day). I remember none of their names
or faces, what they did, or what they wore. I remember
vividly the names, faces, and movements of several boys
of that day.

Taken as a whole, that period of twenty-four hours
seems to encapsulate a good deal that is important about
the development of male identity, masculinity, what males
need, seek, avoid, and honor.

First, anxiety or emotions in general, expressed in the
form of anger, are viewed as acceptable even when they
take the form of physical destructiveness. (This refers to
the late lamented fence, of course.) Females may not understand this, which doesn't necessarily make it wrong in the
eyes of other males. Further, there is among males an attractiveness to male antisocial behavior; it suggests to
many a virile rebelliousness, a strong independent fear-
lessness, and a resistance to containment, restrictions, or
simple dutiful obedience.

Certain crude concepts, such as "might makes right,"
were reinforced. It was shown that self-esteem and social
esteem for males may not be based on character, kindness, sympathy, ingenuity, or generosity. Rather, brute

strength, ability to intimidate, control, and physically dominate were the prized and effective qualities. Granted, this was only fifth grade and even boys often become generally more sophisticated and maturely discriminating about these matters. Yet, for many, a residue lives on and, for some, little changes at all. I know that the big boy who pummeled the little kid in the boys' room ended up battering his girlfriend in high school, the first incident of that kind I can remember being aware of in my own life. The other more diminutive but more charismatic figure continued to struggle with anger and relationships for decades. I do not know specifically what he was like within his love relationships other than to have noted that they were stormy.

The manner by which most males learn and later maintain their senses of self, of masculinity, of self-esteem, of place and security in their world is a long repetitive process directed largely by other males and the institutions and models they have created. The lesson presented, taught, modeled, and taught again in a hundred thousand ways contains, among others, a central theme which is ancient, traditional, and lifelong. Simply stated, it is "Don't be a girl, don't be a sissy, a fag, a baby, a wimp." Don't be emotional unless it's anger. Don't care. Don't cry. Be tough. When I played high-school football, the levels of proficiency for all players were indicated by the label of a designated color. The best players, the starters, were on the blue team. The second team, first-line substitutes, were the reds. The third team was green, fourth team white. At the very bottom, if there were enough players to go so low, were the pinks. Again, just don't be like a female. Watch them and be the opposite and you've got a chance. And don't let them boss you around or appear to control or affect you too much. Furthermore, it is not only critically important for the young boy to not be like a girl, it's important that he not even *like* girls (see cartoon below).

In order to be a masculine boy, a respected boy among boys, he must not have "feminine" characteristics. He must not appear to be too needing of, controlled by, or close to maternal figures either. He must not be a "mama's boy." To be rejecting of them would in fact be preferable. This is what Freud (1925), in "Some Psychical Consequences of the Anatomical Distinction Between the Sexes," refers to as the boy's "triumphant contempt." Later, however, in adolescence and adulthood, when society and physiology determine that males must affiliate with females, have relationships with them, and in some way join their lives with them, many males find it difficult to readjust. They carry old and immature needs and notions into heterosexual love that are incompatible with mature love and establish at the outset a fault line in the relationship that can be the basis from which a dominating, controlling, and abusive relationship can derive.

While Freud, deservedly called a genius, consolidated a revolutionary dynamic for the understanding of the

Calvin and Hobbes   by Bill Watterson

CALVIN AND HOBBES ©1994 Watterson. Dist. by UNIVERSAL PRESS SYNDICATE. Reprinted with permission. All rights reserved.

human psyche, he was nonetheless very much a man of his times and of his culture, conservative in most respects and influenced in his formulations by traditional ideas regarding the sexes. Psychoanalytic theory, at its bedrock level, undisputed even by current theories of gender identity, established that the rejection of femininity is central to masculinity, beginning with the boy's disidentification with his mother.

All children must separate from the complete care and direction of their caretakers. It is essential for the acquisition of necessary cognitive, perceptual, and motor skills that every infant be given sufficient opportunity to venture forth independently as is appropriate for their age. Human infants, unlike the young of most other species, do not arrive on earth prepared to fend for themselves independently. They require the longest period of guardianship and protection, care, and directed assistance. Yet, from the beginning, it is the urge of the young to move toward independence and the role of the caretaker to allow them to safely do so or to pull them toward it if the child is hesitant.

However, for thousands of years, it was the males of the species, by virtue of their superior strength and speed, who had been the ones who physically ventured forth, first in the search, pursuit, and acquisition of meat, later in the defense or acquisition of land and property, ultimately because a male-founded and male-directed religious, cultural, familial, and finally, psychological tradition decreed that that is what males do. In order to maintain and reinforce this distinct identity, role, and power, the emphasis on separation and then difference had to be institutionalized and every individual had to conform. Females, on the other hand, were able to remain with the maternal caretakers, who continued their feeding and caring role to the community, to learn the essential crafts from them.

It has long been established, certainly within our culture, that the male must leave the female in order to be male and that to be male was preferable to, superior to, being female. This came to be believed by females, too.

The male child is propelled in his development toward greater autonomy not only by his natural physical and intellectual needs but by his socialized gender needs as well. He sees and hears it all around him, from the way he is played with to the way his actions are responded to by others. Everyone wants him to separate. Everyone wants him to be "masculine." They are anxious and disapproving should he cling, should his dependency seem too great. In modern times, psychological theory has supported the normalcy and even the necessity of this.

Margaret Mahler (1975), the noted developmental theorist, author of the "separation-individuation" continuum, has described this process in depth. Again, in view of the difficulty many men have in establishing healthy, egalitarian, and empathetic relationships with women, her theories of normal psychological growth can be read as a development toward estrangement from females rather than just "separation;" instead of just "individuation," a negative individualism leading toward difficulty, later on, communing with the opposite sex.

Her theory traces a unilinear track that leads from oneness with the mother to separateness. Her emphasis is on how the self separates and the baby comes to feel not one with the mother. The interdependence and mutuality of their relationship is presented as the ground, with separation the figure in glorious prominence. Mutuality appears as dim background scenery to the triumphant individuality that thrusts forward out of it. Of course, this corresponds to our personal feeling of being the center of our world and to the struggle to enhance or maintain that feeling.

The classic psychoanalytic theory did not see differentiation as a balance but as a process of disentanglement. Thus it cast experiences of union, merger, and self–other harmony as regressive opposites. [Benjamin 1988, p. 46]

Leonard Cohen captures the loneliness and estrangement of this theme with characteristic dark poignancy.

Like a bird.on the wire
Like a drunk in a midnight choir
I have tried in my way
to be free.
Like a baby stillborn
Like a beast with his horn
I have torn everyone
who reached out for me.
["Bird on the Wire" by Leonard Cohen, 1968]

Thus the interdependence or merging of needs between individuals that begins in infancy (or prenatally), which one should *not* grow out of, is given less attention, except to warn of the dangers of symbiosis. Western man has been very late in recognizing the true nature of ecological systems, that all environments in the natural world combine in a non-hierarchical amalgam of non-discrete entities. Nothing is separate; nothing stands on its own. In ignoring this natural truth we have failed to recognize that we have been sending men off on the wrong track, an unnatural and essentially false one. It allows for the possibility in the mind of man (or woman) that domination can be gratifying, absolute, even natural—that it can work. We recognize how far away they have gotten only later when, as adolescents or adults, they cannot pull themselves comfortably back toward a healthy relationship with a lover, wife, or family, when rapprochement is necessary.

It is different for the female, of course. In most societies this kind of separation from the maternal figure is not only less necessary but even culturally forbidden or at least not demanded. Her learning is more likely to stress the importance of empathy, nurturing, and living in cooperative fashion in one's human environment. She is not taught, however, to expect or demand it in like fashion from male mates.

> . . . the girl child is raised and nurtured by someone like herself and, therefore, is more easily able to feel another's pain as though it were her own. For a boy, the path toward development lies not in a continuation of attachment but in *separation* from the early caretaker, and in a definition of himself as different, "masculine," and independent. Often, this translates into different standards of self-control and self-expression, as well as a male ideal of not needing others and the development of a more conflicted response to closeness or dependency. [Browne 1987, p. 77]

THE "TENSION" AND "RISK" OF LOVE AND THE ORIGINS OF DOMINATION

Jessica Benjamin, in her book *The Bonds of Love: Psychoanalysis, Feminism, and the Problem of Domination* (1988), critiques traditional psychological theory of human development. She focuses, as the title suggests, on the problem of establishing a healthy love relationship in the face of cultural forces that from infancy have tended to militate against it. She offers what she calls an "intersubjective" theory of interpersonal development that differs philosophically and in emphasis from traditional psychoanalytic theory. It has much to say about what has gone wrong in male–female relations, what is missing as well as what constitutes a healthy mutually rewarding one.

She states, with regard to infant development,

the issue is not only how we separate from oneness, but also how we connect to and recognize others; the issue is not how we become free of the other, but how we actively engage and make ourselves known in relation to the other. [p. 18]

She draws from the ideas of D. W. Winnicott (1964), Heinz Kohut's (1971) "self psychology," and the expanding research revealing the active, social infant in constructing her intersubjective view.

It assumes that we are able and need to recognize that other subject (person, mother, father, lover) as different and yet alike, as an other who is capable of showing similar mental experience. Thus the idea of intersubjectivity reorients the conception of the psychic world from a subject's relations to its object, toward a subject meeting another subject. [p. 19]

The intersubjective view is difficult to describe and difficult, though rewarding, to live. It presents as a natural given the duality of human existence, separateness from and inextricable relatedness to others. It contends that relatedness is what gives man his fullness, which is as natural and necessary to his growth as the separation–individuation, independence, individuality, and freedom which are the guiding principles of conventional masculine development.

Intersubjective theory sees the relationship between self and other, with its tension between sameness and difference, as a continual exchange of influence. It focuses not on a linear movement from oneness to separateness but on the paradoxical balance between them. [p. 49]

It is from this tension that relationships go awry. The need for domination grows from a feeling of threat and insecurity with this sense of differentness. There comes a realization that one cannot entirely possess that which one loves, needs, and is somewhat dependent on. On the other hand, a fear of being overly dependent, engulfed by, or absorbed by the other can make sameness feel threatening and thus provide fuel to the need for separateness.

It is also true that we in the Western world are unfamiliar with and uncomfortable with paradox. We seek a type of arrangement and organization to our affairs that is constructed as if with bricks, visibly layered, one on top of another, hierarchical, sequential, and linear. Something is either a wall or it is not a wall. It is either finished or unfinished. It begins here and ends there. It can be anticipated, controlled. It will stay where we left it. It will remain the same. We are we and it is it. We are subject, it is object.

Daily in my office I hear people struggling to understand other people and affairs of the heart in precisely the same way. It is difficult and often impossible to get them to see that none of that applies. In this realm everything is fluid. Nothing stays still. There is no beginning or end to be seen. There is no absolute control. Nothing is entirely predictable. One is never finished. Each person is many different, sometimes opposite and contradictory things all at once. Each couple is separate *and* together. Each is both dependent and independent, or should be. Each person's way of being toward the other comes from him- or herself and is created by the other at the same time, together, in proportions that cannot be separated or quantified. There is indeed uncertainty in the realization that another cannot be entirely known. Yet there is an ecstasy in the discoveries that yield communion.

This is not the way we are trained to think, nor is it

how even complex material is presented in history, biology, or even psychology, so it is difficult even for adults to tolerate the tension in the idea that the one we love is both different from us, yet sometimes the same, or that we are separate from the one we need yet at times merged into one. There is terror in the extremes. There is terror in its seemingly capricious variability, like a boom loose on a ship, swinging to and fro and likely to take our heads off. To be separate or different can mean the calming, simplified safety of emotional distance. On the other hand, it can mean emptiness and loneliness, to be cut adrift. To be as one or the same can yield the bliss of feeling understood, validated, recognized by someone whom one respects, not being alone. It can also mean loss of autonomy, freedom, independence, absorption into another, emotional risk, dependency, anxiety over loss.

> Perhaps, also because of a continuing fear that dependency on the other is a threat to independence, that recognition of the other compromises the self. When the conflict between dependence and independence becomes too intense, the psyche gives up the paradox in favor of an opposition. Polarity, the conflict of opposites, replaces the balance within the self. This polarity sets the stage for defining the self in terms of a movement away from dependency. It also sets the stage for domination. [Benjamin 1988, p. 50]

I am speaking primarily of men here but women are included in this too. Some opt for separateness or domination as many men do. The difference is that men are "supposed to" and women aren't. Men can back it up with force that, until very recently in this country, was sanctioned by law. Domination of men by their female partners is a rarer and different matter, one left to some other writer of some other book.

Freud believed that man couldn't tolerate the "tension" and would inevitably either seek domination or accept submission. He did not feel it was within the nature of humans to tolerate the paradox, the delicate balance of mutuality. He believed that ultimately, inevitably, it must give way in one direction or the other.

Benjamin, on the other hand, explains that one is compensated for the loss of absolute sovereignty or specious certainty by the pleasure of sharing and communion with an always somewhat unknown equal. To be recognized and to recognize ourselves in another and another in ourselves is among our greatest pleasures and a natural and distinctly human need. It is a need difficult to satisfy between master and slave.

Recognition is central to the intersubjective view and to healthy relationships.

Recognition is that response from the other which makes meaningful the feelings, intentions and actions of the self. It allows the self to realize its agency and authorship in a tangible way. But such recognition can only come from an other whom we, in turn, recognize as a person in his or her own right. [Benjamin 1988, p. 12]

In other words recognition, to be of any value, cannot come from one who is demeaned, negated, rejected, devalued, or dominated to the point where he or she is a virtual nonentity.

What begins as separation and dismissal of dependency or even closeness to the mother evolves as antipathy toward girls during latency years and reaches an often incomplete and uneasy rapprochement with older girls and women in adolescence and adulthood. The nurturance, caring, and empathy that love at this age calls for can feel like a pull toward feminization to the male. For the dominating male, love can feel like a slide back toward dependency, helplessness, and weakness. It may be countered, when the anxiety or revulsion becomes too great, by a kind of hypermasculinity that features his assertion of superiority, an insistence that *she* be dependent on *him* and a repudiation and devaluation of all things feminine, including most of the qualities necessary for what even approaches mature love or the intersubjective relationship.

The fact remains, however, that the ideal man must also have a female mate. He should be attractive to females and attracted to them. Furthermore, there is expected to exist in the heterosexual male a deep desire to love, be loved, and live those needs out within a committed relationship. So how are these opposing forces reconciled and what does it look like when they are not? It looks like fear, disguised as tyranny. The dominating male is one who has not been able to return to what has been called the "feminine." He has not been able to achieve rapprochement with those giving, sharing, and caring qualities that love requires, nor has he been able to give up enough of his identity and independence to "recognize" another, especially in a love relationship. Instead, he demands that she lose herself entirely within him. He cannot tolerate the tension of intersubjectivity. He cannot tolerate the uncertainties and risks which characterize love. It must be remembered that at bottom, the dominating male is painfully insecure, needy, and lacking in personal strength born of confidence and self-esteem. He believes he cannot survive alone. For him the risk of loss of love, of his one sustaining preserver is viewed as not just very hurtful, as in a normal adolescent, but literally catastrophic. His ability to love is further impaired and distorted by a fearful view of woman as a deadly, dangerous goddess. She is one who may not be completely known or possessed, yet is desperately needed, the source of inexpressible comfort and pleasure yet capable of annihilating him inside and out.

Hindu mythology in all its lush, gaudy, baroque splendor embodies the dual character of love and woman in the figure of the goddess Kali. This description is taken from Joseph Campbell.

> The temple image displayed the divinity in her two aspects simultaneously, the terrible and the benign. Her four arms exhibited the symbols of her universal power: the upper left hand brandishing a bloody saber, the lower gripping by the hair a severed human head; the upper right was lifted in the "fear not" gesture, the lower extended in bestowal of boons. As necklace she wore a garland of human heads; her kilt was a girdle of human arms; her long tongue was out to lick blood. She was Cosmic Power, the totality of the universe, the harmonization of all the pairs of opposites, combining wonderfully the terror of absolute destruction with an impersonal yet motherly reassurance. As change, the river of time, the fluidity of life, the goddess at once creates, preserves, and destroys. Her name is Kali, the Black One; her title: The Ferry across the Ocean of Existence. [Campbell 1949, p. 115]

She is present in every story about the siren whose sweet allure sends men crashing to their destruction, in every song about the attraction and danger of the love of woman.

> Love hurts
> Love scars
> Love wounds and mars
> Any heart not tough
> Nor strong enough
> To take a lot of pain
> Take a lot of pain

Love is like a cloud
Holds a lot of rain

I'm young
I know
But even so
I know a thing or two
I've learned from you
I've really learned a lot
really learned a lot
Love is like a stove
Burns you when it's hot

Love hurts
Love hurts

Some fools think of happiness
Blissfulness
Togetherness
Some fools fool themselves
I guess
But they're not fooling me
I know it isn't true
Know it isn't true
Love is just a lie
Made to make you blue
> ["Love Hurts," lyrics by Boudleaux Bryant]

DOMINATION AND THE INTOLERANCE
OF UNCERTAINTY

One way to protect oneself from the risk of the pain of love is to take love prisoner, to capture and enslave it and never let it escape. All tyrants, dictators, and despots use this type of control to eliminate what for them are the intolerable risks and uncertainties of the relationship between themselves and their people whose adoration they depend on for their existence, invariably crave, then demand. History and the private lives of anonymous men are filled with this struggle. Throughout history, man, particularly in the West, supported by his religions, has believed in the possibility of control and certainty in all things, even in the natural world of emotions and relationships. Men have been, and still are, told that certainty exists in our notions of nationalism and patriotism, and in their respective theologies, and in promises to guarantee absolutely love, now and in the future, in marriage vows.

In 1972 a wonderful series aired on public television. It was hosted by a physicist and philosopher named Jacob Bronowski, a Polish Jew who escaped the fate of most of his relatives by leaving Europe before Hitler's net fell. Later he worked at Los Alamos with the team that developed the atomic bomb. In his television series, *The Ascent of Man*, based on his book of the same name, he described the history of man's growing understanding of his world, his universe, and his place in it. In Chapter 11 (of 13 chapters), which is entitled "Knowledge or Certainty," he brings the reader into the twentieth century and describes man's continuing struggle with the tolerance and acceptance of uncertainty and the tragic consequences of the insistence on absolute certainty.

In 1927 Werner Heisenberg, a German physicist, wrote a paper based on his studies of the properties and characteristics of the electron. In it he said that it is the nature of the electron that it will yield only limited information. Its movements, speed, direction, its starting point or end point, cannot be precisely known. (There's more to it, but this much is enough and already more than I understand.)

Heisenberg called this the Principle of Uncertainty. In one sense, it is a robust principle of the everyday. We know that we cannot ask the world to be exact. If an object (a familiar face, for example) had to be *exactly* the same before we recognized it, we would never recognize it from one day to the next. We recognize the object to be the same because it is much the same; it is never exactly like it was, it is tolerably like. In the act of recognition, a judgment is built in—in an area of tolerance or uncertainty. So Heisenberg's principle says that no events, not even atomic events, can be described with certainty, that is, with zero tolerance. [Bronowski 1973, p. 365]

Bronowski, though, prefers to call this the Principle of Tolerance, and this is why.

All knowledge, all information between human beings can only be exchanged within a play of tolerance. And that is true whether the exchange is in science, or in literature, or in religion, or in politics, or even in any form of thought that aspires to dogma. [p. 365]

Here at the end he is referring to the dogma that was National Socialism and its brutal insistence on absolute knowledge, absolute power that nearly blackened the earth forever.

What quantum physics has found anew is the old but difficult truth that nothing can be known completely and absolutely. There is a degree of uncertainty that must be tolerated, and within degrees of comfort learning can proceed. It is a truth we are not taught and not prepared for. It challenges us most painfully in our closest, most needed relationships, where the stakes are highest and the desire for certainty so great. Yet we cannot have it, other than tolerably. Domination arises when tolerably is not enough.

A dictator behaves much as the dominating and abusive male in love behaves and for much the same reasons. His status, identity, stability, well-being depend entirely upon his relationship with his people. This relationship is usually a good one at first, mutually supportive and generally benign, yet his position is an unsteady one. He is new and he distrusts its instability, and cringes within at the uncertainty of it. He fears and loathes the presence or prospect of rival suitors for the people's affections, so he eliminates them like a jealous lover. His distrust and insecurity, however, do not leave him. As time goes on he feels exposed and sees how far would be his fall if he could not maintain his position with the people. He cannot trust them to keep him so he controls them. The realization that control is always incomplete only causes him to increase his efforts at control. He spies on them with the inevitable secret police. When there are problems in the land they are blamed on others, outside influences or negative or disloyal elements within the people. He grows paranoid. He doesn't stop at seeking to control their behavior and preventing their choosing another; he attempts to control their minds as well through propaganda, a cult of personality, a virtual deification in some cases. Terror and abuse break their will to resist, paralyze them with fear, and demonstrate his unassailable power. In the end, though, he usually ends up alone, isolated by his paranoia and, paradoxically, out of control. A man holds water within his hands best if he supports it gently with open palms. The dominating man believes he must enclose it, must hold it tight, squeeze it to keep it, only to find it running through his fingers and his hands become more empty the more he squeezes. The Chinese symbol meaning "to oppress" also represents "to be in difficulty." It is a truth he is unable to grasp.

For the dominating male and his mate, if he succeeds at mastery to too great a degree he loses essential recognition from the mastered female. His domination will have so diminished her that she becomes a nonentity, and a nothing can provide nothing. As Benjamin (1988) says, "Control, as we have seen, tends to become self-defeating. . . . The master is actually alone because the person he is with is no person at all" (p. 65). Or they are driven away. Such is the ultimate fate of all would-be despots as well as the fate of all the "little men" who would be kings when they refuse to recognize their mate as an equal, independent, and legitimate person, when they fail to give up and risk themselves with another.

There is a lovely Irish myth which tells, in its magical way, the value and the rewards of taking the risk. There are many tales like it in all parts of the world. Its universality speaks of the universality of this dilemma. For females it is the tale of the maiden taking the risk of love and kissing the frog to find for herself a prince and bliss.

This is the tale of Niall, one of the five sons of the Irish king Eochaid, as related by Joseph Campbell (1949) in his great work *The Hero With A Thousand Faces*.

> . . . having gone one day ahunting, they [the five sons] found themselves astray, shut in on every hand. Thirsty, they set off, one by one, to look for water. Fergus was the first: and he lights on a well, over which he finds an old woman standing sentry. The fashion of the hag is this: blacker than coal every joint and segment of her was, from crown to ground; comparable to a wild horse's tail the grey wiry mass of hair that pierced her scalp's upper surface; with her sickle of a greenish looking tusk that was in her head and curled till it touched her ear, she could lop the verdant branch of an oak in full bearing; blackened and smokebleared eyes she had; nose awry, wide-nostrilled; a

wrinkled and freckled belly, variously unwholesome; warped crooked shins, garnished with massive ankles and a poir of capacious shovels; knotty knees she had and livid nails. The beldame's whole description in fact was disgusting. "That's the way it is, is it?" said the lad, and "that's the very way," she answered. "Is it guarding the well thou art?" he asked, and she said: "it is." "Dost thou licence me to take away some water?" "I do," she consented, "yet only so that I have of thee one kiss on my cheek." "Not so," said he. "Then water shall not be conceded by me." "My word I give," he went on, "that sooner than give thee a kiss I would perish of thirst!" Then the young man departed to the place where his brethren were, and told them that he had not gotten water.

Olioll, Brian, and Fiachra, likewise, went on the quest and equally attained to the identical well. Each solicited the old thing for water, but denied her the kiss.

Finally it was Niall who went, and he came to the very well. "Let me have water, woman!" he cried. "I will give it," said she, "and bestow on me a kiss." He answered: "forby giving thee a kiss, I will even hug thee!" Then he bends to embrace her, and gives her a kiss. Which operation ended, and when he looked at her, in the whole world was not a young woman of gait more graceful, in universal semblance fairer than she: to be likened to the last-fallen snow lying in trenches every portion of her was, from crown to sole; plump and queenly forearms, fingers long and taper, straight legs of a lovely hue she had; two sandals of the white bronze betwixt her smooth and soft white feet and the earth; about her was an ample mantle of the choicest fleece, pure crimson, and in the garment a brooch of white silver; she had lustrous teeth of pearl, great regal eyes, mouth red as the rowanberry. "Here, woman, is a galaxy of charms," said the young man. "That is true indeed." "And who art thou?" he pursued. "Royal Rule am I," she answered, and uttered this:

"King of Tara! I am Royal Rule. . . . Go now," she said,

"to thy brethren, and take with thee water; moreover, thine and thy children's for ever the kingdom and supreme power shall be. . . . And as at the first thou hast seen me ugly, brutish, loathly—in the end, beautiful—even so is royal rule: for without battles, without fierce conflict, it may not be won; but in the result, he that is king of no matter what shows comely and handsome forth." [pp. 116–118]

The hero in this case is the man with the "gentle heart," the one who comes with the "kindness and assurance she requires." What makes him a hero is his courage to take the plunge, to open himself to the other and accept the risk and uncertainty of giving himself up. The risks are ugly. But one must be mature and secure to accept that life and death, hard and easy, go together, that true satisfaction comes from giving up as well as taking in and that one can and must lose to gain. An acceptance of all this and the dangers of the quest is the path of a noble king and a true man.

Unfortunately, American mythology includes too few heroes of this sort. Our heroes, rather, tend to be those who have chosen the safer, less bold, more limited course, the "freedom" of the lone wolf, particularly our most "macho" heroes. Like Niall's brothers they have opted out of the game altogether. Their path is one of abnegation. Seldom is modeled for our young the fuller, stronger middle course of open mature love.

Think of the *Gunsmoke* series wherein Sheriff Matt Dillon went decades without a date. The men in *Bonanza*, the father and all three adult sons, lived at home together without women in their lives and with little more than a red-faced, shuffle-footed snickering early adolescent interest in them. Chuck Connors, *The Rifleman*, like Ben Cartwright, had a woman written out of his life by widowhood, thus allowing both to be lone, independent, strong men as well as fathers of sons. Neither Zorro nor the Lone Ranger had serious relations with women. Superman avoided Lois Lane. The Batman of the past remained apart.

In the world of the movies, John Wayne, Gary Cooper, Clint Eastwood, among others, hold all emotions but anger deep inside. Their flat emotionality and solitary stance have been presented as strengths of character, as ideals.

James Bond represents another kind of free male, the type who plays with many women sexually but always dances smirking away before it can become anything more.

Always we are given the impression that if any of these men were to have fallen in love and let a woman into his life fully, he would immediately have been diminished, lost some of his vitality, power, effectiveness, and initiative. The story would have dulled and disappointed us male viewers.

So often we have seen the male lead cast off the clinging female, ignore her entreaties, her influence, and her love in order to venture forth into righteous glory and become, therefore, the hero. It is often the critical moment of the film, particularly the older films, and without it the film could not end in the proper fashion. Triumphant film endings often include both the vanquishing of the evil enemy and the male hero going off by himself, riding into the sunset, as it were, in noble solitude.

It is not always this way of course. In *Rocky*, as macho a film as you're likely to find, Sylvester Stallone's relationship with Talia Shire is clearly as important to him and the development of his character as the big fight. Robert Duvall's Oscar-winning performance in *Tender Mercies* is really about nothing else but his personal growth out of alcoholism, failure, and reclusiveness through a relationship with a woman and her son. In *Moonstruck*, Cher softens the hardened, embittered Nicholas Cage and brings him to life.

Yet it would be wrong to deny that film has given heavy treatment and great honor to the man who is great or becomes great partly because he will not be attached to women or be influenced by mature feelings of love. These are the men who, for generations now, have caught the eye and stirred the heart of American males. As a kid growing up, my predominant image of women in movies and television, when portrayed in situations of danger or crisis, was of a person screaming uselessly or incessantly, falling and spraining her ankle when she and the hero were trying to make their escape, thus encumbering and endangering the hero. It used to annoy the hell out of me even though it was a scene used so frequently you could predict it. And my anger would be at her, not at the manipulative director. Women just always seemed to be in the way of, or a threat to, the man doing the courageous, dangerous, exciting thing. For a man to be a man in America, he must be free of that. He must be as free, to use a country-western term, as the tumbling tumbleweed. Depicting women as whining nuisances helped minimize their attractiveness, reducing their influence on the independence of the male hero. Such characterizations of females as overwrought incompetents also supports the notion that if a man must consort with one, he must and should dominate her, since she certainly can't cope by herself. Domination or disinterest are the two relationship styles most commonly modeled—what Jessica Benjamin (1988) describes as the "negative ideal of freedom: freedom as release from bondage, individuality stripped bare of its relationship with and need for others" (p. 188).

MALE STATUS, SELF-ESTEEM, AND THE PROBLEM OF ABUSE

Much of what troubles the dominating male and what leads him to bring a world of trouble to his female mate has to do with his struggles to achieve and maintain a particular identity and feeling about himself. He is, like most other men in most other times, trying to be something he can live with and be proud of. As a man, he is trying to be a man. As an adolescent male, he is trying to become a man, with a view less and less clear of what exactly a "man" is. At one time this was a relatively uncomplicated and straightforward progression. Men's roles, their positions in society and the family, were set by custom, law, and the social position of the family. A man's choice of occupation was limited and guided within very narrow possibilities. His opportunities for education were limited by class, family status, and money. Often he would simply follow the trade of his father, or become apprenticed in some other occupation that was available within the village, town, or city in keeping with his social class, education, and economic resources. But choices were very few by today's standards.

Men began their occupational careers early. Adolescence was short or nonexistent for all but the upper classes. There was little or no time for a young fellow to languish in uncertainty about what to be. Choices, too, as I have said, were generally either very limited or nonexistent. Aspirations, therefore, were limited and circumscribed as well. The son of a lower-middle-class tradesman generally did not suppose that he would rise much higher than that. He did not seriously contemplate greater wealth, status, or a very different type of life than that of his family of origin. Society was ordered tightly in layers that were very difficult to penetrate or move through.

Nothing like the rather limitless social mobility that exists now in the most advanced of the world's industrial and open societies. Consequently, with ambitions more humble, horizons more limited, and expectations clear, disappointment, confusion, and a feeling of failure were less the plague than they are today.

At home, the man was nearly always either the only wage earner or at least the major one. Economic clout and tradition, backed up by laws regarding occupation, wages, and property ownership, and the very great influence of the church truly made the man the master of his house, if that's the way he wanted it to be. Not long ago a man's wife and children were viewed by law and custom literally as his property, to be dealt with, even sold, as he saw fit. In any case, as with a man's position in the world outside the home, there was little ambiguity or insecurity regarding his position in the home. He did not need to create, within an unstructured vacuum, his own individual role or place. Social law and custom did it for him and helped him to uphold it.

Granted this was a far more restrictive, less free and open world for men as well as women. There was little of this "you can be whatever you want to be if you try hard enough" stuff that the past few generations of American men (and now women) have grown up saddled with. It isn't true, yet it's truer than it ever has been anywhere else on Earth. Nearly everyone believes it.

What one can be has certainly blown wide open in modern America. Few of the restrictions or narrow traditions of earlier times in Europe or the United States continue to stand so powerfully or absolutely. The poor can become rich in one generation. A laborer's son or daughter can access quality education and become a doctor, lawyer, scientist, or professor if their talent allows them to. And no one in America does what his father did for work. While it's still fairly common in Europe, here it seems to be viewed as rather a lack of imagination, individuality, and initiative to so follow.

How one can be has also broadened widely within the past two generations. How a man or woman looks, dresses, behaves, what he or she does for work, hobbies, their sexual preference have all burst their heretofore narrow boundaries and continue to spread ever wider.

These developments, in most people's view, are good things. Our society values, above nearly all else, open opportunities for self-determination. We feel that we all should be able to create ourselves afresh, drawing only from our own abilities, predilections, and interests, to be and do what we feel most suited for rather than what our father did or our village offers or the government needs at the time. This is one of the advantages of life in a free and open society.

However, it doesn't come free. It comes at the price of a lot of confusion, uncertainty, insecurity, failure, and craziness. It is very difficult to decide in which direction to head when so many directions are possible. It is very difficult to know what to be if you can be anything. When everything seems possible it can feel nearly impossible to know what to do. This is why adolescence in this century has gotten longer and longer and is filled with more and more trouble and difficulty. In place of the old strangling predetermination in life and work now comes the desperation and panic of getting lost. Furthermore, as higher education and technical skill have become increasingly a prerequisite for entry into any decently paying occupation, the preparation for independent adulthood has become more prolonged and difficult to achieve.

One cannot so easily take the old simpler route and follow his father into his occupation. While this is still possible in family-owned businesses and within the trades, they are becoming smaller islands in a sea of white-collar occupations. Franchise operations are taking over the family-owned businesses, reducing steadily a parent–owner's prerogative for taking a son or daughter into the business. In a franchise-owned business, they wouldn't have the control to do so.

Still, the idealized image of a man in America is of one who holds a calm and easy control over himself and his surroundings. He's in control of his life, of where he is and where he's headed. He's on top of things and feels little doubt of it. He is strong of mind and body. He is certainly in control of his woman, giving up little of his independence to her. He is moving upward, steadily, inexorably.

Many, if not most, American corporations look with suspicion if not contempt upon any employee who does not continuously strive for advancement. Anyone seeking to simply maintain a position he finds enjoyable and satisfying risks being considered unmotivated. He or she is pushed to advance because it is believed he will inevitably become dissatisfied otherwise. Anyone asking for a demotion from the stress and responsibility of some level of management would, at best, not be believed; at worst, he would be fired.

The ideal male possesses some of the qualities of the finest generals. He prevails in concrete terms with clear-headed and forceful management of his circumstances. He knows his purpose, his goal, and has the control and vigor to carry it through.

In fact, generals tend to merely plan as best they can against unforeseeable eventualities and then react to the inevitable chaos as best they can, relying in the end on luck and the interplay of others. It is much the same for the average man. Few can match the ideal. It is becoming easier and easier to fail, to feel emasculated, out of control and powerless. When the individual male holds to this traditional, unfair, and out-of-date model of masculinity, and then fails to live up to it, he is at risk for trouble. For some, compensation will arise within their love relationships, that world-within-a-world, wherein some men will seek to live out a type of lordship and mastery that they feel they must have but cannot find in the world outside.

The world outside has changed steadily and dramatically around men, yet many have failed to realize it and adjust. Ever since the rise of capitalism and the industrial state, women have progressively succeeded in prying open the door that once only their foot was painfully wedged in, and have entered the world of work, first as subsidiaries but increasingly as the equals of men at many levels. Men no longer hold a monopoly on wage earning. Women are acquiring, albeit slowly and with quite a way to go, access to economic independence. Custom, law, and the church no longer stand in the way.

Men fought this tooth and nail but economics prevailed. Owners saw the wisdom in hiring women at lower wages than men for many jobs since technology was rapidly reducing the advantage or need for physical strength. Women were still paid less than men for equal work, but they were working. Man's only recourse was to say "A woman's place is in the home" and get women to say it and believe it, too.

Since males have historically viewed masculinity as the opposite of femininity and masculinity as superior to femininity, seeing a female doing the same job that he does has been difficult for some to swallow. Similarly, a female's equal or superior achievements in education, earnings, occupational level, or status is seen by some as an intolerable challenge to their own masculinity. For if, as the traditional male view holds, females are by nature inferior to males, it is a sorry sample of a male who is merely equal to or even surpassed in status by his mate. He feels that she is appropriating his masculinity and thereby diminishing him, thereby feminizing him, and that is going too far. This blow to his self-esteem and self-image is particularly problematic to the male who has fallen back upon his love relationship, his relationship with his female mate, as the little world in which he can be lord and master. If it is here and in this way that his self-esteem derives, then the advancement of women becomes a serious, even life-challenging threat. After all, this isn't Salem of 1692. He no longer has the church and state to hold him up by striking women down.

Research on abuse and domination in dating and marital relations adds some empirical validation to some of the concepts being discussed. Surveys of large numbers of college students have found that while female attitudes toward women's social role have changed with the times, men's views of women's social role have not kept pace. Spence and colleagues (1972) surveyed over 1,400 male and female college students and found that males held a significantly more traditional view of women's social roles than the females did. A reassessment of the same survey question carried out ten years later by Bernard and Bernard (1981) found virtually the same disparity in attitudes between the sexes.

Rates of male abuse of female mates have consistently been found to be highest in couples where the female stands above the male in socially important areas. Gelles, in his book *The Violent Home* (1972), reported that the greatest rates of both overall violence and frequent violence occurred in couples where the man's occupational status was lower than the woman's. Conversely, the greatest rates of nonviolence were seen where the man's job was more prestigious than the woman's.

Straus and colleagues, in their book *Behind Closed Doors* (1980), reported severe violence rates two to three times higher against females where the male partner was unemployed, employed only part-time, or disabled. Others have found high unemployment rates among women abusers (Eisenberg and Micklow 1977, Gayford 1975, Hilberman and Munson 1984, Prescott and Letko 1977, Star et al. 1979).

Regarding educational levels, Gelles (1972) found rates of woman abuse highest among men with some high school education (short of graduating), with decreasing levels as level of education increased. He also found a trend for violent male partners to be less educated than their nonviolent male neighbors. O'Brien (1971) reported that 44 percent of violent husbands, compared to 18 percent of nonviolent ones, had dropped out of either high school or college. Comparatively, O'Brien found that 56 percent of his violent husbands were less educated than their wives. Only 14 percent of the nonviolent husbands were less well-educated. The very highest rate of marital violence in Gelles' (1972) large study was among couples where the male was less educated. Carlson (1984) found that in almost 45 percent of 58 couples studied who experienced woman abuse, the man was less educated than the woman.

Clearly, there is a subgroup of men who cannot tolerate sharing or giving up to their female partner an image of superior status in certain socially approved status areas. Their self-esteem as men cannot bear any demeaning suggestion. Their traditional beliefs about sex roles and image consume and discolor much of their feelings within the relationship. Other unrelated aspects of the relationship get sucked in and contaminated leaving, for some, little left to be enjoyed, punctuated by violent episodes.

Men holding and aspiring to traditional masculine identities, who see themselves as failures in the world outside the home, outside their love relationship, often become increasingly frustrated when they see themselves as second-rate to their female mate as well. This is a formula for trouble. Males holding very traditional masculine identities can be trouble even when there is no clear status difference between themselves and their mates.

Bernard and colleagues (1985) surveyed college students in a study called "Courtship Violence and Sex-typing." They found a very strong correlation between traditional male self-image and physical abuse of the man's female dating partner. More specifically, the males most likely to be abusive were those who not only held very strong masculine identities but who seemed also not to possess "feminine" characteristics. Bernard and colleagues stated:

> It seems that those males who chose to endorse those characteristics our culture had traditionally considered masculine while rejecting those considered feminine (e.g., tenderness, compassion, gentleness) were more likely to abuse the women with whom they were romantically involved. [p. 575]

The lack of acceptance of or access to feminine qualities within themselves, even within the context of a love relationship, was as critical an issue as the strong, traditional male identity. In the study findings, the problem this presents was clearly borne out.

The study went on to say that strong, non-submissive females tended to receive the most abuse from this type of male, suggesting that "the more sex-typed masculine male is more likely to respond with aggressive (e. g., abu-

sive) behavior when he perceives that his status is threatened by his partner" (p. 575). Other research, however,
has not generally supported a view that strong women are
more likely to be abused.

How then, given all of this, is the American man to
love? Given the preparation of history, culture, and tradition, how can he come to relate or to love in an attitude
of tolerable safety, comfort, and enjoyment, in a manner
that is mutually respectful and satisfying to both the male
and the female? How can he do so maturely, or inter-
subjectively? How can he be a male, an American man,
and give love to a woman?

American men are raised in a tradition that has taught
that the female is inferior in the eyes of God, poorly constructed in terms of mental ability and emotional balance,
not fully capable of independent existence. She is likely
either to rush mindlessly toward trouble or fall prey to it.
He has been led to believe that she is impulsive, at the
mercy of emotional urges. She's a siren and a temptress,
a hapless victim and a child among wolves. She cannot
be trusted on her own. How then is the man to give up a
belief in the need and propriety of domination? How difficult is it for the woman not to agree?

It is taught to males and females alike that the man is
the captain of his life and of those who are a part of him.
As captain he must keep his head and not be guided too
greatly by dangerous and murky emotions. He strives for
a full, clear sense of the present and future and is uncomfortable with the tension of uncertainty, as any captain
would be. He must avoid vulnerability.

Yet, having cast off as infantile, regressive, dangerous,
and feminine the emotional qualities needed for a loving
relationship, how can he love? What sense then can he
make of the deep, raw, visceral need that rises within him
for love and recognition with a woman? How can he make

use of these feelings, which may seem to be driving him in an uncertain and possibly perilous direction?

If he is unable to loosen and express this swelling tide, to love with the latent "feminine" within him and let go of the mighty masculine dams which contain it, the feelings can find no adequate outlet. They can achieve no satisfying gratification. They rail and rumble frighteningly, persistently, and still only having her brings him any peace at all.

The man who seeks an easing of the tension, who must regain a tolerable emotional condition and maintain his "masculinity" but who cannot give up the woman, will sometimes choose the fateful compromise of domination. He solves the paradox of love and masculinity by the flawed compromise of control. His fears of a love which may give to a woman the opportunity to hurt him, deprive him, engulf or abandon him, gives her a power of emotional annihilation which makes her an awesome and fearful figure—Kali incarnate, holding his hand, dangling him over a cliff. The only way out without actually getting out and riding into the sunset is to take away her power. If he can reduce her, strip her of her self-confidence, she will be dependent on him. She must be made too weak to hurt or abandon him. He thereby calms some of his several fears.

This sounds good on paper, a neat arrangement but an essentially unreal one. The perfect balance, bringing with it the perfect blend of ecstatic love and complete safety, cannot be maintained. For the young man whose self-esteem is particularly low and whose preoccupation with masculine identity is too traditional and too strong, the balance cannot hold. His need for recognition and validation from another will remain strong but his ability to feel in control and effectively dominant will still be lacking. His love will yield him always less than he needs and leave him howling at the moon in anger and frustration.

Then may begin his descent into the dark, obsessive, always unsatisfying whirl of jealousy and possessiveness. In the end he is left thrashing like a desperate child in the waters he has fouled.

Caroline and John II

Caroline sits in her last period class with her head bowed over her open notebook, writing steadily a long letter to a friend away at college. The drone of the history lecture passes by above her. She remains oblivious below it, absorbed within her thoughts and the soothing, focused exercise of writing. It allows her to suspend herself for the time being between the past and the future, between her upsetting morning and what is to be her upsetting evening. The school called her father reporting her late with John again. Suspended as well between a recollection of her relationship's confusing past and its certain-to-be-difficult future, between the image of its beginning and the feared debacle of its conclusion. It takes her away as well from her place and her present, carrying her outward to another place and another existence within the seemingly better and different world of her friend. So she is at ease and writes without pause or effort as page after page fills. She feels that she has flown above herself and is able to look down and see herself, John, their relationship, and the status of her life in general clearly, dispassionately. She can see where it comes from and where it is headed. And she watches herself along the way, happy, like a fool; fooled, like an idiot. She sees what she has and what she's lost. Snapshot scenes click into her mind. And the impotence of her anger, her railings, her complaints, her conversations splashing loudly but ineffectually against his rocky shore, rebound upon her mind. Yet the impact of these memories is little in comparison to the emptiness and terror she feels when she projects herself forward into the scene of a life without him. And for this she despises herself most of all. In a letter to a friend, she writes:

> I have been a fool and I am a fool but I wasn't always. I used to be a good kid. I was thinking about what I was like a year ago, before John, and I was so much better then. Not great, of course, but better, I think. Home sucked, but I was never in trouble. In school I never had a worry. I went, did my homework, hardly studied and got mostly A's and B's. I never got a D yet. I never (hardly ever) lied to my parents. I swam. I had girlfriends (I only miss a couple of them). I talked to a lot of people. It was fun wondering if I liked a kid and if he liked me. It was frustrating that none hardly ever talked to me and I never went with anyone but still it was exciting sometimes. Do you know that I never kissed a boy until 10th grade? Yes, I lied about Frank, and Matt too. Don't tell anyone. I was a big loser, it's true, but it was simple, at least. What else? Well, of course I was a virgin then, too. I'd never been afraid yet of being pregnant (naturally). I'd never had to drive out of town by myself to buy condoms because a *jerk* wouldn't do it. I could go on with this area for another ten pages but I don't want to gross you out. What else. I used to love to go to bed—to sleep. I looked forward to it. I'd hit the pillow, lie there for awhile thinking of things, fun things or things I hoped for or just fantasizing about good things. Then I'd just say to myself, OK, time to go to sleep, and snap, I'd be gone. Next thing I'd know, it was time to get up. I didn't like my alarm then any more than I do now, but at least I'd sleep straight through until it woke me up. I dread going to bed now. It's nothing but trouble and I can't hold a good scene or thought in my head. Then I get mad and that just makes it worse. So I get lousey [sic] sleep, the best part of which naturally comes right before the alarm goes off. I look like hell and it's killing my school. Grades are so-so. I'm worried now that I won't get into the colleges I used to be sure of. I have Mr. Mackey for guid-

ance and he's been on my ass constantly over it. I'm writing you this letter now in Madigan's class. We have a test tomorrow but I can't listen to this stuff. Don't you feel honored that I'm writing to you instead?

You know, I think I liked John at first mostly because he liked me and it seemed he really meant it. Him and his friends were friends with my friends and that made it easier. My friends called him a "geek" but they liked him. He didn't have a bad reputation with girls. He was funny (looking). Actually, he was funny. Also, the Junior Prom was coming up so we could all go together as a big group. So it was perfect. I liked him right away but I didn't really consider him as much more than friend material. But I liked the idea of having a boyfriend for a change. Plus, it got me out of the house and away from my girlfriends when I couldn't stand to be with them. Another thing was that I thought I could trust him completely. I never once thought of him cheating on me and I still hardly ever do, which is good, because I'm a very distrustful, jealous person and I couldn't stand a relationship that gave me any worries like that at all.

After we got started (hope I'm not boring you, because I know you already know some of this but it's good for me to go over it. I know, bring this letter with you to that mind-numbing philosophy class of yours and read the rest of this there. I won't seem so boring then). So after we got started, he constantly amazed me with how much he cared about me. He surprised me all the time. At that time my mother and I were having a lot of trouble with my stepfather (hereafter referred to as Doug, since I vomit at the use of the word "father" in any association to him). That could be a whole letter all by itself. Don't worry! I won't go into it except to say that she was stuck with him but I didn't have to be. So talking to John or going out with him gave me an out. (This is all before I moved in with my father, remember.) This was great because my friends, as you know, were completely unreliable, unavailable, unbearable back then. So it was him and me and that was fine. We saw each other all the time and practically no one else. I couldn't believe it that he could choose me over his own friends just like that. I'd never heard of any guy doing that. As for his looks, I thought he was cute. Not sexy, but I couldn't have handled that anyway because of my jealousy. Plus, he *hated* Doug. I liked that because whenever I complained to my friends about him they'd either go right into their own complaints about their father or stepfather or say "but he seems so cool with that Camaro." My mother couldn't hear any of it because she can't stand any stress and it just made her feel too guilty and depressed or she'd defend him by comparing him to my real father. Besides she always ends up thinking *I'm* the problem anyways. So it was great that John would listen to me about Doug and hate him too, even more than I did. But he'd put down my mother too, and that I didn't like, which I don't understand, since she hates me so much.

You remember the prom story, though. I thought it was so odd that he wanted to leave early. We were all having a great time. He even danced. I couldn't understand why he all of a sudden wanted to pull me out of there. He was actually physically pulling me. I didn't take him seriously. I wanted to stay 'till it was over along with everyone else in our car. I wanted to see who the Queen would be. Afterwards, everyone thought he wanted to get me outside alone to fool around but it was the Queen thing. I never told anyone the truth about that. He was paranoid I'd get chosen Queen and he'd have to stand there alone while everyone in the place looked at me and talked about me. I laughed in his face at the thought of it but he was serious. And then I got picked for the court and that was it. He was cold and vicious the rest of the night and just got drunk and made a big deal out of it and that I danced two dances with Ron, which he hadn't complained about at the time. Then he finally passed out. By the next day he still wasn't over it. He was still mad. But he didn't say much. He'd just give me a shot now and then, like saying how conceited I was or self-centered, call me "beauty queen" or put me down because I only made the court. It was crazy. He never once congratulated me or said one good thing to me about it. Even Doug was happy for me. So was my father. So it was a very strange night with great highs and lows. I can't think back on it without the bad part taking over my thoughts, though. So overall, I guess it was bad. I've been thinking that our whole relationship has been like that. Great highs and lows, but overall, not good. I know you're mad right now reading this because I never told anyone. I used to tell my mother things about him when I'd be mad at him. I told her about the time he caught me walking with Joe and smacked my books out of my arms at school on the stairs and they all went tumbling down the steps, papers everywhere, and me trying to gather it all up and not get my fingers stepped on by the crowds of assholes charging by. That's the last thing I ever told her though, because it just made her hate him and caused trouble for me seeing him. Plus, she'd tell Doug and I absolutely cannot stand taking it from him. So I don't tell her anything and there's less to argue about. I don't tell my father because of his thing with John's mother. [Her father was dating John's mother!] So he probably wouldn't believe me and if he did he'd probably go and kill John. Which reminds me. I'm gonna get killed when I get home tonight after work. John's made us late again this morning for the 54th time and they called my father. So I don't know what he's going to do this time.

What I'm saying though is that I'm afraid I've changed for the worse since you've been gone. I hope you don't notice. But I have to tell someone because I can't figure this out by myself. Well, gotta go. Period's ending. I'll finish this tonight. Bye.

Hi. Well, I'm afraid this is another one of my usual letters that takes a week to write. It's Sunday right now. Sorry I didn't finish this Thursday night when I said I would. It was a bad night. I didn't want to think about it or write about it or live it for that matter. But I had no choice on the 'live it' part.

I worked that night. I got home at 9:15. I was dead like I always am but it's usually worse on Thursday night beause I've had a week of bad sleep and early mornings by then. I had homework still left to do including two biology labs for Rivers (remember her?) and a Spanish test to study for. I'm so far behind. I got home and walked into a war. My father freaked on me. My mother was there, too. She's *never* over. I couldn't just walk away and shut myself in my room. It got real ugly. I was screaming. God, I hate to yell. Then he and my mother started going at it. I ran to my room but they kept at it for another 20 or 30 minutes, screaming as loud as they could. I'd think they were done and then it'd start again. I felt like a volcano. I was walking around my room full speed, talking and saying things. I wanted to explode myself and everything around me. I wanted to destroy everything and everyone. And the whole time the phone keeps ringing and they keep hanging it up. I knew it was John calling, mad that I hadn't called him yet. My mother probably knew it too and that's why she kept hanging up. I have to call him as soon as I get home or he gets jealous because he knows I work with Joe and Sean. Finally, I went to call him and my phone was gone. They'd taken it out of my room. So there was no way to talk to him or let him know what was going on over here. He must have thought it was me hanging up on him. So you know what he did? Now what's the worst possible thing that could have happened next? John came over. I could hear his car screeching around the corner and knew it was him even before he arrived. But I didn't even bother to go downstairs. I let them handle it. John did great. He swore at both of them then went out to the side yard and started yelling up at my window. By now I'm crying. I told him out the window just go and I'd see him tomorrow. He kept yelling at me to come outside. I wouldn't. So he started in on me and my whole family, calling me a baby, etc. Meanwhile, I've got my mother banging on my door, telling me to knock it off and shut the window before she calls the police on "that bum." He left. Not a good night.

So now it's Sunday and I'm grounded. I'm a senior in high school and I have to stay in the house. In a way, I don't mind. I need a break from John which I can blame on somebody else. He still blames me, of course, and says I should just say "the hell with them" and go out. He's been driving by all weekend flashing his high beams at my window or beeping but, thank God, he doesn't stop. Jeannie came by and my father let her in. She said John's been checking around everywhere all weekend making sure I haven't gone out or sneaked out without him. He doesn't even believe I'm in here. I feel bad for that boy. Anyway, it's been boring but peaceful and I've gotten a lot of school work done.

Well, that's enough insanity for now. See you at your Spring break. If you come home, that is.

Bye,
Caroline

3

"PAPER TIGER": CHARACTERISTICS OF THE DOMINATING MALE

The adolescent who is the male half of the focus of this book is one who strives desperately to achieve and maintain (two very different things, in this case) a sense of well-being that can exist only in direct relationship to the psychological demise of his female partner. As his efforts at control and domination progress and her life outside the relationship shrinks, as she is able to obtain less and less pleasure from sources other than through him, as her self-esteem and self-confidence are cut off from all that might bolster them and are steadily ground down, as she grows more unsure of herself and more dependent on him as her only way of feeling good about herself, no matter how inconstantly or unpredictably he may bestow that feeling upon her, from this and mainly this (perhaps only this) may he himself feel expanded, calm, and well. To the extent that she believes and behaves as if he were her only source of oxygen, without which she must gasp, writhe, and die, he is gratified.

On the surface he is many kinds of person. He is handsome and homely, tall and short, well-dressed and slovenly, smart, dumb, an excellent student or a high-school dropout. He may be rich, poor, or anything in between. He may be, to the outside observer, successful, talented, popular, and confident, or he may be blatantly unattractive, a loner, utterly failed and incapable of managing life.

His outward appearance, even his manner at school or work, among friends, family, or on a first date may indicate nothing of what is inside him (or lacking inside him) that propels his need to cajole and force relationships in this direction. Each of these men, however, despite his external manner or the impression or feel of the first thin layers of his personality, harbors a deep and yawning emptiness. It is precisely his lack of a positive, confident, secure sense of self, his hollow self-esteem, his full-bodied dependency on another to make him feel good that causes him to establish this "tin-pot" dictatorship over his female mate.

His efforts may be sly, secret, couched in the words of love and festooned with gifts. His acts will often appear to fall within the bounds of traditional masculine behavior in the eyes of many. Thus his efforts may proceed barely noticed or recognized, even by the girl. Even when it grows clear that he seeks, must have, the power and glory of a king, complete with divine right, it may be accepted with a blasé shrug as his traditional role, or viewed with unconcern as a "benevolent monarchy."

It is when he cannot maintain his feeling of control and certainty that he begins to shake and betray himself, revealing himself as a paper tiger. And he can never maintain himself in his feeling of well-being, no matter how much power he acquires or how much of her personal and psychological territory he usurps. It is at these times, which are both inevitable and increasingly frequent, that he displays something of what he lacks and where he is from.

Though I have just finished saying that these boys and men come in all shapes and sizes, research has been able to give them a rough form. Certain generalities pertain; origins of a particular sort are often found.

It has been only rather recently that the dominating and/or abusive male has attracted any scientific attention at all. For the most part, only the physically abusive adult man within a marriage relationship has been looked at. Abuse and domination in adolescent relationships have received very little and only very recent attention. Nonetheless, knowledge gained from research on domination by means of physical abuse among adult couples is helpful in laying the ground work for an understanding of pathological domination in younger couples. It not only aids in providing an impression of what adolescent domination consists of but serves as an important warning of the worsening conditions that may be not too far ahead. Furthermore, it describes the homes and families that have bred a disproportionate percentage of the young abusers of today and perhaps some of their victims. The modeling of pathological domination and abuse by parents (or other adults) within the home has been shown to play an important role in the development of a similar style of love relationship in a statistically significant percentage of their offspring. Therefore, a review of some of the findings regarding adult relationships is worthwhile. It tells us something of where the younger subjects of this book may have come from, where they may be headed and even what they are like today.

Okun (1986), in his very complete overview of the subject of wife abuse, was able to find only four works in psychology prior to 1970 that directly address conjugal violence. They are the works of Mowrer and Mowrer (1928), Schultz (1959), Komarovsky (1962) and Snell and colleagues (1964). Scattered mention of battering had appeared occasionally earlier, but always as parenthetical or secondary items in works having a different focus, such as homicide or jealousy, or in legal records or newspaper accounts. It was never spotlighted at center stage, yet the evidence of its existence has long been available, and not only through the open windows or thin walls of neighboring dwellings or in the whispered talk of relatives and friends. FBI Uniform Crime Reports carry (and did prior to 1970) annual statistics on homicides by categories, itemizing murders between married and ex-marrieds, showing that a large proportion of assaults as well as homicides take place between family members. This has been evident despite underreporting by police and medical staffs who often record the nature of incidents in general and misleading ways. Origins of injuries are labeled "accidental," "traumatic" or "unspecified." Police reports cite "domestic disturbance," "family trouble," or say simply "assault," without recording who did what to whom and how, often with no arrest. The term "domestic disturbance" suggests a free-for-all started by no one in particular in which everyone gives as well as he gets. A victimless crime, so to speak, or more likely no crime at all. This has begun to change only very recently. Truthful, accurate reporting that can identify the responsible parties and ease the way for consequences is still very spotty and is spreading very slowly through police forces, medical centers, and district courts. In 1976, the first book appeared devoted entirely to the subject of woman abuse, Del Martin's *Battered Wives*. It looked beyond the curtained windows into the often violent lives of American couples and shattered the staid assumption that the average home was necessarily a safe and peaceful place, refuting the blithe assurance of Maccoby and Jacklin's (1974) *Psychology of Sex Differences* that "there can be little doubt that direct force is rare in modern marriage" (p. 121). Sadly, it seemed the *majority* of American marriages experienced conjugal violence.

Yet the men who perpetrated the most damaging and dangerous marital violence were slow to emerge into focus. Earlier writers were often more concerned with the personality of the woman who would receive such treatment, and wondered if she was provocative in some distinctive way. Did she engage in behaviors or attitudes that would drive a man to strike her? Was she a masochist? If she didn't like it or wasn't to blame, why didn't she leave? Even those in the scientific sociological and psychological communities had made the assumption that the woman was the catalyst, at the root of it somehow. Many in the general public still assume this, many women included. Consequently, much attention remained focused on the woman. Furthermore, it was difficult and still is to get men to offer information about their marriages and certainly about abusive behavior by either party. Very few studies reviewed by Okun were able to collect equal numbers of male respondents. In many studies males are absent altogether. We hear of them from their victims only. Snell and colleagues (1964) were commissioned to study wife beaters, but had to settle for studying only the wife of the wife beater. Gelleck wanted equal gender representation for his book *The Violent Home* (1972), but had to settle for only a 17.5 percent sample of men.

So the description of the dominating and abusive male may be flawed and limited in several ways. First, there is an over-reliance on second-hand information, data gathered from another, usually his most regular victim. Second, most of the men studied have been married men. The

first study of abuse in dating relationships was carried out
by Makepeace (1981). Since then the numbers of studies
looking at pathological domination and abuse among non-
marrieds has grown but is still dwarfed, in both the empirical and anecdotal literature, by what is written of
married couples. Finally, nearly all that has been written
and researched deals with the physically abusive male. In
most cases, physical abuse is the only behavior studied,
even though most writers and victims acknowledge that
verbal or psychological abuse is at least as damaging. This
is entirely true of all of the earliest material. Yet the dominating male will always use verbal and psychological
abuse, sometimes adding physical abuse as well. The
forms that verbal abuse can take may vary in their cru-
dity and brutality, being more or less subtle or insinuat-
ing, but they will, must, be present. For some this will
suffice; not all will strike out at their female partner. They
may attack objects instead, or hit nothing at all. However,
the correlations between verbal abuse and physical abuse
are consistently high enough to allow for conservative
generalizations regarding them all. It is fair to speak of
nonviolent dominators based upon findings on physically
abusive dominators. After all, some verbal abusers are
simply future physical abusers who haven't started yet.

  Straus and colleagues' landmark survey and book,
Behind Closed Doors: Violence in the American Family
(1980), reported a strong positive correlation between
verbal and physical aggression, even between violence
against objects and against mates. They found a negative
correlation between physical violence and nonaggressive
verbal styles of conflict resolution. Rates of conjugal violence were found to increase as verbal aggression increased. While not every verbal abuser is a physical
abuser, it is generally accepted that every physical abuser
is a verbal/psychological abuser.

There is as yet no record of a battering relationship free from the linkage of verbal and psychological, in addition to physical, abuse. [Okun 1986, p. 71]

Therefore, while the dominating male may not utilize physical assault, his verbal and psychological machinations serve the same ends and derive from the same needs. A study of him can draw much from what has been learned about those who do use violence against their mates. Finally, and most important, the pathological dominator who does not physically abuse his female mate must be unveiled and held up to public scrutiny. Women and younger adolescent females need an increased awareness of the noxious effects of the abuser who does not hit. They must no longer be placated by the phrase "At least he doesn't hit me."

FAMILY BACKGROUND

All humans feel the need for a tolerable level of control of their lives. We all fear loss and emotional pain, and we all have a capacity for anger, even aggression. The degree to which we feel these things will, of course, vary, as will our capacity and manner of coping with them. The form in which we act out these feelings, how we actually behave, however, is often a function of what we have seen and learned along the way, what we have had modeled for us by significant others. Here our families of origin are most important, followed in some undetermined order by peers and media images.

A large body of research has demonstrated a tendency for men who are physically abusive (meaning verbally and psychologically abusive as well) to have come from violent families where, as children, they either witnessed and/

or received physically aggressive behavior from their parent figures (Browne 1993, Carroll 1977, Fagan et al. 1983, Gelles 1974, Hofeller 1980, Johnston 1984, Kalmuss 1984, Kashani et al. 1992, Rouse 1984a,b, Smith and Williams 1992, Sonkin and Dunphy 1985, Straus et al. 1980, Telch and Lindquist 1984).

Others, led by Straus, Gelles, and Steinmetz's (1980) work have sought to discover how different forms of aggressive behavior within the family effect rates of marital violence. They found that witnessing parents attack each other was associated with a tripled rate of marital violence for both men *and* women. Thirty-five percent of male partners who had seen parental spouse assault were themselves violent in their own marriages during the year studied, as compared to only 10.7 percent of husbands who never witnessed such behavior. For women the figures were 26.7 percent compared to 8.9 percent.

Sons of the most violent parents in the study engaged in 900 percent more woman-beating in a year than sons of nonviolent parents. Daughters of this parental group were 500 percent more violent than their peers with nonviolent parents.

The inclusion of women in their study of conjugal violence is important. Violent behavior by females directed at their male partners is not only a poor form of communication and conflict resolution; it carries with it a very dangerous rebound potential. Most book-length works in this field have ignored this, even though some studies have shown women to be as aggressive toward their male partners as men are to their female partners (Stets 1992, Stets and Pirog-Good 1990, Straus and Gelles 1990, Sugarman and Hotaling 1989).

Feminist literature in particular has failed to deal with this aspect of couples' violence in its laudable zealousness to bring violent males to the attention of the public. However, considerable research and clinical experience has reported both the high incidence and dangerous consequences of female aggression for females themselves. It often creates a rebound effect in which she is the final victim. This matter will be dealt with more fully in later chapters.

Looking at batterers of women, studies report that approximately half witnessed spouse abuse as children in their homes. Pagelow (1981) reported 53 percent, Gayford (1975) 51 percent, and Flynn (1974) "over 50 percent." All of these figures, however, are considered conservative estimates, since the information comes only from wives of batterers whose parents were known to have been violent—those, in other words, who were not able to keep it secret.

Straus and colleagues (1980) looked at the effect of experiencing abuse as a child in an interesting way. They looked for an association between having received corporal punishment from parents as a teenager and later being violent in a conjugal relationship. Those who had been physically punished as teens were four times more likely to be violent against their partner than those who had not been punished in that fashion. The findings were virtually the same for males and females. It is noteworthy that Straus and his associates considered the effect of physical disciplining of an adolescent, since it is during adolescence that dating begins and males and females are solidifying their manners of dealing with one another and with their emotions in general.

However, the vast majority of the research in the field points confidently to the more instrumental effect of witnessing spousal abuse over the acknowledged significant effects of experiencing it first-hand. In the review of the literature by Hotaling and Sugarman (1986), 94 percent of the empirical studies surveyed reported a significant relationship for men between witnessing parental violence and later abusing a partner. Only 69 percent of the studies reported that being the victim of child abuse was associated with partner abuse, while 31 percent did not find an effect.

Rosenbaum and O'Leary (1981) found that men who abused their wives had a higher incidence of witnessing spouse abuse but did not differ from the control group in their experience of child abuse. Kalmuss (1984) found that the transmission of violence tended to be role-specific. For males in her study, witnessing parental hitting doubled the likelihood of husband-to-wife aggression in their later relationships. The effect of having themselves been abused as children had a much less statistically significant result. Similarly, girls are at somewhat greater risk for receiving violent treatment from a male partner in adulthood (or earlier) if they have witnessed violence between parental figures (Browne 1993, Hotaling and Sugarman 1986, Kalmuss 1984).

The consensus then holds that exposure to parental violence as a child is the strongest predictor of later spouse abuse, as well as being a predictor of the severity of injuries suffered by the woman (Fagan et al. 1983). It is even a stronger influence than current life stress on the behavior of violent couples, exerting its noxious generational effect even in the absence of external, identifiable, stressful circumstances (Kalmuss and Seltzer 1984).

Finally, Straus and colleagues cite the compounding effect on those souls who have experienced both aspects of the violent home, witnessing parental abuse and receiving it. Men and women of this background reported four times the rate of violent behavior as individuals fortunate enough to have escaped both experiences. Studies of the family experiences of violent dating couples have duplicated the findings of studies on married couples. Bernard and Bernard (1983) reported that college students who had either experienced or observed violence in their families were more than twice as likely to engage in violence with their dating partners. Other studies have found similar effects (Laner and Thompson 1982, Roscoe and Benaske 1985).

Clearly, men and women do not wait for marriage to replay what has been modeled. Smith and Williams (1992) studied a high-school population and found that teenagers from violent homes had a markedly higher incidence of engaging in dating violence. I know from my own daily work that violence between couples and full-blown pathologically dominating relationships, with or without abuse, emerge in adolescence. For some it begins as early as dating itself, and establishes itself immediately and from the start as the one and only form of relationship some males can engage in. Just this week I was told an outrageous tale by a 15-year-old girl about a 14-year-old boy toward whom she had never been more than friends and then only briefly. Already, however, he is stalking, harrassing, and threatening her in a frightening effort to possess her. He demands to know where she is at every moment. He interrogates her accusingly if he calls and her line is busy. He has pushed and hit her in the school hallways and has threatened to burn her house down at night with her and her parents in it if she will not be his. And he is only 14.

Yet little empirical attention has been turned their way. Nearly all research on dating relationships involves only college students, who may not be representative of their same-age noncollege peers. Only a minuscule amount of research has used high-school subjects in the area of abusive or otherwise dominating relationships. As individuals are now dating longer before committing to marriage and teens begin dating younger and more seriously, the

younger, pre-married population is increasingly deserving of research attention as well as therapeutic help.
Young male teens can hold within them deeply held images from childhood and latent patterned responses that
may spring forth when triggered by the circumstance of
a love relationship.

Bandura's (1973) work has shown that children remember and then imitate aggressive acts that are modeled for them. Boys imitated aggression more spontane-
ously than girls even when not directly encouraged to do
so. Pagelow (1984) demonstrated that behavior modeled
by an adult male was more likely to be imitated than that
performed by women, especially by male children. The
effect was even stronger if the male who was modeling the
aggression was a person familiar to the child. The child
was as likely to imitate a man they knew but didn't like as
one with whom they had a warm healthy relationship.
Jaffee and colleagues (1989) reported results indicating
that latency-aged children exposed to wife battering have
more pronounced inappropriate attitudes about violence
as a means of resolving conflict than children not exposed
to violence. They also presented a greater willingness to
use violence themselves compared to peers not exposed
to wife assault.

Certainly then, adolescence is an especially vulnerable
age to experience problems with abusive relationships.
Young men can carry with them into their first relationships time bombs of anger, aggression, and tyrannic
control that may explode upon the unprepared and
inexperienced psyches of young girls, who may carry into
adolescence their own vulnerabilities and susceptibilities
for becoming involved and be ill-equipped to understand
or handle what is happening. The boy who witnesses a
significant adult male abuse his female partner will likely
be struck by a more profound and influential realization—

it works. Sonkin and Dunphy, in their book *Learning to Live without Violence: A Handbook for Men* (1985), draw from their clinical experience with male abusers in describing the concrete and brutal efficacy of violence. In the short term, it "puts a quick stop to an emotional argument or situation that is getting out of control" (p. 3). It allows the perpetrator to take control, to gain mastery and domination over others. He is listened to. He gets his way. The riveted eyes of a child will take this in and store it up.

Boys grow to teenagers and into men in a society where males are encouraged to be forceful, aggressive, and master of their surroundings. The expression of anger is tolerated. Qualities of conciliation, adaptation, or the willingness to admit to error, apologize, and submit are viewed too often as less manly, perhaps even weak. A quick look at how most politicians operate will provide ample validation.

Children who have grown up experiencing the chronic anxiety and terror of parental abuse are later on apt to find emotionally charged situations very difficult to tolerate. Conflict with a dating partner may give rise to such internal discomfort that they may find themselves using aggressive force to stop it and in so doing cool for the time being the distress boiling within them.

Children (or adults) who have been held powerless in the face of traumatic experience, such as that of the boy or girl witnessing the humiliation or beating of their mother, unable to intervene or have any effect, may later on feel compelled to relive the experience with the tables turned, with themselves as the active agent. It seems madly incongruous that a child who has been abused or been sexually molested would ever grow up to do the same thing to another child. It would seem that they would be the least likely perpetrators. Yet we know that the converse is true.

In the 1978 movie *The Deerhunter*, Robert DeNiro and Christopher Walken are American soldiers in Vietnam who are captured and forced by their Viet Cong guards to play Russian roulette with loaded pistols while their captors bet on the bloody outcome. The atmosphere of fear, rage, and powerlessness is overwhelming, difficult to watch even though it is only a movie. DeNiro and Walken escape but are later separated. Sometime later, in Saigon, DeNiro discovers Walken playing Russian roulette with real guns and live ammunition for money in a back-street dive. Why would Christopher Walken's character do this? The scene baffled and seriously annoyed many people I know and really turned them off to the whole movie. They said it didn't make sense, but it did. Walken was turning the tables. He was reenacting the traumatic event of his life, this time feeling that he was in charge. He was seeking mastery of the experience that had left him feeling frightfully obliterated, so impotent in his rage. It *is* pathological, but it does carry its own special logic, too.

Abused and molested children and, as research also shows, child witnesses of parental domination and abuse are similarly affected and some, males particularly, will find themselves later on reenacting the part, this time with themselves in charge.

The family of the child who has witnessed conjugal violence, especially wife abuse since it is such an unequal conflict, is much more than simply a home where Dad berates and/or hits Mom sometimes. It is also a home that must necessarily model poor impulse control and unhealthy management of emotions. It is a home wherein the most powerful figure is immature and dishonest, a home that maintains a high level of stress and anticipatory anxiety, where unpredictability reigns. When the one who is wrong wins and the victim apologizes and submits, right and wrong, real and unreal, become mixed and confused. In this environment, in addition to a whole host of pathological behaviors modeled with powerful impact by adults for children, there is the absence of a positive male role model and perhaps the destruction of a positive female one as well.

Children in the homes of violent men witness an inadequate and severely compromised quality of effective, healthy, mature problem-solving behaviors. They do not see their fathers engage in a nurturing, empathic, supportive relationship. They do not see stress or conflict being coped with in strong, calm, productive ways. They do not see equality in the relationship or mutual respect between a man and a woman. Later on, as the boy grows to become an adolescent, as he moves smoothly among friends and within the worlds of school, work, sports, and activities and ultimately enters the heated realm of love relationships, then may be reaped what had been sown.

DEMOGRAPHICS

Demographics, when useful, can be read as clues. They offer little truth in and of themselves but can provide relevant information. When combined and analyzed, a picture sometimes will emerge in which something real is contained. It is so with the demographic and socioeconomic data regarding abusive and excessively controlling men. The findings on race, employment status, income level, and so on tell us little of value on their own. In fact, the information they provide can be dangerously misleading, inaccurate, or meaningless read at face value. It tells us nothing that will help us understand the dynamics of the man's behavior. It will not help his female victim to understand what it is she's up against, nor will it help us develop treatment plans for male abusers. However, the material is far from worthless. Aside from describing something of the context that may help give rise to the abusive controlling personality, it can also tell us something of what *isn't* true. The data can help to clarify and dispel some of the myths and misconceptions about the people who live their lives in this manner.

Again, as with most research in the field, adult marrieds constitute the bulk of the studied samples. A few studies of college student populations exist. Virtually all of the data is based on males (and females) who are physically abusive. We must extrapolate to consider younger men, unmarried men, and men who do not include physical aggression in their arsenal of domination tactics.

Finally, the confounding problem of underreporting of the incidence of abusive behavior by men in general and certain class groups in particular is a serious problem. Results of studies and surveys must be carefully considered and conclusions cautiously derived. The areas in which underreporting seems to have been most in evidence will be acknowledged and explored.

RACE

Race as a factor is often reported in the literature without any elaboration as to its causal role or meaning. Straus and colleagues (1980) present the only findings on racial rates of violence embedded in a larger context of meaningful data. They found the rate of woman abuse to be triple and the rate of husband abuse to be double for blacks relative to whites. They acknowledge, however, the possibly critical impact of class level, income, and more candid responses by blacks than whites upon the findings. Racial findings may have been to a significant degree an artifact of those factors plus the psychological by-products of poverty, frustration, and lower social status, which may cut across racial lines. Rather than signifying any biological or even cultural differences between the races on this criterion, these findings may instead say something about the effects of particular living conditions upon self-esteem, perceived status, and adequacy. The influence of these psychological states upon male abuse of females may be of the utmost significance. There is much in the field of demographics which would lead us to think in this direction.

RELIGION

Findings on religion as a variable are very thin, due in part to apparent lack of interest and the notion that perhaps it plays no significant role on its own. Gelles (1972) and Straus and colleagues (1980) both found mild tendencies for assaults to occur in couples of mixed religious affiliation as compared to couples of the same religion. Both found marital violence more common in couples wherein one member professed no religious affiliation at all. Straus and colleagues found couples sharing a religion designated "other" had a higher incidence of conjugal assault than those couples sharing any combination of Protestant, Catholic, Jewish, or none. Jewish couples had the lowest rate of all groups, while Protestants were lowest in husband abuse.

SOCIOECONOMIC FACTORS

The variables of class status, income level, employment status, education, and occupational status are closely related and largely mutually dependent. In a real sense they cannot be studied or understood separately. Every statement that can be said of one draws from the effects of the combinations of the others. Together they make a powerful statement but not about money, class, and education per se, for these are not the keys, only clues.

However, this is an area which has received a good deal of attention. Reviews of the literature by Hotaling and Sugarman (1986), Okun (1986), Pirog-Good and Stets (1989), and Straus and colleagues (1980) are fine sources. Numerous studies have looked at various pieces of the picture, sometimes with conflicting results. In some respects the state of comparative research in the field is a mess. Plagued by methodological inadequacies, insufficient samplings, and survey groups that are incompatible with others for the purposes of comparison, many studies add little of value to the body of information as a whole.

While most who have studied the question have found a significant effect from the variable of class status, *most* is not *all*. Flynn (1985) and Owens and Straus (1984) found class to have no effect whatsoever. Komarovsky's (1963) findings on working-class couples do not differ from the general national rates found by Straus and colleagues. Davidson (1978) and Walker (1979) held that the middle and upper classes have the greatest incidence of woman abuse.

Most others are of the opposite opinion, based on research results that show the highest rates among lower- and working-class couples (Goode 1971, Hotaling and Sugarman 1986, Steinmetz and Straus 1974, Stets and Straus 1989, Whitehurst 1975). Okun (1986) found more violence by both male and female partners in the working class as compared with the middle class, with an effect far more pronounced for the husbands. Levinger (1983) reported that divorcing wives of lower-class status cited physical abuse far more often than did divorcing wives of higher classes (and so did lower-class divorcing men).

The well-established finding of significant levels of underreporting among the upper classes raises some havoc with all of the data on class status and related areas. It seems that the higher the class level, the greater is the underreporting, which, of course, also means the higher the income level the greater the underreporting and, to some extent, the higher the occupational status and level of education the greater the underreporting. Clearly this has implications for variables such as race as well.

Okun (1986) reported results demonstrating a pronounced tendency on the part of middle-class parents to underreport violence compared to working-class parents. Reports of children were compared to the reports of their parents. Working-class fathers admitted to committing 64 percent of the violence that their children report about them, while middle-class fathers only confessed to 30 percent of the conjugal violence that their children say they witnessed. Middle-class fathers confess to less than 23 percent as much reported violence as working-class fathers. Similar class effects were reported regarding the violent behavior of a mother of either class when compared to their children's reports. Okun concludes that despite middle- and upper-class underreporting, the body of evidence supports the position that lower-class couples engage in the highest levels of spouse abuse.

Underreporting is also a function of sex, the degree and type of violence engaged in, and whether one is the perpetrator or victim. Males admit to perpetrating far less violence than females compared to the reports of their victims or witnesses (Okun 1986). Henton and colleagues (1983) found this to be true among high-school-age couples. Lane and Gwartney-Gibbs (1985), as well as JeJeune and Follette (1994), obtained comparable results among college students.

It is a consistent finding that the person who does the attacking is increasingly less likely to admit to it as the severity of the acts escalates (Henton and Cate 1983, Okun 1986). The perpetrators of the most violent acts are, more often than not, males (Lane and Gwartney-Gibbs 1985, Okun 1986).

Many other physical means of domination and intimidation are often omitted from surveys of violence between couples. Behaviors such as abducting, carrying, choking, suffocating, physical restraint and rape (all especially male behaviors) are often not among the choices of behavior available for a respondent to a battering questionnaire. Threats of bodily harm, an almost exclusively male form of effective intimidation and control, is also not included in any of the empirical data on dominating relationships.

Income as a variable has been studied by several investigators, yielding results that are not surprising, considering findings about class. They indicate higher levels of violence among lower-income couples. Such were the overall findings of the two largest surveys to date (Gelles 1972, Straus et al. 1980). Sugarman and Hotaling (1989) reported the same association for college student dating couples. O'Brien's (1971) research, however, hints at what is probably a critical factor associated with male violence and, in this case, income level, and it is a psychological factor. He reported that the *attitudes* of the partners toward their level of income may have had a more powerful effect on male violence than the quantity of money earned. The wife was dissatisfied with the husband's income in 84 percent of the violent marriages in his sample, but in only 24 percent of the nonviolent marital couples. Straus (1974) found that as students' judgments of their mother's satisfaction with the family income rose, the level of reported marital violence diminished. It is odd, however, that the wife's attitude was studied rather than the husband's. Both studies were done in the 1970s and may reflect the still strong notion that battering of the female is somehow instigated by the female. Nonetheless, pursuing the role of psychological dynamics was a step in the right direction. Attitudes and levels of satisfaction are among the understudied but key psychological factors that cut across class and income groupings.

Occupational status was among the many factors included in Straus, Gelles, and Steinmetz's (1980) landmark study. They found that the rate of severe violence is double among blue-collar couples. Gelles (1972) had found that 82 percent of violent husbands were of lower occupational status than their nonviolent male neighbors. O'Brien (1971), again looking deeper than the rest, discovered that violent husbands were more dissatisfied with their jobs than nonviolent husbands *and* were of lower occupational status. This raises very nicely the question of which is cause and which is effect and again pushes forward the prominence of psychological factors.

The associations between employment status, education, and the rates of marital or couples violence were reviewed in Chapter 2. Unemployed, underemployed, and disabled men were far more likely to be reported as violent than men employed full-time.

Men with less education, or men with less education than their female mates, tended to be more violent than men with higher levels of education, particularly if theirs was higher than their female partner's. People of both sexes who had not graduated high school were most likely within their gender to be victims of conjugal abuse. Women with bachelor's degrees were the most likely to have avoided being subjected to abuse (Straus et al. 1980).

In reviewing the findings on socioeconomic factors, the circumstantial evidence seems to lean heavily in the direction of underlying and highly active psychological variables as the most important influences on abusive behavior by males toward females. It appears very clear that it is not class, money, education, employment, or occupational status that really influences men's abusive behavior. To believe that it does is to fall into believing in stereotypes and prejudices. Rather, it is the way various manifestations of these factors make one *feel* that provides the real motivational thrust that expresses itself in the abusive treatment of women. Viewing it in this light helps to smooth out the inconsistencies among study findings, accounts for the presence of abuse among the wealthy, the high of status and education, as well as the absence of violence among many of the relatively poor, the lowly of status and the unemployed. Gelles (1972) reported that the most violent couple in his entire study was the wealthiest. These irregularities are reconciled by looking below the socioeconomic surface as O'Brien did. Racial differences are also understood differently.

The common denominator is to be found in the effect certain living conditions (and how society views those living within those conditions) have on how the man feels about himself. In Chapter 2 it was pointed out that males whose masculine identity felt threatened by their relatively low status or their female partner's higher status tended to be more abusive. I would add that any conditions which result in a lowering of self-esteem, perceived status, or a sense of personal adequacy may cause some males to become distressed to the point where they fall back in desperation and frustration to aggression and woman abuse in a final effort to dominate with visceral, gratifying efficacy the last bastion of their existence. This could hold true for an adolescent, within his world, as well as for an adult. Any male, of any age, even those at the highest levels of social or academic success, can struggle with intolerable feelings of inadequacy and failure. They are so common, in fact, that any of us can think of a person we know or have read about who seems to have so much yet is not satisfied, who feels insecure, threatened, unhappy, and failed.

Okun (1986), after acknowledging the consistent findings that lower class status is strongly associated with higher rates of woman abuse adds:

> Rather than a reflection of lower-class attitudes or norms, any positive incidence rates of conjugal violence and lower socioeconomic status could be interpreted theoretically into terms of frustration, low self-esteem or oppression. [p. 48]

So, in identifying, treating, or avoiding the abusive male, it is far more important to know what he is like and how he feels than where he's from, what he drives, or what college he's headed toward.

AGE

The available research yields widely varied findings on the matter of age, due mainly to the differences between and limitations of the populations studied. There appears, however, to be consensus on a few relevant points.

The incidence of domination in the form of physical violence by males toward females appears to progress with age along the path of the well known bell-shaped curve, skewed toward younger age groups. As with all other forms of violent behavior, young men will have the highest rates. Murphy and O'Farrell (1994) found that younger men in newer marriages had the highest rates of marital aggression. There is no survey data on age as a factor in nonphysically abusive but excessively controlling relationships. There is no consensus on the actual rates at any particular age or on the placement of specific age levels along that curve. It is important to note, however, that conjugal violence when it exists tends to escalate in its severity and in the frequency of its occurrence over time (Okun 1986). Physical abuse of women partners is more common when the male partner is three or more years older than his mate (Gayford 1975, Pagelow 1981, Star et al. 1979). Gelles (1972) also found a higher proportion of violence in married couples where husbands were older than wives and the greatest degree of nonviolence when the woman was older. A disturbing and increasing body of research has documented high rates of couples violence and abuse of females within the dating relationships of teenagers and young, college-age students. Since Makepeace (1981) first opened the lid on this dark aspect of early-stage male/female relationships, many others have come forward with empirical results to back up the clinical experiences of others in the field that domination and abuse in all its forms starts young.

Makepeace (1983) found an even higher rate of male violence among his college-age dating sample than Straus and colleagues (1980) reported in their study of older married couples, with 13.7 percent of college males admitting abusing a female partner, as compared with a rate of 12.2 percent in Straus and colleagues' group. This is not to suggest that younger unmarried men are more abusive; no other survey has reported results that would support that position. It does say, however, that marital abuse may be a well-established practice well before marriage arrives.

Lane and Gwartney-Gibbs (1985), in a detailed exploration of male- and female-perpetrated violence and abuse in college dating couples, add further to this unpleasant picture. Referring to college-age males, 31 percent in their study admitted to having used threats of violence against a date. Twenty-six percent admitted slapping, kicking, biting, or punching a female with whom they had a dating relationship. Seventy percent reported using verbal abuse. These numbers are very close to those reported by Laner and Thompson (1982), the one significant difference being their finding of 59 percent of males admitting using verbal abuse. Knowing what we do about males, class status, and underreporting, we may reasonably speculate that these rates could be even higher.

Sexual coercion as a form of domination and abuse has been reported by college-age unmarried females at rates varying from 20 percent to 50 percent of respondents surveyed (Burke et al. 1988, Kanin and Parcell 1977, Korman and Leslie 1982, Koss and Oros 1982). Fifteen to 25 percent of young male respondents have been reported as admitting to using sexual coercion in dating (Burke et al. 1985, Kanin 1967, Rapaport and Burkhart 1984, Wilson et al. 1983).

Data on specifically teenaged, high school populations are limited but disturbing. NiCarthy and Davidson (1989) state that 25–40 percent of teenagers have already been in at least one violent dating relationship. Sugarman and Hotaling (1991) reported an incidence of 28 percent. Henton and colleagues' (1983) and Berman's (1992) groups, which were a bit younger, reported rates of 12.1 percent and 15.5 percent, respectively, percentages perhaps lowered by the more limited dating experience of the samples. Henton and colleagues' female group reported having first experienced abuse at the average age of 15.3 years old.

Finally, Roscoe and Benaske (1985) cast some further light into the semi-private world of young peoples' dating by finding that 49 percent of the battered wives in his study had been in physically abusive relationships while dating. The authors went on to state that the reported dating experiences of abused college females and the recalled dating experiences of battered wives were quite similar.

> These findings are of interest as they suggest behaviors which occur in dating relationships may establish expectations and patterns of behavior which continue in later marriages. [p. 423]

The media, popular publications, the press, and schools have done well in bringing the issue of date rape into open discussion. Consciousness has been raised (one would hope) regarding the incidence, dynamics, and process of date rape. Females have been warned, taught appropriate defenses, and instructed to think clearly and fairly on the issues of self-blame, guilt, and the meaning of the word "no." They have been helped to see that certain forms of force, control, or coercion, along with the verbal judo that accompanies the physical, are wrong and should be identified quickly and not tolerated. Many young males, too, have been clearly told what date rape means, the harm it does, and the fact that it is illegal. A concerted effort is being made to teach men and boys that girls and women don't really like to be roughed up and that the myth which says "when she says 'no' she really means 'yes'" is rarely true.

The same cannot be said of nonsexual domination, abuse, or assault. To my knowledge, and I work with young people full-time, this area has been virtually ignored. Young men, often drawing from experiences within their families, bring directly into their first adolescent relationship a complete array of abusive and dominating responses to the feelings a relationship brings to life in them. Fortified by their intense needs to fulfill the role of a usually traditional male or macho identity, living as they do saturated with media violence and crude images of idealized male/female relations, it is no wonder they veer off toward this kind of relationship.

Judging from the findings thus far reported, verbally and physically abusive and dominating relationships are common among high-school and college-age dating couples. Experience has demonstrated to me that, qualitatively, abusive teenage relationships can be just as confining and damaging to younger females as abusive marriages are to older women. And they are always progressive—they either get worse or they get better—they don't just sit still. Usually they get worse. It is hard, however, for the young to understand, to appreciate what it is that they are involved with. Hard for the victims to understand, to believe that they are in danger. They are not taught that pathological domination is wrong, unhealthy, and dangerous. Most seem to believe that excessive jealousy and control simply mean they are loved and needed. They believe that as long as they are not being hit hard, the relationship is okay. Even if they are hit they can and usually do make the mistake of explaining it away, rationalizing it a dozen different ways.

Battering and domination are common in the young. It leads directly to more serious and sometimes deadly battering and abuse for those trapped by the responsibilities of marriage and children. Studies have been quite consistent in describing results that suggest that one should not expect a teenage boy who is abusive to simply grow or mature out of it. On the contrary, he is more likely to get worse before he ever gets better. Yet young men and women, those probably most at risk for developing unhealthy relationships, are not effectively forewarned.

PERSONALITY CHARACTERISTICS

Research and experience clearly indicate that the dominating male is the active agent in the instigation and development of a pathologically dominating relationship with a female. The female cannot create single-handedly her own pathological domination and abuse. Even if she wished for it, she would still need a zealous, active participant to do the dominating. That drive and need can only come from within the male. It is unlikely to be placed within him by his mate. In young relationships in particular, even a strong, independent, confident female can become entangled in a dominating and abusive relationship from which it can be very difficult and dangerous to extricate herself. This can be the case even when she realizes and takes action against her situation fairly quickly. Nonetheless, it is also true that many adolescent females enter their teens vulnerable and susceptible to participation in, even attracted to, love relationships that may quickly degenerate toward unhealthy domination and abuse. Even they, however, need a boy who will make it happen to them. In this section the personality characteristics of such a male will be described. The characteristics and contribution of the female who participates and submits will be discussed in the following chapter.

Few males are so inept as to come stomping into a new relationship making heavy demands and insisting on completely arranging the life of a new partner. Few males will initially feel the need to. It is usually only when feelings grow, become serious, and "love" of some sort is felt that the need to control begins. It is only when feelings and dependency have reached a point where a particular kind of male senses that the emotional stakes have grown high, the possibility of loss is intolerable, and the anxiety created by uncertainty is too great, that the compulsion to control will be triggered in some men. Many of these men never even see it coming. They do not anticipate it, desire it, or even recognize it when it has arrived and they are in it. Few plan it from the start with style and stealth, though a few probably do. Most are swept along, never able to admit or identify what has moved them or what they are doing. Most find ways to blame the woman for any excesses that cannot be denied. There is a lot of support for this belief available to them.

When a man goes overboard with jealousy, possessiveness, control, or even abuse, almost immediately speculation or outright accusations begin regarding the role of the woman in creating the situation. "She drove him crazy," many people will say. Women are notorious for their alleged capacity for tormenting the hearts and minds of men. Lacking the physical strength of men, women are thought to relish opportunities to yank men around emotionally instead, using their feminine "charms" and wiles as a cruel and powerful magic against them. The old ideas of the female as witch and siren have not left us. The disturbing and destabilizing effects that women are blamed for having on men are caricatured in a million cartoons depicting males in either human or animal form reacting with bulged out eyes, smoke blasting out their ears, tongue falling to the floor, head or eyeballs spinning around, panting, gyrating, in a trance, or having a seizure at the very sight of an alluring female. And so women are believed to have a devilishly strong effect on the emotions and behavior of men, certainly strong enough to make them lose their minds or lose control. In reality, it tends to work the other way around within the relationships discussed here.

Self-esteem has been found, in numerous studies, to have a very strong and consistent association with male needs to control and abuse female partners (Burke et al. 1985, Deal and Wampler 1986, Goldstein and Rosenbaum 1985, Stets 1993, Stets and Pirog-Good 1990). Abusive and controlling men have been found to have significantly lower self-esteem than noncontrolling and nonabusive comparison groups. Sometimes this has been associated with low status socioeconomically, educationally, or occupationally. The common denominator, however, has always been low self-esteem.

Men with low self-esteem have been shown to be more protective of their notion of male identity and more sensitive to perceived attacks upon their male self-concept and status and more likely to use aggression in defending it (Goldstein and Rosenbaum 1985, Stets 1993). Men with lower self-esteem are reported to tend more toward excessive control of female partners (Kalmuss and Straus 1982, Stets 1992, Stets and Pirog-Good 1990). Excessive interpersonal control and aggression have been found to have a "very strong relationship" (Stets and Pirog-Good 1990).

Low self-esteem and the experience of having witnessed marital violence in childhood are the two most solidly researched and highly correlated factors in the studied lives of abusive and controlling men. They are traits that the man brings into the relationship with him. It is the circumstance of a serious relationship with a woman that, for these men, activates the behaviors and intentions carried out to protect that weak and fragile self-esteem. Nothing else in their lives stimulates their feelings about themselves, defines them, or gratifies them like their love relationship. In some cases this is because they have few, if any, other relationships or friends. Their jobs may offer little if any status or satisfaction. They may even be unemployed or, if of school age, a failing student or a dropout. They may be frustrated by many real or perceived failures and view their relationships as their final repository of self-respect and therefore may hunker down within it in obsessive, clinging desperation.

Frequently, however, much of this is not so. The person (by most people's standards) is not a failure, has a certain status, apparent friendships, and gives no sign in those areas of his life of the painfully insecure and uncertain condition of his self-image. He fools his peers, his mate, and himself. When things go awry within that other world, that of the relationship, it is easy for everyone to suppose that it was the woman who somehow wrought this condition and its consequences within the man. The woman is likely to think so too, particularly if she is young and relatively inexperienced.

The dominant male's overreliance upon the defense mechanisms of denial and projection serves to protect his already low self-esteem and negative self-image from any further damage. They shield him from what would be the devastating and overwhelming effect that a clear and honest view of his immature, unfair, cruel, and abusive (verbally or otherwise) practices would have upon him. He cannot accept blame, only give it. His image of himself is already too awful to bear—it won't stand the light of day. It is the reason for his need to control, for his jealousy and his possessiveness. He thinks so poorly of himself that he labors under the constant belief that he isn't good enough, adequate enough, or lovable enough to keep his mate. He believes that she can easily find someone better, concluding that that is precisely what she is thinking of doing. Since he has no faith in himself and does not believe he can sufficiently improve himself, his only protection is to fence her in, and while she is contained, ruin her self-confidence and capacity for independence to the point where she no longer is able to leave him. His defenses keep him unaware of the true nature and purpose of these designs. His denials and projections confuse her and keep her in the dark as well. Finally, they are true markers of the elemental immaturity of this type of man's emotional development. And it can be present in all classes and races of men.

The pathologically dominant man is very immature and is severely (and in some cases permanently) limited in several areas that are critical to fashioning a healthy relationship. But, again, these deficiencies may not be evident in other areas of his life, areas which are not affected by the supercharged feelings that serious relationships provoke. Furthermore, few occupations or endeavors demand the level of maturity that healthy love does, and consequently might not reveal limitations so readily.

One feature of his immaturity is an enormous self-centeredness. He is egocentric in the extreme, childish in this regard as in others. He lacks objectivity, especially when emotional, and sees things only from his own perspective. He often views himself as deprived and wronged by the world, "screwed over" as it were. He tends not to believe in the vicissitudes of luck. When bad things happen he is likely to believe it was somehow intentional. When bad things happen to him he seems to subscribe to some crude magical notion that things are out to get him. There is a grandiose self-reference to most of what he perceives. When a guy cuts him off on a busy street he may imagine the guy did it on purpose to emasculate him personally, that the guy thought about it, thought about him, looked him over, sized him up, planned his move, and, with a demeaning grin, cut him off. He does not check on these perceptions. He doesn't self-observe. He doesn't consider that maybe this guy's act had nothing to do with him at all. Maybe he was daydreaming and never even saw him. Or maybe he's in a hurry and is sorry but he's really got someplace very important to get to. Instead his view is self-referential, defensive, and sometimes aggressive.

I have a friend who drives me crazy, occasionally, with his cynical attitudes regarding sports. When I was a kid, I first heard the idea that professional teams in a championship series, if they were ahead, say, 3 games to none, or 3 to 1 in a seven game series, might sometimes lose a game or two on purpose in order to prolong the series and make more money for themselves, the ticket-selling team owners, the TV networks, and the advertising sponsors. When I was a kid this sounded reasonably possible. Now it seems mean-spirited and ridiculous. I now know far too much about sports, human unpredictability and inconsistency, to believe it. While scandals are not unheard of, they are *extremely* difficult to achieve in the area of team sports. Besides, today's players are far too well-paid to need to bother with such a risky venture. Knowing as we all do that truth is stranger than fiction, the crazy failures and stupendously unexpected victories seen regularly in the world of sports are nothing more than the always surprising and often spectacular fancy of nature at work, nothing more. Believing that upsets are rigged and a star who had a terrible performance at a crucial moment was bought off is like believing that a tornado or a flood or a drought is the work of the Mafia or, if this were the 1950s, the Communists, or in the Middle Ages the devil, or in 1692 in Salem, witches. But this is how my friend thinks about many things, from sporting events to politics. He seems to believe that some invisible group of smart guys is out there running things in just such a way to aggrandize themselves and make him feel stupid, weak, and disappointed. Part of this need within the dominator to be in absolute control comes from distrust and anxiety at the risk of being controlled by others. He does not view others as generally benign and well-intentioned. Not to be in control is, therefore, to be in serious jeopardy. It is a gloomy and bitter outlook.

For some controlling men, feelings of inadequacy and low self-esteem are reinforced by unrealistic expectations and demands. They might be thwarted in their aspirations by a need to start out at the top. They may be intolerant of step-by-step advancements, unable to bear the lowly image it suggests to them and impatient for it to improve. They may demand and expect what they are unprepared and unqualified to receive. They behave and think at times very much like the overly demanding or spoiled child who acts brazenly entitled and feels betrayed, furious, and righteously indignant at any refusal. In their love relationships, they quickly reveal unrealistic and immature expectations for attention, reassurance, and intimacy, but are unable to reciprocate, nor do they feel they should.

Even when apparently successful, some men are not satisfied. A highly negative self-image can make one devalue and demean what one has accomplished, as if to say, "If I did it, or have it, it can't be that great." All of this may be covered up with veils of bravado and bluster, only disclosing its darker aspects within the privacy of a relationship.

Another feature of the immaturity of the pathologically dominating male is his very rudimentary or even nonexistent capacity for empathy. This, of course, is related to his expansive subjectivity. Stets (1992) found that college men with low scores in interpersonal empathy, referred to as "low role-taking," showed a stronger tendency toward high levels of "interpersonal control" in their dating relationships than young dating men with higher role-taking scores. Furthermore, levels of role-taking and interpersonal control were found to be far better predictors of physically abusive relationships than any socioeconomic variables studied.

Her follow-up study, also on college dating behavior (Stets 1993), demonstrated that poor "perspective taking" by men led to a need for increased levels of control in their dating relationships. Men who perceived that they had insufficient control in the relationship experienced lowered self-esteem and increased feelings of stress. Stets speculates, wisely I think, that the tendency of highly controlling men to be less willing or less adept at taking the perspective of another can lead to a feeling of being out of touch internally with a much-needed individual and consequently out of control and vulnerable, leading to increased efforts to externally control the other. Pathologically dominant men, almost by definition, embody this dynamic and build their love relationships upon it. Whereas most women tend to seek security and easing of stress and uncertainty in a relationship by finding out as much as possible about the inner states of the man she is with, by finding out about how the other thinks, sees, feels.

Men, in general, are often said to be less in touch with and more intolerant of most strong, unpleasant emotions, such as sadness, insecurity, and fear; dominating men show an extreme aversion. For them, most emotions are anathema. They strenuously resist awareness or acknowledgment of such "feminine," "weak" feelings. Instead, they appear in the form of anger, the only feeling that is tolerated and righteously expressed, usually in the direction of the person or thing that he believes has provoked the unacceptable feeling. He is, for the most part, incapable of introspection, self-critique, or self-criticism. He externalizes nearly exclusively. Everything that hurts or distresses him, every setback and misfortune, is viewed as having originated from some external source. He rarely sees his own role in it. When such a realization does break through, he is unable to hold onto it or use it, and it quickly fades away. This is one of many reasons why it is so difficult for him to change or improve. Because of his general distrust of people and institutions, he determines that the external source is ill-intentioned. Problems are not viewed as consequences of misfortune, accident, coincidence, or his own behavior. They are seen as the purposeful results of malevolent and unfair persons and conditions. When all else is eliminated from consideration there is really nothing left *to* think. Frustration, anger, and an unceasing drive to control and disable whatever can hurt him most are his only available responses. He feels fully justified.

Since love produces the most intensely felt and unpleasant feelings, it is within love that his angry and controlling responses find most of their release. These men experience love as far more distressing and anxiety provoking than pleasurable. Their distinctive quandary is that, nonetheless, they are extraordinarily needy of and dependent on it.

How this all plays out within a serious male/female relationship will be described in later chapters. For now, it is important to emphasize the existence of a host of personality features and characteristics that are carried into a relationship by the pathologically dominating man and act as catalysts for the damaging and dangerous relationship that is likely to ensue. While it can be shown, empirically, that men of this type are represented in greater or lesser proportions in one socioeconomic group or class level, race, religion, or age group than in another, this kind of survey data is of no real value to the individual. It is of no help to a young female seeking to identify such a man and thereby avoid him. It is of no predictive value to a parent or counselor helping a young couple avoid tying themselves together in such unhealthy fashion.

The individual dominating male is likely to be out of touch with and rejecting of the "feminine" within him. He is unable to comfortably provide nurturance, support, or empathy. He is unlikely to possess a capacity for honest introspection, self-appraisal, or objectivity. His internal emotional life is incomprehensible to him. He will have minimal capacity for insight into and understanding of the internal feelings and thoughts of his female mate. He is uncomfortable with emotions and cannot identify any of them except anger. He has very low self-esteem, a wretched self-image, and a gnawing feeling of inadequacy and insufficient status, regardless of superficial appearances.

He may ascribe to a highly rigid and traditional masculine sex role, but in the end it is his lack of complementary feminine qualities which limits him. He is self-centered, blameful, and fundamentally immature. He cannot adapt or accommodate either to the needs of another or the dictates of difficult circumstances without great stress and a feeling of being diminished. He may feel emasculated by compromise, by giving in, giving up, or even giving to.

None of this places the dominating and/or abusive man in any common and distinct diagnostic category of mental disorder. They will not be found in the *DSM-IV* under a label inclusive and specific unto themselves. Many, if not most, would appear "normal" upon psychological evaluation, as they would in most areas of their life and even in the early stages of a relationship. Sadly, it is usually only when a relationship with a female has become serious that the more unequivocal features of his personality are unsheathed. By then, unfortunately, both may be held captive.

4

CHARACTERISTICS OF THE DOMINATED FEMALE

It has been possible to describe some of what the male half bring to dominating relationships. They share certain historical and characterological traits often enough for one to be able to make generalizations about them. While it would not be quite safe to say they all fit a certain type, one gets a sense that the character is a recognizable one. You can formulate a picture in your mind of what he is like. There is a core to him that is much like that of other men with the same problem in love relationships. Though the exteriors may vary infinitely and enormously, the core, when it becomes visible, can be recognized as familiar and much the same.

This cannot be said for the female half of the pathologically controlling relationship. Research and experience bear this out. Generalizations do not apply so well; they have no common core. Their histories and experiences do not seem to lead them toward victimization with anything near the power of the particular history and experience that influence the controlling/abusive male.

It had been thought that female partners of abusive men were more submissive by nature, more inclined toward a traditional sex role, had lower self-esteem to begin with, and were more likely to have patterned this abusive adult relationship after the experience of having been abused as children or to have witnessed spousal abuse than women who were not victims of dominating/abusive male partners. The stereotype does not hold. As Okun stated in his 1986 review of the available research and literature on battered women,

> No one has yet presented convincing evidence of factors which predispose women either to be battered or to abide in violent relationships. . . . This point seems to be less true for perpetrators. [p. 66]

The general public and many writers have at times been misled into believing in a female victim's stereotype by focusing on similarities in the effects abusive relationships have on women. In this regard there are a great many common effects and conditions, psychological and behavioral, which tend to ensue. However, unlike the men who are the causal agent in the dynamic, women going into it do not seem to have much in common. Caution must be used in drawing firm conclusions regarding these women from the findings of the existing surveys and research on the subject, since they are derived largely from samples of male batterers and their female partners, who in most case studies have been married couples. What may be true for them may not be true of non-married couples, younger couples, and/or couples where a damaging dominating relationship exists but physical abuse is absent.

In the past (until very recently), it had been generally assumed that female victims of battering had been prepared for such treatment by particular childhood family experiences, causing them to be more accepting of violent treatment and victimization in general, perhaps to even seek it out. While this may not be generally true, it certainly may be in some cases. Research on incest victims has indicated a strong tendency for them to be revictimized. Mayall and Gold (1995) found that women with a history of childhood sexual abuse are at greater risk for sexual assaults as adults, showing a rate of victimization two times higher than non-abused women. Russell (1986) and Wyatt and colleagues (1992) reported even higher rates of female re-victimization. A history of childhood sexual abuse may later on impair the normal adult mechanism for self-protection in dealing with later relationships. Similarly, childhood physical abuse may have the effect of making a person less confident of their capacity for self-protection, less sure of the integrity of their personal boundaries, and more apt to accept victimization as a part of a flawed personal belief system and self-image. This may also be true of a female growing up watching her mother be physically or verbally abused and dominated by her male partner over an extended period of time.

The result can be an attraction to relationships that will recreate the childhood scenario, either due to a misguided desire to seek mastery of it in adult life or to passively succumb to it as an accepted lot in life. Nonetheless, this dynamic offers only a partial explanation that applies only to some dominated women rather than all. It certainly is not relevant to the many women who would seek an escape from domination as soon as they identify it.

The issue of female masochism is closely related. It provides an explanation which has strong appeal and seems to be widely believed. Psychoanalytic theory and the writings of Freud (1933) and Helene Deutsch (1944) are particularly responsible for the modern-day promotion of this idea. However, there have been many other contributors.

> The victim can always be assumed to have played a crucial role in the offense, and may have directly or indirectly brought about or precipitated their own victimization. [Schultz 1959, p. 72]

> If it is not safe to let oneself be dominated, it is not possible to be fully feminine. . . . The nagging, aggressive woman is often unconsciously demanding that which she most fears. By irritating a man, making unreasonable demands and criticizing, she is really trying to evoke a dominant response. . . . Her aggression . . . is [both protecting] against male dominance and, at the same time, demanding it. [Storr 1979, p. 134]

Masochism (in the strict sense of the word) is the term for achieving sexual arousal and/or orgasm through experiences of humiliation and/or physical pain, and it is by no means a phenomenon exclusive to women. The life of T. E. Lawrence, better known as Lawrence of Arabia, serves as a notable example of male sexual masochism (see *A Prince of Our Disorder: The Life of T. E. Lawrence* by John Mack). In a more general sense, it is the direct enjoyment of painful stimuli. No one has ever been able to demonstrate that this condition is anything but rare, or that it has very much to do with abusive relationships. A more purely psychological level of masochism could be described as an inclination toward martyrish tendencies, of taking pleasure in self-castigation and abnegation, a predilection for placing oneself in a position of suffering and/or victimization. In orthodox psychoanalysis, this level of masochism may include such personal characteristics as unhealthy submissiveness, passivity, and inordinate self-sacrifice in the service of others to the detriment of oneself. This type of masochism was thought by Deutsch to be an attitude innate to females, as described in her book *The Psychology of Women* (1944), and by Freud in his New Introductory Lecture on Psychoanalysis *Femininity* (1933). Karen Horney (1933) extended the breadth of the principle of feminine masochism by equating the mere experience of suffering with a lust for suffering.

It is a very short jump indeed from these notions to the effortless acceptance of an association between some fundamental quality of femaleness or female experience and the condition of abuse victim, that a woman who becomes an abused and dominated partner is likely to have carried the seeds of that eventuality into the relationship with her. The observation that women remain in these relationships, sometimes long after it seems obvious that it is harming them, has always been the most incriminating evidence in support of the idea that female victims are either living out a pathological need or simply being women. The fact that most women *do* leave abusive relationships, and that leaving is extremely difficult and dangerous, is often overlooked.

The psychoanalytic view, based as it is on archaic and traditional sex roles and a philosophy of male-domination and superiority, has, nonetheless, provided the bedrock for popular and scientific beliefs on the subject of dominating and abusive relationships, as it has on so many other issues regarding human behavior and relationships. As in many other areas, its position here is, at best, controversial and is unsupported by empirical or clinical evidence. Certainly, there are cases which do fit criteria described by psychoanalytic theory. Masochists do exist and some are female. Martyr personalities exist. Some individuals do find themselves drawn to adult situations and relationships that recapitulate childhood experiences, even harmful, pathological ones. Some of these individuals are women. Yet to suppose that these are *likely* dynamics, to *expect* to find them at work guiding the relationship, is to be misguided most of the time.

Regarding family history, Okun (1986) found that a group of shelter women (victims of spousal abuse who had left their relationships) did not differ from adult American women in general in the prevalence of violence in their families of origin. He further found that women who were the daughters of abused mothers were *more* likely to leave their abusive relationships than women who did not have violent parents. Speaking of his own findings and those of others which were reviewed, he stated,

> These findings tend to contradict analyses that view battered women as women susceptible to entering violent relationships due to processes such as transference, unconscious identification, modeling, vicarious reinforcement or the assimilation of family values regarding conjugal or family violence. [p. 227]

The balance of research now weighs heavily on the side of this position (Bowker 1983, Dobash and Dobash 1979, Rosenbaum and O'Leary 1981, Star 1978). Pagelow (1984) reported findings in agreement with Okun's. Women who had been abused as children had a tendency to leave relationships that had become violent more quickly than women who had not been abused as children. But even leaving early isn't easy. Women who'd had no exposure to significant levels or types of family violence in the past often failed to understand the danger and likely chronicity of violence in their adult relationships. They had a greater tendency to view incidents as isolated occurances due to external circumstances or problems. They tended to focus more on their own behavior as a way to cope with or control further incidents.

Rosenbaum and O'Leary (1981), in a study of marital interactions, warned that there are serious problems with models that look to the wife/victim for reasons for her victimization and urged more inquiry into characteristics of the husband/assailant. Hotaling and Sugarman (1986), in reviewing the findings of investigations from the fifteen years prior note that the main factor in the victimization of women is the simple fact of being female. They found, on the whole, that characteristics of the male half are far better predictors of a woman's likelihood of being victimized than are the characteristics of the woman herself.

It has been suggested, and by many others presumed, that dominated or abused women bring to their relationships a submissive personality type, very low self-esteem and a belief in traditional sex roles of the strong dominant male and more passive subservient female. Okun, in a section of his book entitled "Characteristics Common to Both Batterers and Battered Women," presented descriptions of battered women gathered from his review of the literature including "low self-esteem," "negative self-image," feelings of "inadequacy," "shame," "self-contempt," "extremely dependent," "impulsive," "jealous," "socially isolated," and "generally expect their men to be dominant, the head of the household" (p. 67). He wisely points out, however, that many (if not all) of these characteristics, when legitimately found, may have been the results of abuse rather than preconditions for it. Few studies have effectively investigated this critically important distinction. While it has often been found that abusive males appear to favor traditional sex roles, including a clear male dominance in heterosexual relationships, their female victims and partners often do not.

Bernard and colleagues (1985) carried out research intended to investigate, among other things, the presence of traditional sex-role beliefs, including characteristics such as passivity and compliance, in the wives of male batterers. Their clinical experience with men being treated for wife abuse had called into question the stereotypical pairing of dominant/submissive extremes described in the battering literature. In their experience, the wives of their men tended to be assertive, sometimes actually aggressive, and as "anything but the passive compliant individuals one reads about in the domestic violence literature" (p. 574).

Their findings bore out their hypotheses that while the male college students who were physically aggressive to their female partners did hold strongly traditional sex role beliefs, their female mates tended not to. They were found to have high levels of assertiveness, self-sufficiency and competitiveness. The authors speculated that when men of this type become serious with women of this type, their masculine self-image becomes fearfully threatened and they cannot bear it. They then may turn to physical violence in an attempt to right the scales they feel to be intolerably unbalanced. Physical violence and effective and consistent domination can be two different things. Self-esteem may play a role in the latter, if not the former.

Susan Forward, in her book *Men Who Hate Women and The Women Who Love Them* (1986), a best-selling and generally excellent self-help offering for those in need, devotes a chapter to the issue of what the female may bring to the dominating relationship. "How Women Learn to Love Women Haters" goes into the childhood, parental, and family influences. She describes modeling, identification, and the effects of physical and sexual abuse in sections called "Learning to Take the Blame," "Controlling Fathers and Adolescent Daughters," "Turning Anger in on Yourself," "When Mother Models Submission," and "Repeating Patterns." Her writing is based on her extensive clinical experience and she knows what she's talking about. I too have seen many examples of the meek, worth-less-feeling, weak-of-spirit female fall seemingly without resistance deeply into the darkness of the controlling/abusive relationship. It is also true that adolescent females in particular tend to struggle with problems of self-esteem, self-image, and adequacy that can make them vulnerable to dominating relationships. But, I, like the Bernards and others, have seen many that do not fit this picture at all, teenage girls and young women with strength, character, ability, and confidence, who enter a relationship in one condition and are shrunken and twisted into another, who commence in laughter as competent equals and slowly begin to feel increasingly confused, responsible, fright-ened, and lost, their lives consumed in a ceaseless battle to make something good out of something which is get-ting worse and worse. Some see it coming or sense it; they stay away or, having entered, try to get out quickly. Even for the latter, there can be great difficulty and significant danger. Little is known about these women or what it is they see that others do not or what enables them to get out before becoming seriously entangled. Those who do get caught seem to be of many types and are trapped in as many ways. Perhaps they are more attracted to the appeal of the serious relationship or at least are less afraid of it. Perhaps they are more responsive to the man's enor-mous need for them and find his great involvement in her life gratifying. Maybe it's timing. He comes along at a moment in her life when she is more vulnerable to his distinctive offering. Or she may be drawn to the challenge of the difficult male who finds it difficult to love; a boy or young man who is clearly flawed, but to her a man with clear potential. She may seek to create him, unaware that *she* will be created by him.

    She may be uncertain, without direction, confused as to who to be or where to head. She may welcome his certainty, his firm, confident opinions. His dominance, perhaps gentle at first, seemingly born of love, could feel comforting and calming, as would any healthy guidance. If he is older, he may seem wiser.

Once involved, she may remain despite hints of trouble because she doesn't want to be a quitter or a person who is incapable of working at a relationship. She may need to prove to herself and others (and there are always others) that she can "do" a serious relationship. Even teenagers feel this pressure and they feel it strongly. I have known many who fear there may be something wrong or lacking in them because they haven't had a long-term relationship in high school yet. Long gone are the days of "playing the field." That is an old person's term now. Girls who "play the field" are considered flighty, untrustworthy, emotionally immature, and usually are seen as "sluts" by other girls and boys. The big push is for serious monogamous relationships even in high school.

Consequently, even when the relationship begins to be trouble, there are various powerful motives to stay in it. There is the belief in the myth of "one true love" and only one in the lifetime of each person, and the fear that if this one is lost there may never be another. There is the belief that the male will grow out of his immature, needy, demanding, jealous, possessive, and tempermental ways. Among the most commonly held attitudes is the one that says, "We have put so much time into it. It would be stupid to end it now. It would mean that all of that time was wasted." When the relationship is also a sexual one, the bond, especially for the young, will be a much harder one to break. Probably they have never had the experience of ending a love relationship, surviving, recovering, and finding a new one, and being able to do so may be hard to imagine.

Some of the women who become entangled will be relatively submissive types. Some will have low self-esteem and a negative self-image. Some will believe in, or find natural for them, traditional sex roles in their relationships, wherein the male is expected to be dominant and superior and the female subservient and secondary. Yet none of these types, styles, or conditions need suggest any pathology within the female, nor any provocative predispositions, nor even any generally shared personality characteristics. And none of them can make a man work so hard, so obsessively, to dominate or abuse her so harmfully.

While their male counterparts share several core dynamics, which powerfully predispose them to create pathologically dominating relationships in much the same form with every female partner, the female half appears, at the outset, to fit no general mold. They are enormously varied, and only begin to look somewhat alike when time and the more uniform effect of the abusive and dominating male has pressed them into a shape that then becomes recognizable as the dominated and abused woman.

THE ONSET OF ADOLESCENCE:
VULNERABILITY TO SUBMISSION

> Go go go go now out of the nest
> It's time to go go go now
>   Circus girl without a safety net
> Tuck these ribbons under your helmet
>   [from "Mother," by Tori Amos]

Adolescence in our culture is a stage of challenge, stress, and jeopardy for all children, but for females in particular. That age is not kind to girls. A large body of research has consistently described female adolescents as experiencing significantly greater problems with depression, anxiety, self-esteem, body image, suicidality, eating disorders, health problems, health concerns, and somatic disorders than their male adolescent peers.

During the elementary school years, boys hold the clear edge over girls in behavior and emotional problems. By age fifteen this state of affairs is largely reversed. For growing girls, changing bodies and developing sexuality thrust them, ready or not, into a new role and a new way of being perceived, judged, and related to. As a consequence they are heavily influenced by both the microworld of their immediate surroundings and the macroworld of the surrounding culture and its ubiquitous media messengers to perceive, judge, and relate to themselves in a whole new way. It is often a harrowing experience and one which can shake the confidence of even the strongest girls. While both boys and girls perceive the changes that boys go through as positive changes, girls view the changes in themselves at adolescence as negative (American Association of University Women 1991b). It is understandable that so many will seek to cope with the awkward transition of female early adolescence by means of various unnatural contortions, each intended to shorten or avoid altogether the most difficult period of adjustment. Some will seek to leap past it altogether by taking on a form of pseudomature, precocious sexuality in an overdone attempt to establish themselves, at least superficially, as if the outer trappings might somehow alter the inner uncertainty and meet the external challenge with bold confidence. Others may retreat instead, hiding out in various ways from the push of time, appalled and intimidated by the new land their changes are leading them to. Some will fortify their efforts with eating disorders, which offer the additional side effect of retarding sexual development. Still other girls strive to deal with the problem by avoiding it—they decide simply to be boys instead. I worked for a time in a junior high school and still work in a high school that includes eighth-graders. Girls at this age go through a stage of dressing like boys, with far less diversity in style than will be seen as they get older. The emphasis is on sneakers, pants, T-shirts, sweatshirts and big coats, often bearing the logos of athletic teams, pro or college, made famous by males—in short, whatever the boys are wearing. They break out from these narrow boundaries as they move through the grades. Skirts and dresses appear, more colors, increasing diversity of style and individual inventiveness and, for increasing numbers, a clear sex difference. But not at first. The girls with the very lowest self-esteem, the greatest degree of uncertainty, will be among those girls seen trying to graft themselves onto the most macho of boys, the "bad boy" delinquent types. They idolize the boys who have what they do not possess: power and the freedom to desire. They may express their admiration in relationships of overt or unconscious submission to them, to experience these things second-hand. You will not, however, see the most insecure boys emulating girls.

Many girls at this age change from children who desired to adolescents preoccupied with being desirable. They give up internal and familiar sources of approval for unreliable external ones. Our culture's heavy-handed emphasis on the value of external appearance for females as compared to males decrees this. The girl's changing body is her signal that the time has come for her to scrutinize herself as meticulously and critically as she is told others will. The stress and strain on her young confidence and self-image is terrific. "America today is a girl-destroying place. . . . Many girls lose contact with their true selves and when they do, they become extraordinarily vulnerable to a culture that is all too happy to use them for its purposes" (Pipher 1994, p. 44).

Diderot observed ruefully, "You all die at fifteen."
Today, it may occur sooner. Children leap early from the
support and influence of their families in an age where
parental and familial influence may be at an all-time low
to begin with. The idea, "It takes a village to raise a child,"
is very popular right now, yet it is a plea more than a
reality. Children are seldom raised with the help of the
extended family, supported by strong, respected, and coherent community values. Half spend part of their childhood raised by only one live-in parent. Nonetheless, they
shed this more or less adequate holding and building environment at an early age. Those from deficient environments flee from it earliest with the least internal resources,
unaware that those inner strengths, the toothpick structure of their self-image and identity, will be severely tested
in the inconstant, unforgiving, rough-and-tumble world
of adolescence. Their susceptibility to a risky and unhealthy overdependence on the world of their peers, particularly dating partners and lovers, is thereby formulated
and increased. This is especially dangerous for girls.

The average age of sexual initiation dropped steadily
in the 1980s. Some studies have found that 53 percent of
middle and junior high school students have had sexual
intercourse at least once (Orr et al. 1989).

The American Association of University Women Educational Foundation's *AAUW Report: How Schools Shortchange Girls* (1992), of which we will hear more, estimated
that 28 percent of children engage in intercourse before
they are 14; of those the average age of sexual initiation
is 12.

The onset of adolescence, like the onset of some perilous disease or affliction, carries with it, for girls, not only
the primary effects of physical and psychological change,
but often a weakening of the person's ability to cope with
other conditions as well and, for our purposes, a signifi-

cant vulnerability and susceptibility to entanglement in dominating and abusive relationships. There is much in the process and effect of this stage which seems tailor-made as a preparation for such an eventuality. For, if to effect a domination of another, the controller must have his subject first be lacking in self-esteem and self-confidence, dependent on external sources for approval and a sense of adequacy, uncertain, confused, within a culture that approves of female submissiveness, accommodation, and dependency on male approval, then adolescence is the perfect situation.

As girls enter adolescence they experience a marked increase in psychological problems and disorders. McGee and colleagues (1992) in their longitudinal study of a group of boys and girls from age 11 to 15, showed that while at age 11 boys outnumbered girls in ten of twelve diagnostic categories, by age 15 that finding had been entirely reversed. As 11-year-olds, males had outnumbered females by a ratio of 1.3:1 in diagnosable disorders. By age 15 the male-to-female ratio had changed to 0.7:1. Males continued to lead only in the categories of aggressive conduct disorder and attention deficit disorder. Girls were particularly high relative to boys in depressive and anxiety conditions. Overall, females showed a 1 1/2-fold increase in disorders from age 11 to 15 while the male incidence remained stable. Girls, therefore, showed both an absolute and relative gain in difficulties upon entering adolescence.

Kashani and colleagues (1989) studied the incidence of psychological problems and symptom clusters in separate groups of 8-, 12- and 17-year-old children and reported similar findings, including a rise in conduct problems for boys and affective problems for females. Concerns about body imperfections and inadequacy increased with age but only for girls.

Offer and Schonert-Reichl (1992), in a review of relevant research in this area, state, "Before adolescence, girls are mentally healthier, whereas after adolescence begins, an opposite pattern emerges" (p. 1008). Absolute and relative (to males) increases were reported in depression, nervousness, headaches, sexual problems, health concerns, physical problems and illness, sleep problems, suicidal ideation, and loss of appetite. Girls' health concerns were found to be related to body image and social relationships. Overconcern with personal appearance was a predominately female problem. Dubow and colleagues (1990) found that 53 percent of the girls in his study were distressed at feeling overweight compared to only 16 percent of boys.

Central to these phenomena for girls entering adolescence of increasing physical and psychological distress and problems with domination and submission in relationships is self-esteem. Numerous studies have pointed to girls' self-esteem as the major casuality to the onset of adolescence. Low self-esteem has been associated with a host of psychological problems.

Peggy Orenstein, in her very effective and moving book *School Girls: Young Women, Self-Esteem, and the Confidence Gap* (1994) has made the fall of female self-esteem the cental theme of her study of the lives of a group of eighth-grade girls. "Although all children experience confusion and a faltering sense of self at adolescence, girls' self-regard drops further than boys' and never catches up" (p. xvi).

The American Association of University Women (AAUW) reports provide the largest and most recent body of research on teenagers that exists in support of this statement. Nearly half of boys aged 15 strongly agree with the statement, "I am happy with the way I am," compared with less than a third of girls (AAUW 1991, p. 4). Boys are also more likely, by a margin of 18 percent, to reject the assertion, "I wish I were somebody else" and 10 percent less likely to say, "Sometimes I don't like myself" (AAUW 1990, p. 17). While the adolescent gender difference in self-esteem is disturbing, the female adolescent's drop in self-esteem is alarming. From age 9 to age 15 the number of girls responding positively to the statement, "I am happy with the way I am," drops 33 percent for white girls, 38 percent for Latina girls and 7 percent for African-American girls (still a gap of 18 percent between themselves and African-American boys).

Self-esteem and self-image have been found to have a strong association with varying levels of depression, suicidal behavior, sexual behavior, and the incidence of experiencing physical and sexual abuse for adolescent females.

McGee and colleagues (1992) found self-esteem and depression to be significantly associated. Their study suggested that "adolescent girls may be more vulnerable than adolescent boys to threats to their self-image" (p. 57). Depression has a well-established and strong association with suicidal behavior. The reported rise in incidence of depression among adolescent girls and the relative difference between themselves and boys in this diagnostic category is reflected in their rates of suicidal behavior as well. Though males continue to outnumber females by approximately 3:1 in committed suicides, in rates of attempted suicide, a vastly more common form of suicidal behavior among adolescents of both sexes, females are estimated to outnumber males by a ratio of anywhere from 4:1 to 10:1 (Curran 1987).

Stets and Pirog-Good (1987) found that female college students rating higher in self-confidence and independence were less likely to have been physically abused by dating partners.

Regarding sexual involvement, sexually active adolescent girls as a group appear to have lower self-esteem than their non-active peers. The same association does not hold true for boys (Coles and Stokes 1985). This is an especially painful finding but one that comes as no surprise to people working with and familiar with teenagers. The brutal irony is that for many sexually active girls, sex is their way of coping with low self-esteem, a sense of inadequacy, and questionable desirability, their way of seeking a quick fix of acceptability, togetherness, and approval. What is well known to the rest of us, however, is that it usually drives the girl down even deeper, as she is usually bitterly disappointed by the boy and censured by her female peers as well, earning their contempt in a failed effort to bolster her self-respect. Nonetheless, some girls get stuck in a neurotic and devastating repetition compulsion involving the use of sex, in a persistent attempt to ease their pain and right themselves. They are the "sluts" (though nearly every teenage girl is called that at one time or another), the promiscuous girls, the "easy" ones who pathetically give everything they have from the very start in the sad belief that anything less will insure their quick rejection. They have so little regard for themselves that they have adapted how they present and relate to others to feature only their physical, superficial, sexual self. They have come to believe it is the only aspect of themselves that has any value or appeal only to find over and over that even that is insufficient. Meanwhile, their real self, their old self, shrinks and withers.

There is a firm consensus among researchers that there are important differences in the criterion upon which male and female self-esteem is based at this age and that therein lies much of the problem. Using the concept of adolescent self-esteem put forth by Harter (1990) and Rosenberg (1989), two factors are paramount:

How a person views his or her performance in areas which are subjectively valued and important, and second, how a person believes he or she is perceived by significant others.

Male adolescent self-esteem has been found to be largely based upon features of performance and talent—in short, on what and how they *do* (AAUW 1992, Ostrov et al. 1989, Williams and McGee 1990).

Boys are twice as likely as girls to name their talents as the thing they like most about themselves. Girls, on the other hand, in study after study, cite an aspect of their physical appearance as their most important feature (AAUW 1992, McGee et al. 1992). The AAUW Executive Summary (1991) reports that 21 percent of girls mention an aspect of physical appearance as "the thing I like most about myself" compared with 12 percent of boys (p. 6–7).

Orenstein (1994) recounts an eighth-grade class assignment involving the assembly of a time capsule. Each student was to contribute a one-page description of an object that in their opinion would best represent contemporary culture, as he or she saw it, to people in the year 3000. A few wrote of social issues and problems such as AIDS, drugs, or violence. "Overwhelmingly, though, the boys in each class have chosen computers, CD players, VCR's, guns and sports equipment to epitomize the 20th century. The girls, meanwhile, have chosen clothing, hair-care products, and make-up" (p. 62). The boys wrote of things they use and things they do, of what they enjoy themselves, of action and mastery. The girls wrote of passivity, of appearance, and of how they wish to look for others.

Body image is a far greater concern to adolescent females than to adolescent males and they feel far less satisfaction about it (Dubow et al. 1990, Kashani et al. 1989, Offer and Schonert-Reichl 1992, Ostrov et al. 1989). Adolescent female disatisfaction with weight and body image has been strongly associated with increased levels of depression, anxiety, somatic disorders, and, of course, lowered self-esteem and a reduced feeling of competence (Offer and Schonert-Reichl 1992). Making matters worse, two-thirds of adolescent females appear to have distorted body images, perceiving themselves as larger ("fatter") than they are (Tolman and Debold 1994). Our culture, through media and marketing messages, has effectively induced a delusional condition in large numbers of girls and young women, especially middle- to upper-class white women, through whose images the message is delivered and to whom it is largely aired. Twenty percent of female college students have eating disorders. The overall incidence of eating disorders among adolescent girls is seen as being on the rise (Orenstein 1994). The *DSM-IV* (1994) reports that 95 percent of those afflicted with anorexia nervosa are female. Its cultural origins are clearly indicated by the significant absence of self-starving in non-Western societies and before the modern age of ever-thinning models and beauty contest icons. Within our own culture, in our own time, African-American girls are less affected, reporting lower rates of eating disorders and healthier body images than white and Latina girls. In high school, 58 percent of black girls strongly agree that "I like the way I look," compared to only 12 percent of white girls and 11 percent of Latinas (AAUW 1990). Black girls show far less of a drop in self-esteem on entering adolescence than white and Latina girls, as well as higher overall ratings of self-esteem. The interesting implication is that black girls are spared certain unhealthy influences from the culture by having been less included within it.

Dominating relationships can only thrive in an hospitable environment. Adolescence contributes to the hothouse nature of that environment by weakening those qualities and inner resources that girls need to establish and maintain equality and independence within their love relationships.

Girls who have psychologically detached themselves from their families too early, too fully, having taken with them too little in the way of self-confidence and inner strength, enter adolescence in serious jeopardy. The vicissitudes of adolescence will probably weaken them further. They are susceptible to overreliance upon external sources of approval to maintain tolerable feelings of well-being, adequacy, and self-esteem. Their own truly personal desires and needs may melt away and be forgotten, replaced by a greater need to be desirable to others, perhaps on their terms. They may find their self-esteem held in the hands of others rather than within themselves. For many girls, that external other will be a boyfriend.

Left with a diminished sense of self, she will find it more difficult to be alone with herself and her own thoughts and feelings. Inordinately, good feelings may exist within her only when placed there by another, not a warmth she is able to reliably kindle within herself. Similarly, bad feelings seem able to be removed only by someone else rather than herself. She is vulnerable to overdependency. Weakness and dependency do not produce domination or necessarily a pathological state of submission; they are merely prerequisites.

Deficits in confidence, independent sources of self-esteem, and assertiveness contribute further to a girl's preparation for unequal and controlling relationships. Boys, in the AAUW Report *Executive Summary* (1991b), were found to be twice as likely to speak out in class and also two times more willing to "argue with my teachers when I think I'm right."

Orenstein estimated that in the suburban eighth-grade class in which she spent time, boys outnumbered girls five to one in the frequency with which they called out answers.

Sadker and Sadker's (1985) observations of one hundred classrooms in four states found that in the typical classroom setting boys overwhelmingly dominate the procedings, initiating contact with their teachers with a frequency eight times greater than girls. By adolescence, boys have taken a clear and growing lead over girls in initiative, confidence, self-esteem, and assertiveness. They are learning to master their surroundings. Girls are giving away opportunities to receive praise, to feel good about themselves through their own efforts, to experience the value of venturing forth, taking action and risks, of asserting themselves. Our society generally is not disturbed by this lack of development when it involves girls. We tend to become concerned only when boys demonstrate this passivity, uncertainty, or weakness. We accept without thinking that by adolescence girls have learned to "get along" while boys are learning to "get ahead." Girls have instead been assigned the "lesser" tasks of caring for, nurturing, and maintaining relationships with others, often at some cost to their own self. These qualities are both valued and derided. They are valued for their manageability and the comfort they provide for others. They are denigrated for their suggestion of weakness and dependency.

Sport serves as a perfect example of an exercise in the maintainance and strengthening of all the personal qualities that adolescence can threaten in a girl. Adolescent females who play sports are found to be less depressed than their peers, have a more positive body image and higher self-esteem, and were more willing to take risks on and off the playing field (Jaffee & Manzer 1992, Women's Sports Foundation 1988).

Hotaling and Sugarman (1986) concluded that the main factor contributing to the victimization of women within relationships with men was being female. We might add that being an adolescent contributes even further. The adolescent effect appears to be twofold: first, by weakening female self-esteem and fostering a greater dependency on external sources of psychic sustenance; and second, by eroding the feelings of competence, independence, mastery, and assertiveness needed to meet one's own needs and to insist that significant others consider those needs as well. Adolescence for some girls renders them more susceptible to submission in the face of attempts at domination from males.

Chapter Three looked, systematically, at various factors in the origins and characteristics of dominating males. Factors such as family background, race, age, and socioeconomic factors such as income, educational level, and occupational status were considered. The leading conclusion, however, was that psychological factors were the real common denominator among these boys and men. Psychological and personality factors are also of paramount importance for girls and young women but in a more complicated fashion that does not lend itself nearly so well to generalization. While only a certain type of male will demonstrate a powerful pathological need to dominate in a love relationship, many kinds of females can fall into serious difficulty with a male who emerges as a dominator. Personality characteristics may contribute to how the female handles this difficulty and to how much she gives up and submits. They will offer very little help, however in describing the type of girl who is likely to simply become involved. Involvement alone can be a serious, even dangerous, problem to a girl. Managing such a problem, even with help from others, whether her desire is to improve the relationship or leave it, will require confidence that her perceptions and feelings are right, a level of self-esteem which allows her to feel entitled to consideration and having reasonable needs met, a belief that she is competent to achieve her goal, and the independence and assertiveness needed to actually carry it through. This is a prodigous challenge to any person and certainly to any adolescent. It can daunt even the strong. The inexperienced, the confused, the unsupported, and the weaker will be at even greater risk.

5

EARLY WARNING SIGNS

It is probably safe to say that all relationships begin differently and that at the outset it is usually impossible to tell how they will develop. This is what helps keep fortunetellers in business. Speculation in this area is a long-standing human tradition and has never progressed to anything like an exact science. Only the most deviant and inept individuals will give early in the relationship unequivocal demonstrations of how their pathology will become a threat later on. Most people enter new and uncertain territory with caution. They restrain their more negative urges, restrict their demands, and sheath their sharp edges. Their expectations normally are more modest. Their emotional involvement is (or should be) less. They are keenly attuned, to the extent they are capable, to the attitudes, feelings, needs, likes, and dislikes of the other and generally attempt to present themselves, to behave, in a way compatible with that person. At the very least, the other person is recognized as a separate entity who must, to some degree, be accommodated to if the relationship is to even begin. Many men who later emerge as exceptionally controlling in fact begin relationships as exceptionally accommodating. Her every wish is responded to as his command. He may be spectacularly attentive, showering her with gifts and consideration. It may even seem that he is willing to suspend all other interests and relationships of his own in order to fall fully into her life. It may seem at a surprisingly early point that she is all he cares about. Paradoxically, what may later become an inability to accommodate to her can begin as an apparent desire to be assimilated *by* her; he may begin his enslavement of her by offering himself as captive to her, but it is a Trojan Horse he is offering. I try to explain this to young clients and end up telling the story of the Trojan War too often without effect. I guess it's time to pick another analogy.

At any rate, the preceding scenario is just one example of the great difficulty in identifying the pathologically controlling/abusive relationship in its early stages. Particularly for young people, inexperienced with relationships, detection is likely to be extremely difficult. Even when the signs of a dominating attitude and behavior are present at the start, widely held traditional notions of appropriate sex-roles may obscure the female's view of what may be signs of danger. Finally, the enormously broad concept of what constitutes "loving" behavior will sometimes mask even aggressively controlling or abusive behavior in the guise of "love." Nonetheless, there are things that even an inexperienced woman is likely to see, if she looks for them, in the early stages of a relationship that should indicate the presence of this particular type of pathological potential. Therapists must also be alert to these signs in order to be in a position to quickly diagnose the danger and intervene effectively.

NEEDINESS

Much of what the controlling male does in his love relationships is fueled by neediness of some sort, though it may be expressed in enormously varied ways and cloaked in forms that may make him appear to be anything but needy.

It should always be a red flag and a source of concern when the male seems to need the relationship too much too soon. How much is too much? How soon is too soon? I don't know—there is no tape measure for this kind of thing. However, if the girl or woman feels there is a marked and uncomfortable difference between how much she feels she needs the relationship compared to how much he seems to need it, if she feels pulled or surrounded by his need in a way that makes her feel a bit like leaning back from it, then she *should* lean back from it. After that she should pay close attention to how he responds, to how much frustration, anger, or hurt it produces within him.

Gifts that the woman considers expensive or offerings that feel too large or too frequent, given at the the very start, can be a bad sign. Expressions of deep love at the start of the relationship should be cause for concern (e.g., cards, letters, flowers, etc.). The reactions of friends and family to his gestures will be of great help in assessing such acts. Therapists should ask about the impressions and opinions others have in order to broaden the scope of their information and perspective.

Men who either have no other interests, activities, goals, or sources of pleasure or satisfaction but the new relationship, or men who precipitously discard all else to focus exclusively on the relationship, signal trouble. While some women may find this attitude intensely flattering, it will not come free, and the cost is likely to mount quickly. While there may be appeal in the security it seems to provide, it may soon be *his* security that is served. The great neediness of dominating males will have many facets that will be more or less visible early on. Dependency is a bedrock term in the psychology of these men and boys. It will always be there and will always reveal itself sooner or later. It may seem that his self-esteem and general feeling of competence and well-being are inordinately dependent upon the status of his relationship. Since he "needs" to feel good, he needs the relationship and he needs it to feel good to him at all times. Consequently, he needs her to be happy and content with him at all times. If this feels like a burden and a pressure to the girl, she should pay attention to that feeling and consider its meaning.

It may seem that his entire psychological and behavioral equilibrium is dependent on the status of the relationship. When it fluctuates, as all relationships must, his state fluctuates. He may become depressed. He may become irascible, short-tempered, or violent at home, school, or work. His performance and achievement in the world may have no solidity. His grades or school attendance may plummet when he feels there is trouble in the relationship. He may not go to work, he may not eat or sleep, or he may drink or use drugs to cope. This may tempt a girl (or woman) with the lure of power and control, or appeal to her sympathy, caring, or guilt. A troubled boy (or boy-man) is a great attraction to some females, and a likely source of exhaustion and ruin as well.

On the other hand, the male may express his need for the maintainance and deepening of the relationship in entirely opposite fashion. He may react to minor natural ripples on the pond by pulling back coldly on his overt feelings. He may withdraw like a sea anemone, seeming to disappear within himself. He may pour himself into other activities and ignore her, make her chase him, make her restore the secure and constant placidity he needs. She is left wondering what happened, but feeling it must have been something she did. Again, friends and family can help the girl or woman to objectively assess the situation. If it does appear that the behavior is due to his "sensitivity," that she must walk on eggshells, even early on, in order not to upset him, then she must regard him as perhaps not ready for a serious relationship.

I knew a girl, a senior in high school, who, out of kindness and pity, decided to include one particular boy among the classmates to whom she would give Valentine's Day cards. She handed them out, dozens of them, in homeroom and in her various classes that day, as did many other students. It was a well-known tradition at the school and all in good fun. She and he were not friends. They had never been at any social gathering together. They had never even spoken, not even to say, "Hi." She gave him his card with a smile and without fanfare, saying simply, "Here."

The next morning he walked up to her in morning homeroom and gave her a red heart-shaped box of chocolates the size of home plate, an oversized and expensive card, and a small, carefully wrapped boxed gift. He beamed exultantly at her and took his seat across the room.

She came to me during first period, immediately after homeroom. She was intensely distressed, confused, and even frightened, carrying all these gifts. She plopped it all on my desk. I could tell it wasn't for me. She said she couldn't explain what had happened.

"Just read this, then I'll tell you what all this is about." She handed me the huge card and I read it. It was a profuse and overflowing testament of love, not so much gratitude or appreciation for her simple thoughtfulness, but raw, beseeching love signed, "Tom." I knew her life extremely well and there was no "Tom" in it.

"Who is Tom?" I asked, bewildered.

"Tom—!" she exclaimed, wide-eyed. I knew him.

"Why?"

"I gave him a valentine," she said, apologetically. I was surprised.

"Well, what did it say?"

"Nothing. It was just Happy Valentine's Day, with some silly sappy saying and I just signed it 'Jen.' Not 'Love, Jen.' Just 'Jen.'"

"And you got *this*?" I said, gesturing to the things overflowing my desk.

"What am I going to do?" she asked nearly in tears, panicked at having to see him and deal with him. She felt guilty, too, feeling she'd somehow toyed with him, led him on. She must have, she said, to have had him react this way, yet she knew, on the other hand, that she hadn't. I assured her that she hadn't. She couldn't have anticipated the effect it would have on him, but now she was going to have to take the initiative to calm him down. She had to call him and thank him, but explain that accepting all that he had given would give the wrong impression. She had to explain that she had a boyfriend whom she loved and that her valentine to him was intended as a friendly act, which she is very sorry carried a much larger message to him. Her goal was to lay this to rest clearly, kindly, but firmly, which she did, and no more was heard from him by her on this matter. Here was a fellow giving off some serious warning signs.

POSSESSIVENESS

Almost anything is okay in moderation, but possessiveness is a problem when present to any degree. A lot of possessiveness is a very big problem; a little possessiveness is a small problem, but it is still a problem. Any time one person seeks to contain, confine, or control another person to satisfy his own needs at the expense of the healthy and legitimate needs of another, an unsavory situation exists. Whenever one person attempts to enclose the life of another within his own life, the autonomy and the very self of the other will shrink and may eventually be entirely consumed.

Possessiveness will almost always be evident from the start. Like anything else, however, it can take many forms. The man may give the impression of wanting to be with the woman all the time, or at least all the time he has available. For teenagers, this may truly amount to nearly every waking minute, including before-school time, in-school time, afternoons and evenings, seven days a week, with phone calls in between and the clear expression of discomfort or unhappiness of some sort whenever circumstances force them to be apart.

He may seek to accomplish a near-total merging of their lives by including or intruding himself into as much of her life as he can, and/or discouraging her from continuing or engaging in activities that place her apart from him. He will try to make her friends his friends, or he may seek to pull her away from her friends altogether in various ways. He may denigrate them, say that they are bad in some way or bad for her. They will be called losers, snobs, sluts, or whatever. Time spent with them or even positive attitudes toward them will be perceived as disloyal, stupid, selfish, inconsiderate, foolish, or evidence of a problem with her character or personality. His attitude may be directed at her family as well. He may say very little, just pout. However it is expressed, the female will feel her life growing smaller. At first, she may not notice or mind because the rapture and excitement of a new relationship, a new love, may outshine all other interests, but eventually it will begin to cause problems. They may be experienced externally, at first, in the form of complaints and pressure from family, friends, and other commitments. It may be felt internally as frustration and confusion over what is right or wrong, fair and unfair, and where her time and energy should be spent. He will show very little doubt or confusion about this. He will seem sure and, in the face of this, it may be difficult for a girl or woman to hang on to a clear idea of what is going on in the early stages of an attractive relationship. Once ground is given, however, it is usually hard to regain it.

On his part, he may indeed have given up friends or other activities, seemingly all other thoughts, for her. He will point this out to her and expect the same. If she does not reciprocate he will question her love, her caring, her ability to "handle a relationship," her self-centeredness, even her maturity.

When he isn't with her, he may demonstrate an extraordinary need to know where she is, who she is with, and what they did to a degree that, if a parent acted that way, a teenager would be indignant and angry. He may spy on her, or have others do so. He will not call it spying—he may call his unexpected or uninvited presence coincidence, or say that he was in the area and just decided to stop by. But it may feel strange to the woman, and if she is with others at the time it may seem even stranger and more innappropriate to them. He may be the only boyfriend to visit an all-female sleepover. He might be the guy who shows up at his girlfriend's lunch period in the school cafeteria though he does not attend her school. He may be seen following her in his car or showing up to see her at work at a job where visitors are not appropriate and he has no important or pressing reason to be there. He may intrude into her family matters, entering into decisions or disputes or their familial relations in a way and to a degree that will disturb most members of most families. The girl or woman may feel that she is not without him in any part of her life.

Phone calls may be excessive, too. He may seem to need contact that feels like reassurance or supervision almost constantly. He calls immediately after having just left her. They have been at school or on a date or work together; they separate, go home, and he calls right away or expects her to. Certain phone conversations soon feel obligatory—for instance, a good night call nightly, an afternoon or after-school call daily, even when they've been together at the same school all day.

When out together socially as part of a larger group, he may appear to need to be at her side at all times or expect her to be at his side constantly. He may even insist on an actual physical attachment throughout, holding hands, arms around waist, sitting on his lap. They give the impression of not being separate people. Friends often find this extremely annoying, and they will be more or less articulate in saying so. They will feel and express frustration at the unavailability of the individual self of their friend. They will say, "You change when you're with him." They seem to be in a world of their own and when making contact with others it is in an inhibited, affected, limited way that lacks something genuine and free.

Sara, a senior in high school, was telling me about a problem she was having at parties with her large group of boy and girl friends. She had just begun seeing a boy named Carl, who was part of this large group and a good-looking, funny, and popular member. She had received little attention from guys during her adolescence though she was 17 and very pretty, probably due to her shyness, which may have made her look inaccessible. So she was pleased and flattered by Carl's attention. Though they hadn't had any actual dates, she looked forward to seeing him in school and enjoyed hearing about the nice things he'd told friends about her. She would feel excited about seeing him on Friday or Saturday nights when they'd all gather at a park or woodland hideaway to talk, flirt, drink, or otherwise carry on, but she felt that a problem was developing. She was having a hard time, though, making herself clear on what the problem was.

"When we go to the bonfire," (a regular hangout) she complained, "I have to sit on this big rock the whole time. Sometimes Kerry will sit with me. I stay there and people visit me."

"Okay." I'm thinking, *What's the problem and why do you have to stay on a rock all night?* So I asked her.

"Oh, I don't *have* to stay on the rock. It's just better if I do," she said. "Because of Carl."

"Why? Does Carl tell you to or make you?"

"No."

I was not getting this at all. I had to chuckle out loud at the incomprehensibility of it. I leaned closer to her from my chair. "Okay, now Sara, tell me why you stay on the rock if you'd prefer not to. What happens if you just walk around and talk to different people? I mean, if you step off the rock, do alligators get you, or what?"

She was smiling, too, the ridiculousness of the scenario not being lost upon her. "If I'm off my rock and walking around to talk to other people, in two seconds Carl comes up behind me and picks me up and carries me over to where he is, and when I leave to talk to other people he does it again." She was laughing now. "So I either walk around fast and say 'Hi' to people and keep going, all night, or I stay on my rock and people visit me."

"And that's okay? He doesn't mind that or get mad?" I asked, smiling as she was.

"Oh, he doesn't get mad. Even when he'd carry me around everywhere he never got mad at me. He would get mad at people I talked to or at our friends for laughing at him, but not at me."

"What about on the rock?"

"That was fine. I guess because I wasn't going up to anyone, they were coming up to me. I don't know. But that's pretty weird, huh?"

"Oh yeah, that's pretty weird all right." I had a lot more to say but had to save it for another time.

Carl's almost comical, literally physical, possessiveness was predictive of more serious problems with control and neediness. More disturbed and ominous tendencies eventually emerged. Fortunately for Sara, she did not love Carl and got entirely out of the relationship soon after it began. Not, however, before she had to witness him drunk at a party, punch *himself* in the face, knock himself down a flight of stairs in response to feeling ignored by her.

Possessiveness, like neediness, can hold a strong appeal for many girls and women. Obsession may look like exceptional thoughtfulness. His need for public clinging may mean, to her, that he is simply proud to be seen with her, and she may feel the same way about him. She may be unaware of the change it creates and angry at the perceptions and reactions of friends or family. His calls, visits, and attentiveness may be gratifying for various reasons as well. It is impossible, however, for two separate people to function always as one. We all have other things to do, places to be, people to be with. The overly possessive male will have difficulty tolerating this fact. Here is where the female will feel, at the very least, stirrings of a sense of trouble. She may feel outrage, too, but if she does, she is likely to forcefully knock back his demands and that will either be the end of the problem, if he can adjust, or the end of the relationship. Other women may feel much less certain. It may be hard for them to judge or gauge the appropriateness and normalcy of his needs and to sort out what she feels from what he and others say. Her affection and attraction for him, of course, make it even harder to understand how she feels and what to do. She likes to be with him. She likes to be liked and needed by him. She is proud to be with him. She is happy to be in his thoughts, to be wanted, to be so important to him. It can be thrilling, but when it is excessive, it will show.

It will show in the difficulty she will have in excercising routine independence, even in instances where she *must* be separate. It will show in the strain that will be felt in other relationships, with friends and family. It will show in the pull she feels on the time and energy she must devote to school, work, and other hobbies or activities. She may feel pressured or even guilty about simply going to class or home or work or music lessons or to the gym or to read a book. What may have begun as bending to his wishes can stiffen into a requirement to yield to his demands. Soon she will find herself fighting with those who see the trend (if she hasn't), fighting with him if she has, or fighting with herself if she is very confused. Often she will find herself fighting with all three.

JEALOUSY

There is probably no greater single force driving the pathologically controlling male than jealousy. It is often the first feeling to reveal itself as excessive, the first to become problematic, the one most likely to drive him over the edge. It is also the condition most likely to place the woman in the greatest physical danger. Roscoe and Benaske (1985) listed jealousy as the number one reason given by battered women for having been assaulted by their husbands or boyfriends. Only alcohol came close among the eight reasons given. Makepeace (1981) reported virtually identical findings in his survey of violence between college-age dating couples. Male sexual jealousy is considered to be the leading cause of spouse battering and homicide across cultures worldwide (Daly and Wilson 1988a,b). Society has acknowledged the overwhelming power of this force in love relationships. Further, it has supported the righteousness of such an act. Murder provoked by jealousy has traditionally been legal under certain circumstances. It remained legal in Texas and Italy within the past thirty years. Only a few years ago a young woman was publicly beheaded by order of the state for adultery in Saudi Arabia.

On the other hand, everyone has a capacity for jealousy. It is unlikely, if not impossible, that anyone who has ever desired another has not felt jealous at some point. Particularly during early stages of a serious relationship, when it has reached a point where feelings and attachment have grown strong but time and experience have not established an adequate degree of security, jealous feelings can be quite normal if not inevitable. We can more easily imagine losing our loved one to another. We may, therefore, experience greater anxiety and discomfort with sharing that person with certain others. We may be more prone to worry during periods of separation. Depending on the style of our partner, the nature of the relationship, our capacity for trust, the level of our own self-esteem and self-confidence, we may experience more or less distress in our jealous thoughts and fantasies. One's ability to deal with jealousy and the possibility of loss, more than the mere presence of those feelings, can tell a great deal about an individual's view of himself and his ability to handle a serious relationship. In the real life of the natural world, nothing can truly be guaranteed in advance. No state can be held absolutely constant. Things naturally move, fluctuate, grow, shrink, and shift. The possibility of loss and pain cannot be eliminated. The future cannot be proven.

It cannot be proven with absolute certainty that loss will not occur, it can only be dealt with by a kind of faith. This, as I have said before, is one area where the pathologically controlling male has a great deal of trouble and, consequently, where he gives his mate a great deal of trouble. For jealousy's central element contains the bottom-line fears and blackest imagery condensed into the single scene of a loved one in the arms of another—and it only gets worse from there. To him there can be no greater or more complete statement of utter rejection and personal inadequacy. His own deep-seated feelings and perceptions of himself cause him to be more expectant of this outcome and less able to bear its possibility. He is tormented obsessively by a possibility he cannot disprove. Faith, which can only be maintained by self-esteem, is absent. It becomes a serious problem for his mate when he cannot calm himself through purely internal processes. He cannot evaluate and analyze his situation with a clear eye and an orderly, reasonable mind. Instead, he sees, hears, thinks, and feels in a paranoid fashion. He fits his perceptions to his fears. He adds two and two and gets ten, and isn't able to check his work.

Jealousy and possessiveness go hand in hand. Possessiveness is an outcome of jealousy, a way of coping with the distressing thoughts and feelings that jealousy provokes by cutting them off at their source. The source, in his view, however, is the woman's freedom to have other relationships and contacts outside of himself. Indeed, it is the view of some evolutionary psychologists that male sexual jealousy evolved as a solution to the problem of uncertain paternity over the offspring of mating partners (Buss et al. 1992). In order to insure the furtherance of his particular progeny, the male must establish exclusivity of sexual relations with his mate. This need is observed in numerous species, including lions (Bertram

1975), bluebirds (Power 1975), doves (Erickson and Zenone 1976), many insect species (Thornhill and Alcock 1983) and non-human primates (Hrdy 1979). Since parental investment is greater among humans than in any of the other two hundred species of primates (Alexander and Noonan 1979) the pressure of this need might be expected to act most strongly on human males. Sexual infidelity, more than emotional infidelity, is the focal point of male jealousy (Buss 1989, Buss et al. 1992). Sexual territoriality, for some men, remains a primary and overwhelming preoccupation that can only be maximized by ever-present control. Since supervisory physical control is limited to opportunities for a physical presence, effective control must be emotional as well, yielding domination through possessiveness. Rather than seeking to cope with his feelings, fears, and insecurity by means of work focused on himself, he makes it her problem. She must adjust, rather than him. Instead of looking into himself in order to study, evaluate, limit, and correct his perceptions, thoughts, feelings, and behavior, he casts his eyes immediately outward toward what he views as its external source and attempts to deal with it externally. He studies, evaluates, limits, and corrects *her* thoughts, feelings, and behavior. He seeks to calm himself by controlling *her*. She is made to be the problem.

Again, most people have struggled with jealousy, at least in the form of feelings, if not with its actual behavioral derivatives. What indicates danger and the likely development of an excessively dominating and controlling relationship are factors such as timing, reality of perception, strength of affect, nature of behavioral derivatives, and whether the issue is dealt with primarily internally or externally.

Strong jealous feelings at the outset are always inappropriate and a sign of a strong need for proprietorship and control in a relationship that is likely to grow quickly if it isn't quickly quelled. It is an indication of powerful neediness and deep insecurity. If it also seems that the distress can only be calmed by external means, that is, the control and accommodation of the other party, then a serious problem exists. It would be a problem whenever it emerged in the development of the relationship, but the earlier it emerges, the more significant it is, the more powerful are the feelings and the less capable the person is in coping with them. Furthermore, early signs of powerful and poorly contained jealousy are suggestive of poor judgment, faulty perception, a strong tendency for self-reference and subjectivity, and an insufficient awareness and acknowledgment of his mate as a separate and independent individual with her own needs.

Reality of perception and the ability to test that perceived reality refer to the external justification for the jealous thoughts and feelings. In other words, does he have any legitimate reason to be jealous? Is it reasonable that he should feel at risk for losing his mate to another? What is the nature and strength of the evidence? Are his perceptions rational and objective? Has he considered other possible interpretations? How much is inferred? Is there even any evidence, or is his jealousy provoked merely by a lack of absolute proof to the contrary? Is his mate often viewed as guilty until proven innocent, rather than the other way around? It will be very difficult (if not impossible) for his mate to defend herself against suspicions and accusations if they are prompted more by his internal state than by objective reality, particularly if his internal state is unknown and inaccessible to him, as is often the case with the pathologically dominating individual.

This perceptual problem is so unruly and problematic because it has broken loose from the system of checks and balances that the executive function of the ego should be imposing on it. The emotions seem to be fed directly. Perceptions are not passed first through the evaluative screening, testing, weighing, and measuring of a strong and vigilant cognitive entity. His perception of reality is not sufficiently tested or placed in its proper perspective. His deficient self-esteem and self-image have constructed within him an ever-present answer to which his pre-influenced perceptions gather confirming evidence, unchecked by a faulty or subverted consciousness. Reason and logic cannot appease him, for it is not a rational problem. His inner doubts and fears must be addressed and bolstered directly, so that the girl or woman may find herself needing to offer a great deal of reassurrance of her love and steadfast and constant fidelity. She must bolster his inner self. Unfortunately, in the excessively controlling relationship, words will not suffice. He will need concrete, physical evidence, reassurrance, and proof. He will need to actually have her with him to be sure he has her, and he will need to have her physically separated from others to feel tolerably assured that he is not losing her to another. This is where jealousy becomes extreme possessiveness and the basis for excessive control and domination. If we accept the capacity for or the presence of jealous thoughts and feelings as a given within us all, yet acknowledge that most relationships are not destroyed or twisted into perverse shape by them, then it becomes evident that there are healthy ways of handling jealousy.

Therapists working with men or women with problems in this area, or with men or women whose partner has a problem in this area that is harming their relationship and threatening them, should be be able to evaluate the quality and potentialities of that dynamic. The negative manifestations will be reported, and much has been written of them in the preceeding pages. Positive signs, however, must be considered as well.

Since, at this point, I am speaking only of the early stages of a relationship and early signs that it carries dangerous features and possibilities, *any* strong and unreasonable displays of jealousy that are poorly supported by external evidence and that result in attempts at excessive possessiveness and control of the other in the early stages of a relationship are a very significant negative sign.

On the other hand, if the individual shows an ability to wait and check his (or her) perceptions, thoughts, and feelings so that his emotional and behavioral responses show objectivity, appropriate restraint, and a willingness to work on his feelings internally as well as externally, the picture will be considerably brighter. He must demonstrate that he can talk about it. He must demonstrate that he is able to test reality and see fairly clearly through the influence of emotional pressure. He must show a desire to build greater trust or faith. He must *want* to diminish and ultimately extinguish problematic, jealous thoughts and feelings, rather than maintain them with an attitude of righteous entitlement. He must demonstrate that he can tolerate and accept uncertainty as a natural condition, with comfort rather than debilitating distress. Above all, he must not seek to deal with his jealousy by forcing his partner to do all the changing, or by exclusively external modifications. He must demonstrate that he can and will work on his jealousy within himself. I emphasize the use of the word *demonstrate* because in this area, as in most others, deeds, rather than words, are what count. Promises and apologies in the absence of actual behavioral change are worth very little.

The focus of this book is on the problems of the pathologically dominating and controlling relationship for the male and female who are harmed by it. The literature (this book included) features the jealousy of the controlling male as a central and particularly dangerous aspect of that type of relationship. I must make clear that this is not to say that women have negligible problems in this area. I have no reason to believe that their capacity for or incidence of difficulty with jealousy is any different from that of men. I have had many female clients who have sought help primarily and specifically for just this problem. However, there appear to be several differences in their typical way of handling their jealousy and in the way the issue plays itself out.

First, women seem far more willing to view their jealousy as, at least partly, their own problem and are far more likely to want to work on it internally. Second, related to the first, they are far less likely to attempt to assuage their inner distress by external control of their mate. Third, society is far less supportive of a controlling female and a dominated male. There are few epithets which describe a dominated woman but many for a dominated male. He is called a "cuckold," "hen-pecked," "whipped," "tied to his wife's apron strings." It is a most odious and unmasculine position to be in. Women strong enough to achieve such dominance are not viewed favorably. However, when the reverse is true, neither appears to be in such dissonance with their sex role. Consequently, neither looks as bad and there is far less societal pressure against their taking or accepting such unequal positions of dominance. Fourth and finally, the jealous male is able, due to his superior physical strength, to back up his accusations of infidelity or his insistence on his partner's restricted independence with threats or actual physical violence, which carry a menace which few women can match. While there have certainly been many celebrated and not so well-known instances of female vengeance provoked by her partner's real or imagined transgressions, the data is very heavily in favor of the male as the one who, through his propensity for domination and aggression, must be stud-

ied with intensity and greater concern regarding the issue
of jealousy.

   The three characteristics mentioned as bearing possible early indications of a developing pathologically dominating relationship are neediness, possessiveness, and jealousy. They are separated for the purpose of descriptive
clarity, though in real life they always live together, merely
different aspects of the same entity. It is not so much their
mere existence but their strength and intractability that
partly determine their symptomatic quality. Many distin-
guishing features have been noted and some distinctions
drawn between pathological signs versus more healthy
manifestations and coping. I would like to add one final
note. A critically important diagnostic issue and important early sign of trouble is the individual's response to
challenge and frustration of his needs within the relationship. How does he deal with a girlfriend's resistance to his
needy demands and confining jealousy and possessiveness? The most hopeful and healthy reaction, of course,
would be an open-minded consideration of ways to accommodate to the style and needs of his partner if, in fact, he
wishes to stay with her. One looks for an ability to deal
with issues such as the amount of time spent together, time
spent apart, other relationships, differences in interests,
friends, needs, and decisions on sex, among other things,
without provoking a level of anger, anxiety, depression,
or emotionality that overwhelms and contaminates perception, cognition, objectivity, and mature recognition and
accommodation. Can he learn and adapt without problematic distress? Without becoming enraged? Without threatening, stalking, harrassing, or spying? Without sulking,
withdrawing, withholding, or suicidality? Without fighting back with jealousy games that seek to frighten his mate
into submission by appearing to pursue other women in

place of her? Anger, guilt, and confusion-inducing accusations and threats are common responses of the dominating male when his needs are frustrated and he is made to feel insecure and fearful of abandonment. His conscious focus is entirely outward, external. He steadfastly insists he is right and fair and justified while she is being selfish, callous, disloyal, immature, bitchy, slutty, and whatever else comes to mind and seems to have effect. If that doesn't work, or if his style is different, he may take the nonaggressive approach of "loving": pleading, crying, throwing himself at her feet, and placing full responsibility for his precarious well-being in her hands, hoping to seduce her by flattery, empowerment, confusion, guilt, or fear, engaging in a kind of emotional blackmail that can and often does effectively trap a person.

Some men will use a variety of stratagems, looking for a soft spot until one of them works. Once firmly hooked, even if by demonstration of his need and dependency on her, he will quickly revert to efforts at greater control and domination.

Some men will be more subtle. They are able to quickly judge the danger of rushing too hard too fast. When their control is challenged forcefully they back off. They will make peace for the time being, seeming to adjust to the needs of their partner, but they remain crouched always at the very edge of her tolerance, straining to accept it and always, always ready to press again. They wear a false smile in compromise. Their relentless return to the same point in the same way ultimately reveals that they have not changed in the least and have learned nothing. These men will wear a woman down, and they are much harder to identify early on. Their nature may be most evident to a perceptive woman by the strained control they appear to maintain over their temporarily frustrated possessiveness and neediness. Psychologically, they are perpetually biting their tongues and gnawing at their knuckles rather than maturing and enjoying mutual recognition and growth.

The early stages of any potentially serious relationship are not characterized by intellectual analysis or cerebral scientific testing of the qualities or characteristics of the object of one's affection. There is, rather, a more emotional, visceral appeal, the features of which cannot be logically assessed or empirically measured. We cannot even effectively or fully explain an attraction to another. What can be explained are aspects surrounding an ineffable center. And the center is the all. It is essential, and without it the rest does not matter. It explains why So-and-so, wonderful and beautiful as he or she may be, can only be a friend, while So-and-so can never be anything but a lover. In this state, rational danger can be difficult to see. Giving up and giving in may be done with joy and independence little valued. The importance of friends, family, personal interests and activities pale in comparison. The self may be gradually encircled, squeezed, and diminished without making a sound. Eventually, though, the emotions will begin to shift and groan under the stress. Things won't feel quite right. Others will point at and complain of the change. Conflict, tension, and the debilitating effect of the growing pain and work of the relationship will increasingly take away from the joy in the relationship. Love and hate, bliss and agony, hurt and help, real and unreal, caring and abandoning, respect and contempt rail together into a swirling and incomprehensible mix. Young people, in particular, are often completely unprepared to understand or make a decision about something so inconstant, parodoxical, and chaotic. We have grown up to believe that a thing is a thing and one thing only. We are not taught that a thing can be many things at once, even opposite things. We are led to believe that a thing can only be one thing at a time and find it hard to understand that a thing, regardless of its present manifestation, can carry other things with it that, though not always visible, are equally present. Mostly we are not taught that love can carry hate, harm, selfishness, domination, and even death. More than half of all women murdered in the United States during the first half of the 1980s (52 percent) were victims of partner homicide (Browne and Williams 1989). Analyzing all criminally negligent homicides from 1976 through 1987, Browne (1993) found that women are more likely to be killed by their male partners than by all others categories of persons combined.

Despite all of this, and the frequent reminders in the media and the press, most young people continue to believe that if it is called "love" it must be true and it must be good. The early signs of unhealthy love or need, in the form of pathological domination, are, therefore, more easily ignored, misinterpreted, or minimized. Warnings are more likely to be discredited, overlooked, or disbelieved. When the feel and look of it does begin to change, they are ill-equipped to find their way out of the confusion which increasingly fills them because it has snuck up on them. Supported by a traditional culture and history which has always supported the roles of dominant males and submissive females, disguised by simplistic beliefs in the basic goodness of anything someone has called love, held to it by the pressure of peers, unresolved confusion, and, for some, the bond of sex, growing dependency, and the fear of loss and loneliness, an excessively and pathologically controlling relationship can begin to be established.

6

THE ONSET OF DOMINATION: SEX, LOVE, AND THE "SERIOUS" RELATIONSHIP

Whether by development or design, excessive levels of domination rarely come to life in the earliest stages of a love relationship. Research and clinical experience show that attempts at pathological domination and control, as well as physical and sexual abuse, within young people's relationships usually begin only after the couple has come to view the relationship as serious. As was described in Chapter 5, one would have to be a fool, grossly inept, brazen, and rash to try to take such control at the outset, which is not to say that some males don't begin in just that manner and sometimes succeed. It is not the usual pattern, however, nor is it the initial intention of many young, ultimately dominating men. It is only when the emotional stakes have become high, when one comes to perceive a loss as unendurable or at least excessively painful, when emotional dependency has become powerful, and when the internal problems of low self-esteem and inadequacy trigger the dominator's obsessive morbid fear of abandonment that the compulsion to control will begin to grow to unhealthy and dangerous heights.

This is the point at which a serious problem exists for both parties. Even if the relationship is viewed as serious by just one of them, especially if it is the male, the other can find herself the victim of severe pressure to submit. Resistance or, worse yet, threatened or actual separation can precipitate desperate measures on the part of the panicked and perhaps destabilized other. The feeling of responsibility thereby thrust upon the young female can be dreadful, particularly amid the inevitable confusion of the situation.

When both parties view the relationship as serious and believe that they are in love, the problem quickly becomes a dilemma wherein to remain in the relationship is unhealthy, but to leave is frightening and unbearable. Here is where the couple becomes stuck in a way that I have found extremely difficult to extricate. The longer it goes on, the worse it gets. The damage, psychologically, is progressive, the risk in leaving more profound. When the relationship has been sexual, which in serious adolescent relationships it usually is, the bond, the emotions, and the problems become supercharged.

Research has consistently found that violence, when it occurs in dating relationships, develops *after* the relationship is perceived to be a serious one. "Serious" is defined for the purpose of most studies subjectively by the individuals themselves, from a group of choices. A few studies (Stets 1992, Stets and Pirog-Good 1987) have included the component of "time spent together" or have considered the length of the relationship (Deal and Wampler 1986). Some have linked a young couple's designation of their relationship as one of "love" to attempts at domination and to violence. As with much of the research in this field, the presence and incidence of the male's physical aggression is interpreted as an indication of a need for excessive control. While the one doesn't always equal the other, the association has effectively been shown to be strong enough to warrant that presumption. Stets and Pirog-Good (1990), in a study of college dating couples, found a "very strong relationship between the two dimensions of interpersonal control (attempting to control and successfully controlling another) and aggression" (p. 385). Their study, like many others (Stets 1992, Stets and Pirog-Good 1990, Straus and Gelles 1990, Sugarman and Hotaling 1989) showed that females were as guilty as males in initiating and using violence against their partners. Henton and colleagues (1983) reported further that violence by one increased the use of violence by the other. However, female attacks were less severe, caused far less injury, and seemed to bear a different instrumentality. The young women were more likely to inflict aggression when *attempting* to control, while the young men used more violence for the purpose of *maintaining* control. Stets and Pirog-Good (1987) found that control in dating relationships was associated with a need to keep serious relationships stable and predictable. We see here, in action, the intolerance of uncertainty. Violence as a means of control has been found more likely to occur in serious dating relationships by many (Cate et al. 1987, Henton et al. 1983, Laner and Thompson 1982, Stets and Pirog-Good 1990). Laner and Thompson reported that 86 percent of the young couples in violent relationships described their relationship as serious, while only 14 percent of the "casual dating relations" reported experiencing or using violence. Browne (1987) reported on research on college dating, finding that 72–77 percent of the couples' physical aggression developed only after the couples were seriously involved, were engaged, or were living together.

For Henton and colleagues' (1983) high-schoolers, 76.9 percent had become serious before the violence began. It has been found that couples who spend more time together have higher rates of violence (Stets 1992, Stets and Pirog-Good 1987). Deal and Wampler (1986) reported that persons in more longstanding relationships held more accepting attitudes toward violence within the relationship. Male sexual aggression was found more likely to occur the more serious the relationship had become (Russell 1982).

Sex is a key factor in what makes individuals within a relationship perceive that their relationship is a serious one and that they are in love. This is probably particularly so in young persons' relationships. They basically believe what they have been told: sex means love; love means sex. You don't have sex unless you are committed to each other. Sex means you *are* committed to each other. True, adolescents do not always act on all or any of these beliefs. Still, the myths are strong and often exert a powerful force, certainly when it is in their interest to embrace them.

Peplau and colleagues' (1977) college couples were found to base their perception of whether their relations were serious or not on whether they were having sex. Cate and colleagues (1982) reported that among the high-school-aged couples studied who experienced violence, the aggression first occurred after the relationship had become sexual in 83 percent of the couples.

For many young couples, sex makes it serious. Sex and serious relations both develop earlier today than ever before. Certainly their peer group supports, if not promotes, more serious monogamous relationships very strongly. Speaking of peer pressure in this regard, Barrie Levy, author of *In Love and In Danger: A Teen's Guide to Breaking Free of Abusive Relationships* (1993), writes, "They are judgmental and critical of girls who are not seeing one special guy. A girl feels pressure to be in a relationship even if it is not good for her" (p. 53). Sex is the major link to problems with jealousy, possessiveness, and ultimately to attempts at excessive control for males and females. Males are generally able to back up those needs with more power and more effect. Young people entering adolescence with low or diminished self-esteem, unmet dependency needs, and depleted ego strength have enormously powerful attachment needs. Their apparent detachment from parental figures only means that the needs have been transferred, often to other adults, usually to peers, frequently to a love object. Many unwisely funnel all these needs into a single relationship. In doing so they invest the relationship with absolute power to provide for his, her, their, total sense of well-being, self-esteem, personal adequacy, competence, desirability, and approval—in short, life itself, in the present and in the future. This scenario is so frequently seen in adolescence that, while it is often a matter for concern by adults and even by peers, it is considered normal. Most can deal with its existence and ultimately its dissolution without suffering any significant upheaval or harm. Some cannot.

As was described in Chapter 5, many young people are sexually active practically from the moment they become adolescents. For girls, in particular, this is not a positive development. Aside from the medical risks, such as pregnancy and an ever-growing list of curable and incurable STDs, the psychological risks are significant. Sexually active girls tend to have lower self-esteem than abstaining girls (Coles and Stokes 1985). Many girls engage in sex *because* of low self-esteem. Many find their self-esteem lowered in the aftermath of a sexual experience—it hits them both ways. Coles and Stokes found no association between sex and diminished self-esteem for boys, which is not surprising considering our culture's continuing double standard in this area, one that is alive and well among teenagers as well.

As with adult and married couples, sex was found to be the major source of conflict between adolescent dating couples (Lane and Gwartney-Gibbs 1985, Makepeace 1981). Sex is not only substantially responsible for making the relationship serious, for instigating development of excessive possessiveness and jealousy, and indirectly provoking a greater need for control, it is a major battleground in and of itself. Conflict immediately arises between the boy and girl around the issues of frequency, location, type of sexual acts, the when, where, and how of sex, as well as the perennial question of whether to have sex at all, which our culture has kindly left up to females to decide.

Most girls have not found their first sexual experience to be a pleasant one (Orenstein 1994). Neither have most boys, but they have far fewer misgivings about keeping at it. Girls, on the other hand, are immediately deluged in an internal backwash of societal, religious, and personal admonitions, not to mention the difficulties of peer-group reactions, the reverberations of the often disappointing and painful physical experience, and the fears of pregnancy or disease. It is typical then for girls to hold very mixed feelings about sex and what it means to them personally and within the relationship, and for that ambivalence to manifest itself in an irregular desire or acceptance of sex.

Boys have far more consistent feelings about it and find the girls' inconstancy difficult to understand and, in most cases, more or less maddening. Here is where girls are called "fickle," accused of manipulation and "mind games." Here, too, is where sexual coercion and downright aggression are born. Domination of the interior as well as the exterior life of the female often go hand in hand.

Yet sex equals love in the minds of many and, so, much is tolerated. Many young women are uncertain of their right to say no to sex within a "love" relationship, especially if they've said yes even once. Girls sometimes believe that if they have excited a guy they are then responsible for his condition and therefore *must* satisfy him. Guys lie and tell girls that if they don't "get off" they will suffer excruciating pain ("blue balls"). In any case, adolescent relationships often become entangled in the bonds of sex, fortifying the problematic bonds of "love."

Beliefs, in particular myths of love, serve as powerful forces holding a young couple together even when one or both of them senses serious trouble with the now serious relationship. Again, Henton and colleagues' (1983) study of high-school relationships is most informative. They write that partners believe there is only one person in a lifetime with whom they can fall in love and that they are and should be inseparable. Men, in particular, have been shown to hold to a belief that love is forever. Peplau (1983) observed that "men are more likely to endorse 'romantic' beliefs such as that love lasts forever and comes but once" (p. 242). Support for this finding reported by others (Okun 1986, Rubin et al. 1981) may be found in the greater difficulty men have been reported as having with breaking up or the unwanted termination of a love relationship (Peplau 1983, Stets 1993).

The power of love's bond is evident in how couples will perceive and interpret problem behavior and what they will tolerate from each other. In the first study of dating violence, Makepeace (1981) noted that 44.7 percent of the relationships which had experienced physical aggression had remained intact. Twenty-nine percent reported the belief that their relationships had actually improved. Cate and colleagues (1982) reported very similar results, with 53 percent of the violent high-school relationships intact and 37 percent reporting improvement. Finally, Henton and colleagues (1983) again, writing of high school couples, found 41 percent still dating, with 36 percent feeling the relationship had improved.

In Cate and colleagues' study 29 percent of abusers and abused viewed violence as an act of love. In Henton and colleagues 26 percent of the victims and 31 percent of the aggressors interpreted the violence as deriving from love. Very few (41 percent of victims, 3 percent of aggressors) viewed it as a form of hate.

The point is that once a relationship becomes serious and is perceived and felt to be one of love, particularly if tied tighter by the bond of sex, in adolescence the relationship has become a difficult one to break, a difficult one to leave, a difficult one to bear losing. Males are found to have the greatest difficulty. Peplau (1983), in discussing research findings on this subject, writes, "Boyfriends were less sensitive to problems in their relationships, less likely to foresee a breakup, less likely to initiate a breakup, and tended to have more severe emotional reactions to the ending of the relationship" (p. 246). Writers in the field of battering and severe spousal abuse are unanimous in stating that an abused female partner's threatened or attempted breakup places her in the greatest physical and mortal danger from her male spouse or partner (Browne 1993).

We have, at this point, a relationship which is established and close. There is a significant degree of mutual dependence. Loss would be a hardship. There is the perception and feeling of love. Each derives from the other a special feeling that they may get from no one else. It provides some of the best feelings each has ever experienced. They may be sharing many firsts together. They may believe that they are each other's one and only. It may, therefore, have occurred to them that without each other they would be doomed to a bitter loneliness. They include each other in thoughts of the future. Perhaps they have never allowed anyone to know them as they are known within this relationship. Would, could, anyone else know and then accept and love them like this? They know secrets of each other's lives, feelings, and bodies. These intimacies are unique, exhilarating, and bonding.

In the face of all this and more, it can be difficult to see, identify, and acknowledge serious problems. Certainly, conflict and pain will be present and felt, yet there may be strong resistance to seeing them as a problem. More often, couples will simply want the troubling episodes to pass and will do anything to simply make or let them go away in order to get back to good feeling and away from bad as quickly as possible. Denial and avoidance help. Apologies are accepted and believed to signify change. Each may strive mightily to perceive and interpret words and deeds in the most positive, hopeful light, going to terrific lengths and the most outlandish of cognitive contortions to support a view of their partner and their relationship as good and good for them. It is in their interest to do so to the degree that good perceptions maintain good feelings. Depending on their tolerance for distress, or for bad feelings in general, good thoughts and good feelings may need to be supported against all indications to the contrary. For those whose weak and fragile self-esteem and sense of personal adequacy and desirability is largely, if not totally, dependent upon the belief that they are loved in a particular loving relationship, this view may need to be defended against any and all detractors, be they external or internal. Outsiders simply don't know, don't see, the good. Doubts from within are often buried or converted. Problems, therefore, may be difficult to accept, the beginnings of domination difficult to identify and still more difficult to combat. Within the emotional context of a love relationship, perception, judgment, reality-testing, and assessment will be hard pressed to do their jobs well. Friends can play a critical role in helping a friend fairly, truthfully gauge what is happening within and around them. They may be in a position, as trusted witnesses, to hold up to their friend pictures of what is happening. They also can provide emotionally support-ive alternatives to a relationship that may be going bad. In the end, however, if the truth is bad, hard, and scary, and presents a threat and a challenge to one's internal and external well-being, the truth may waver. The profound impact of loss of a key relationship on teenagers is seen in the finding, reported by many, that loss of this kind is the leading precipitant to adolescent suicide attempts (Curran 1987).

Identification of the problem, then, is not a simple matter for those involved. Nonetheless, if bad things are happening, troubling feelings will usually exist, though they may not be appropriately linked to their actual ori-gins. Instead, they may be experienced as confusion, gen-eralized anxiety, depression, or some combination of vary-ing unpleasant emotional states, few (if any) ascribed to the appropriate etiology. For females, much of the distress is likely to be internalized. They will scrutinize themselves for the causes of their troubling feelings and discontent. Having adopted this perspective, trouble will not be hard to find, and will take the form of self-blame, guilt, and second-guessing in a potentially unhealthy and often inaccurate array of self-castigation. The absence of any absolute right or wrong in much of the world of interper-sonal relations leaves most of what is done open to sub-jective interpretation. Young women without a very firm and positive sense of themselves may be unlikely to judge fairly and judge well. Yet it is just that sense that adolescence weakens in many girls. It is difficult and for some, impossible, to judge what is selfish of them to demand, need, and expect and what the self is entitled to in the absence of a somewhat healthy and solid image of self to refer to. And it must be a self held in fairly positive regard, otherwise it will not be viewed as deserving or well provided for.

One of the saddest statements I ever heard came from a nearly 18-year-old girl whom I was recently asked to evaluate. Her background is a wretched one, having included nearly all of the worst that can happen to a child, from the start, including repeated physical and sexual abuse from more than one parental figure, addicted, mentally ill parents, a disorganized, unpredictable environment with many moves and separations. It wasn't long before all of this bore fruit in the form of serious conduct problems and self-injurious behavior. From the age of 11 Jean had been held in one form of residential program or another with only brief and unsuccessful visits home. Runaways, prostitution, suicide attempts, and substance abuse were later added to her history. Her relationships with others became more disordered and, from males, abusive. In all that time, up to the present day, she had never attended a regular school, sat in a regular classroom, been inside a high school even for a single day. She'd never had a date, gone to a teenage party, a dance, a prom, or a game.

She was responding to a TAT card, picture 8gF, which may be described as a young woman sitting with her chin in her hand gazing off into space. Her face shows no expression. It may be read many ways, as a good projective image should, yet she is clearly pondering. All the action here is taking place in her head, in the view of most people who respond to it. It is usually a quiet card, eliciting inner thoughts and feelings regarding aspects of a person's life, wishes, and self-image. It requires effort, imagination, and openness to produce significant material for this card.

Jean dove into it, at first, without hesitation. "She's thinking of her future and she can find nothing in it for her. She hates herself for that." Then she pushes the card away. "I don't like that one." I asked her if she could look at it a little further and add a bit more about this person. "She hates who she is and who she isn't, everything about herself. . . . People do like her, but those who do, like her only because she puts up a front. They tell her to try, that she can do it. They say, 'Do it for yourself.' But she has no self to do it for."

Caroline, also a 17-year-old with a slightly less horrific history, had been a top junior swimmer. Between the ages of 10 and 14, she had been one of the country's best. The dissolution of her family, their subsequent lack of support, and the demise of the own confidence, focus, and strength led to the slipping away of her involvement with the sport. When she was 15 she met John, and he became her life. His will flowed into the void of her own. She welcomed it. It gave her shape and purpose. So when she revealed to him one day what she had hidden or denied to all others, that she had been sexually abused as a child, and he spit in her face and called her a slut and said she'd probably liked it, she tolerated it. When her friends and all other activities and connections melted away, replaced by nothing or by him, she considered it, in balance, an acceptable trade.

Now she was 17 and she was beginning to change. In therapy, which she entered and remained in without telling him, she exercised and allowed to develop a new perspective, or rather, an old one, a growing consideration of self. Yet it was small, weak, and unsure. For instance, she could not, on her own, decide if it was right to attend the rare family function against the opposition of John.

John hated her family, not for what some had done, but because they were rivals for her thoughts, attention, and time, and had a capacity for making her sometimes feel good about herself, which he alone wanted to control.

She had decided that she would like to begin working out again, even to swim again, not necessarily competitively, just for exercise. Reflection upon herself and her past had led her to choose this as the focal point of her burgeoning effort to revive herself, to get stronger. Yet she struggled mightily with the feeling that to do so, to do for herself, was to betray John, whom she felt she needed and who had done so much for her. When she safely checked her wishes out with him by making joking, apparently nonserious references to exercise clubs and swimming, he would rant about the showoffs and whores in slutty exercise suits displaying themselves to everyone in sight and to the predatory men and instructors they attract. As for swimming, that meant bathing suits, and only he could see her in one. He ridiculed her past successes as kiddie-pool competition and teased that with her large breasts she'd be plowing through too much water to make any time anyway. Furthermore, the desire to win would be more selfish showing-off. So she never told him.

Yet she could not be comfortable with her efforts. She joined an aerobics class and swam nearly every day but did it early in the morning and kept it from him, careful always not to let it slip. Though her conditioning improved and her strength and speed in swimming increased so fast it amazed even her and drew much praise from astonished onlookers, she could hardly muster any feelings of pride, no internal feelings of greater strength or happiness. It seemed to add little to her care or consideration of self. Instead she continued to be harassed by guilt and shame for lying to him, for displaying herself, for her limited pride, ambition, and "selfishness." She actually had to ask me if she were being fair. If you have to ask, if you have to actually think about something such as this that should, in a healthy self, be effortlessly clear, you are in big trouble.

This kind of reasoning has nothing to do with intelligence. Jean, for instance, was one of the brightest persons I've ever evaluated, with a tested IQ at the 99th percentile. Caroline was an A and B student all through high school and maintained that level through her first year in college. Yet where self is concerned there is a hole in their thinking. Their selves are too insubstantial to be properly weighed in the balance when considering what is fair, what they need and are entitled to, and what selfish is.

Nonetheless, when an individual becomes aware that a relationship is becoming or has become uncomfortably and excessively controlling she must take initiative and act. She must act strongly and persistently in word, but especially in deed. She must present her controlling partner with at least the appearance of a firm resolve not to back down on important issues such as sex, having other friends, interests and activities, time spent together either in person or on the phone, physical aggression, or whatever else seems important. She must have faith in two things in order to hold her ground or to win back lost ground: one, that since he does love and need her too, that he will change if he has to; and two, that she will survive without him.

Unfortunately, for a girl or young woman to effectively cope with unhealthy domination once it has been identified, she must rely upon strong reserves of just those qualities that adolescence itself may have seriously diminished. She must be assertive—she can not lay back in simple defense. This assertiveness must come forth from a confident belief in the rightness of her feelings and needs. She must value herself enough to feel deserving and worthy of consideration and care whether from herself or from him. She must view herself as lovable in order to believe that she is loved and that therefore, he may change to keep her. Finally, she must believe that she exists, can exist, will have a self or others to fall back upon if they part. The adolescent female's frequent lack of a coherent, tangible self-image held in positive regard is her greatest liability and is largely responsible, along with the pressures of love, for her falling victim and prey to confusion and inaction. Ostrov and colleagues (1989), in a study of gender differences in adolescent symptomatology in a nonclinical population, found that 20 percent of the girls (between ages 16 and 18) reported feeling confused most of the time, more than twice the percentage for boys.

THERAPEUTIC IMPLICATIONS

The therapeutic implications regarding a controlling male or an increasingly dominated female at this stage are several, and it is at this point that distress levels will become high enough to either bring a person into therapy or to present the relationship as problematic material in therapy that has already been established—if the client is female. A male who is seeking to dominate a female is very unlikely at this stage to feel that there is a problem. To the degree that he feels uneasy in his relationship he will simply respond by exerting more control. He will view his problem as external to himself.

It is at this point, however, that, unless she effectively resists or leaves, a young woman in a pathologically controlling relationship will begin to shrink as a person, to have her spirit slowly crushed. As for the young man, he has begun his self-defeating course, which, if he succeeds, will either destroy or drive away that on which he will increasingly depend. Both will be wasting the last best chance that adolescence provides to strengthen and mature critical aspects of their character and their way of living and relating in the world in preparation for adulthood, marriage, and parenthood.

Young men or boys who are already in therapy and present unknowingly as dominators are unlikely to respond to their therapists' urging to beware of that path. In the absence of any internal distress they are not apt to feel any great motivation to take the great risk of loosening their grip, particularly if they do not sense any great distress or resistance from their mate.

In work with the female half, however, one of the first things I am concerned about is sex. If she hasn't started, I emphatically suggest that she not begin. I explain the reasons for this, saying that if the relationship becomes sexual, it will immediately be much harder for either of them to end it. I warn that the boy is likely to make things particularly difficult and messy and greatly increase the chance that he will haunt and harass her if she leaves. "You have told me and showed me that there is trouble here. You can be sure, absolutely, that sex will increase it."

Depending on the range of her present activities and associations, I seek to maintain her self-stated awareness and appreciation of their value to her and the pleasure they give. If some of her interests and good friendships have already fallen away, I look for any little hook into her feeling that she misses them and try to pull those feelings out and display them before her. I encourage her to regain them, to be a larger, more varied person, and warn her of the risk of basing one's life on any single person or thing. If she recalls having felt better, had more fun, slept better, done better in school, gotten along better at home, or in any other way perceives and feels that she is worse off now than before, I first strive to keep these impressions alive in her consciousness and support their validity (if they do seem valid) and second, help her to see the causal links that may exist between her unhealthy relationship and these subsequent changes.

I am in favor of her distress so long as it can be directed fairly at the relationship rather than in unfair ways toward herself. It is only her distress that can motivate her to take the hard course of either changing it or leaving it. Her distress is also a sign that she cares about herself enough to feel bad that she is being harmed, that she has a self that exists, has life, and is crying out in dismay against its oppression.

In matters of the heart I have little faith in the weight of empirical or intellectual measures in one's ultimate decisions. For this reason, I don't give much credit to lists of pros and cons, good and bad points, healthy and unhealthy qualities, in helping a person to decide upon a matter such as a love relationship. Experience has shown me that you can have twenty things on the bad side of the list, but if on the other side there is the one ineffable spark still aglow that had drawn her to him in the first place, that had placed him without question within the boyfriend rather than friend category, then the twenty items on the other side just seem to crumble.

Nevertheless, I do want her to hold in her consciousness all that she has told me and all that I have drawn from her and held up for her to see, if not in the form of a list, though she may keep one if she likes (I have my notes), then at least maintained in a repeated spoken form. And these points must be repeated, over and over again, for her rumination. I advise keeping a journal, though unless one is a journal keeper one usually finds it hard to start. A journal ensures that material is kept in consciousness and is critiqued by the higher, most objective levels of reasoning. Change and trends, both positive and negative, are recorded and may be reviewed. It is harder to bury,

dismiss, or forget. When the time is right the conversations, the internal lists, the dual and solitary reflection and
deliberation, which may have lain latent and passive, may
then come to life and in one quick burst support the positive action she now believes she can and must take. After
all, that is how all great discoveries and insights are arrived
at, how all new ideas are born, through a burst of revelation arising from a prepared mind. We therapists merely
prepare the mind—the realization that creates change
comes when it will. So I try to prepare (and keep prepared)
my client and wait for the trigger to bring to life what has
been well stored. I do not urge a break-up. To do so before
she is ready would be ill-advised for several reasons. It
would, of course, be getting ahead of things. It would risk
a shutting off of material or a change in what was presented in order to avoid the therapist's disapproval and
disrespect, and cause the client to feel disobedient in the
therapist's eyes. She might also terminate. The therapist
would be safest and most productive by listening to and
supporting the client's own thoughts and wishes in that
regard, keeping present the reasons she has given for the
value of such a move, using her own words and ideas as
much as possible. The therapist's own strong feelings must
be subdued, his or her own hopes, expectations, anger,
and enthusiasm held in check lest impatience and frustration show through. We must expect the process to be
slower than we wish. One should not think that simply
because the girl has said, in the supportive, somewhat
artificial atmosphere of the therapist's office, "That's it,
I'm breaking up with him," that she will really walk out
and do it. It will probably be much harder than that. Statements such as that are usually no more than an essential
form of mental and emotional rehearsal for the real thing.
She must first imagine herself doing it. She must try on
the thoughts, feelings, and imagery of it before she can

be reasonably expected to actually do it. In fact, if the client openly muses on the possibility, I encourage it, urge her to take the thought to its furthest limits, making it clear that I am only thinking of it as practice or rehearsal, rather than give the impression that I expect her to immediately follow through. The active management of breaking up from a pathologically dominating relationship will be discussed in detail in a later chapter.

Presuming (for the sake of the book's organizational needs) that the relationship is likely to be ongoing, that neither party is ready to consider leaving it, attention must be returned to evaluating it, coping with it, and changing it if possible.

Once it is mutually established that the girl accepts that the relationship is harmful to her in specific ways and that she needs to change it and the way she has come to live her life, specific plans can be jointly developed. Here the therapist must become far more active. Having chosen an area or areas where pressure should be brought to bear, therapist and client can then collaborate on strategy. It is essential that the challenge chosen be reasonable and suitable to her capabilities, that it be something she stands a good chance of holding her ground on. It will often be necessary to start small—a night out with friends, for instance, maybe more than she can handle if it will provoke a reaction from her boyfriend that will overwhelm and defeat her. Instead, she may need to begin by carving out time for herself for less pleasurable activities, to work, to nap, to do her homework. These are less likely to propel him against her, fueled by the force of jealousy. They are more likely to be viewed as necessities and commitments that do not stand either as rivals to him or alternate sources of pleasure for her. Consequently, she is less likely to be weakened in her resolve by guilt or confusion.

Clearly, these are small things and she deserves far more, but we are held to her pace, whatever it may be. In any case, he is being forced to adapt, to accommodate to her, forced to tolerate separation. This is good for both of them. It would be wonderful if he were to use that time productively. As for our client, simply having asserted herself effectively has been a healthy exercise that now must be repeated regularly. Furthermore, by doing so she is already building a life to fall back to if she is able to gain increased freedom from him, and she is preparing the ground for herself emotionally if they should part altogether.

None of this will work, however, if she lives in constant fear of utter oblivion should she anger and then lose him. She must be gradually prepared to spend time away from him, even if it means to be alone, and learn to tolerate it, to fear it less, hopefully even to fill that time with other things she loves.

Each challenge against his control is valuable in two broad areas. The first includes those therapeutic goals just described, which may be referred to as effective assertiveness, building the self, and practice and preparation for separation. Each challenge also stands as an exercise and test, not just of the female's fortitude and resources but of the controlling male's reaction and response, and this is the second area. The therapist must help her to observe those responses and find the significance in them. What feelings do challenge and separation provoke in him? How strong are they and what behaviors do they produce? Can he adjust? Can he be objective, empathic, and try to see her side and her needs? How distressed is he by even slight diminution of his control? What level of dependence and desperation or rage does it reveal? And what does all of it mean about the character of his love and care for her and their prospects for the future?

As we can see, this is not a problem that will easily lend itself to the brief therapies of modern managed care. This may be one explanation for the finding by McGee and colleagues (1990) that most of the adolescents in his large general population sample who were in counseling had gone to school counselors. The other advantages of school-based therapies, besides their potential for long-term free services, are the opportunity for self-referral and the possibility of confidentiality and privacy from the client's parents. The adolescent, if he or she is in high school or college, can usually access therapy without needing to go through an adult to get there or pay for it. A girl doesn't need to tell her parents that she is having trouble with her boyfriend in order to get help.

Regarding parental involvement, I am all in favor of a parent forcefully prohibiting a son's or daughter's harmful relationship, but they won't hear about it from me unless it's life-threatening. They will have to find out on their own and usually will. They rarely, unfortunately, have the power to stop it. The days of sending daughters off to a convent, or sons to the army, are gone. For better or worse, the young people will have to work it out largely on their own and perhaps with the help only of those they choose.

The problem with parental involvement at this point is that, out of love or their own need to control, they will almost always rush their child and succeed only in adding acrimony and turmoil in the home to that already existing within her and within her relationship.

If they are aware of it, however, they are under no obligation to help it. Peace at home is very important. Home should be a haven, and it is impossible for parents to maintain that and fight the relationship at the same time. They explain to their daughter that from what they have seen and heard from her and perhaps from others (using her own words and actions that they themselves have heard and witnessed as much as possible), the relationship is bad for her. As parents they may not be able to prevent it but they are obliged not to help it. Therefore, he cannot come into the house. She cannot use their car to see him. Certain rules may have to be adopted to encourage time spent doing other things rather than with him. There are innumerable options here and a therapist working with a family or with parents in this predicament can offer much specific guidance on these matters. Parents must be urged not to play games with this. For instance, they should not look for trivial pretexts to constantly ground their teenage daughter as a blatant subterfuge to keep her away from him. Nor should they attempt, in most cases, to *force* her to become involved with other things, since it is usually wasted effort. Instead, they should merely open doors and reward her for going through them, reward her for doing all the things that are good for her to do. They must accept limited control over what isn't good for her to do. Such is the lot of the parent of any adolescent.

I am sure it is easy for the reader to imagine all sorts of problems in this scenario, and there are many. Lying, deceit, continued struggles for control, very nasty battles may become part of home life. If the girl is 17 or older she may even move out. Nonetheless, unless the parents are exceptionally powerful, there is little else they can do.

Finally, in cases involving physical abuse, stronger measures may be required. (There will be more on this topic in later sections.) Parents should consult with local police and the district court's district attorney's office and, if they exist, battered women's groups on the laws and practices of the police and courts in their area. In some states and counties, police are instructed to make arrests even if the victim denies the attack, so long as there is strong evidence that one has occurred. Parents will need expert help in pursuing legal actions in such cases where they themselves may not have witnessed the assault. They should get advice on restraining orders and statutory rape laws, depending on the ages of their daughter and her boyfriend. In this way, they may help bring additional pressure to bear upon the unhealthy relationship.

7

OUT OF THE BLUE
AND INTO THE BLACK

Our composite couple is now seriously involved, in love and very much wishing to remain so. Thoughts of parting fill them with dread. But they want it to be good and it's a growing realization within at least the female that it isn't. Leaving is not a serious consideration or wish. Yet what she has come to depend on and look to for most, if not all, of what feels good and is valued within her and around her is also causing her great pain, distress, and confusion, among other unpleasant and unwanted effects. Increasingly, she feels hung on the horns of a dilemma. She is in love, perhaps more intensely than she has ever been in her life, yet she sometimes feels worse than she ever has in her life and it is clear that the thing that makes her feel best also makes her feel worst. But she cannot leave. Often she feels that she understands nothing, is sure of nothing, can explain nothing. She is older but she does not feel wiser. Primarily, she cannot make sense of, in any firm or solid way, nor reconcile the opposites which seem to exist for her love, within her male partner, her relationship, and perhaps herself. It seems to her impossible and certainly incomprehensible that such polarities of good and bad, loving and hating, care and abuse, apparent empathy and obvious neglect can exist together in one person and one thing at the same time. And it is unlikely that anything in her background or experience has prepared her to understand. Our Western tradition and form of thought ill serves us in comprehending the common mutuality of apparent opposites, despite their omnipresence in the natural world. We, the intellectual offspring of the Judeo-Christian and Aristotelian traditions have been raised in the belief that good and bad truly are separate entities and phenomena. These were new ideas in the world 3,000 years ago. They carried with them the notions that man and nature, god and man, and even man and woman are separate and exist on different hierarchical planes, ideas that have caused us a great deal of trouble and that we are slowly struggling to shed.

Consequently, when an adolescent girl with a pathologically abusive and dominating boyfriend struggles to discern the meaning of his vacillating love and predict its course she will often find herself unprepared and unable to grasp the nature of the problem. She is often unable to simply, quickly, and clearly just see it and leave it as some might expect.

I find adolescents (and people in general) mightily resistant to accepting that good and bad are full members within a coherent whole, that the "opposites" are not so much separate, but merely different manifestations of one system. His contemptuous abuse, vicious jealousy, self-centered possessiveness, as well as his tenderness, desperate neediness, and protectiveness, are all demonstrations of a deeper dynamic involving dependence, insecurity, and fear of loss. All of his "good" and "bad" love emanates from a central wellspring and thus is all of a whole. It is a form of mental trickery to artificially simplify and separate this concept. It involves a form of psychological splitting wherein the "bad" is set aside and she bonds powerfully to the "good."

Some grasp this instantly and intuitively with a type of intelligence not measured in tests nor, unfortunately, much valued in society. Most, however, persist in trying to separate the two, and frustrate themselves trying to make sense of a problem while using the wrong method. Though their outcomes will continue to be inconclusive, their motivations for pursuing them in this misguided manner are compelling. In various ways the bad parts are split off, discarded, denied, rationalized, or minimized in order to protect and preserve a positive and viable image of a much-needed relationship, a much-needed person, and an unsteady and vulnerable self.

Simple methods include writing incidents or conditions off to various transient or chronic external forces, or to divide incidents into isolated, unrelated, one-time events that, therefore, fail to carry the meaning of a pattern of behavior. He blew up at me because he's stressed by the home or because he was drunk or because he misunderstood what I was saying or doing. He won't let me hang around with those girls because they really do have sort of bad reputations and I could get one too. He puts me down because his parents and teachers always put him down. He doesn't mean it. He had a bad day. He has emotional problems that aren't his fault. He thought I was talking to Jim about something different. It was a misunderstanding. Maybe I did look slutty. He's had bad experiences with other girls so he doesn't trust very easily. He just has a temper. Over time, the dominated woman may give up her notion that the good and the bad are separate and discrete entities, but the dominator is likely to hold tenaciously to this perspective.

Many young women will look to themselves, to their own behavior, for explanations for their problems. They will search within themselves for triggers to his abuse or mistreatment. Henton and colleagues (1983) reported that in one-half the cases of physical abuse in high-school couples, victims felt or shared responsibility for the assault. As a byproduct of a particularly female degree of adolescent self-scrutiny and their oft-cited tendency for internalizing anger and blame, adolescent girls are especially likely to view themselves as a part of the problem. In some cases this may be due to a desire for empowerment in making the relationship better. If you are part of the problem, maybe you can be part of the solution. It can give a feeling of control to a situation which might otherwise appear frightfully out of control and unpredictable. Usually, inappropriate sharing or taking of responsibility comes from a negative self-image and low self-esteem that allows the individual to easily feel that they may be the one who is wrong, bad, or a problem to others. I must emphasize the word *inappropriate* here, since an attribute of maturity and good mental health is the capacity for introspection, self-study, and a vigilant observing ego. It is only when self-critique becomes unduly, unfairly, and inaccurately critical that it becomes inappropriate and unhealthy.

In a related dynamic, her taking onto herself responsibility or blame for the relationship's problems helps her to preserve a positive, idealized image of the person on whom she has come to depend and to love. To view him otherwise would immediately confront her with a very unpleasant and frightening crisis and deal a blow to her perhaps already damaged or wavering self-esteem. For her to be loved by someone she has labeled good helps her to feel better about herself than if she were to view him as bad.

Nonetheless, the inadequacy of all her answers and images breaks through to her nearly every time a new problem arises, her needs are squashed, or defiled, or his mastery is thickly imposed. At these times she may fall victim to the confusion that adolescent females have been shown to be particularly vulnerable to. It is a confusion which breeds self-doubt, a loss of confidence, and a discrediting of one's thoughts and perceptions. It incapacitates the confident assertiveness she needs in order to fight back. Furthermore, it opens her up to the fear that perhaps she is the crazy one. She feels that she has lost the capacity to make sense of things. She loses faith in her ability to think, reason, and come to an understanding of things. She feels she has become mentally and emotionally weaker. This is particularly disturbing if he presents as unassailably certain of all that she is confused about and reinforces by his statements and actions her sinking state. The pathologically dominating relationship practically defines what he will and must do. This type of male will externalize his problems and turn the tables excessively. He will deny, project, and avoid responsibility, and it is critical to his need for control that he weaken her desire and ability to resist. It is then a short step from confusion, self-doubt, and the inappropriate sharing of responsibility to self-blame.

The fact that the pathologically dominating male is often, albeit rather unpredictably, good, loving, and attentive in his way serves only to baffle and stultify his mate even further. His benevolence is as capricious as his abuse. It appears to follow no pattern that can be anticipated, improved, or controlled. Changing oneself has not seemed to help. Changing him is forcefully rejected and even dangerous to suggest.

Benjamin (1988), Browne (1987), Okun (1986), and Serum (1979) have all emphasized the dramatic power of intermittent, random, positive reinforcement upon human behavior patterns. It is well accepted that this system of reinforcement produces the most persistent behavioral response. The subject becomes intensely dependent upon the reinforcer. Since the positive reinforcement is bestowed in a random and irregular schedule, it is persistently expected and hoped for. It is the power behind gambling addiction, for example. In behavioral terms this viewpoint would predict that remaining in such a relationship would be a behavior very difficult to extinguish. Serum listed ten phenomena that were found to occur both in battered women and concentration camp prisoners. Their applicability to even non-physically abused victims of domination and abuse and to the specific vulnerabilities of adolescents is chilling.

1) guilt feelings, with an attendant sense of deserving the victimization
2) significant loss of self-esteem
3) detachment of emotion from incidents of severe violence, and extreme reactions to trivial incidents
4) failure to observe the controller's rules because of the arbitrariness of punishment
5) extreme emotional reactions
6) difficulty planning for the future and delaying gratification
7) fear of escaping the coercive control situation
8) child-like dependency on the controllers, and identification with them
9) imitation of controllers' aggressiveness, and adoption of their values

10) maintenance of the hope that the controller is kind and just [cited in Okun, p. 87]

Drawing upon the work of earlier writers and researchers, such as Bruno Bettelheim (1980), Jay Robert Lifton (1961), and Edgar Schein (1961), who studied the effects of concentration camp experiences and Chinese thought-reform techniques upon inmates' personalities and their relationship to their captors, close parallels are found to the experience and coping style of battered and systematically dominated women. Okun (1986), in reviewing their work concludes, "All consider the ambiguity induced by random, non-contingent rewards to be a very important influence contributing to the breakdown of the battered woman" (p. 129).

Lenore Walker, author of the landmark study *The Battered Woman* (1979), considers this tactic to be the means by which the batterer induces "learned helplessness" in his female partner. Lifton (1961) considered this process crucial to the effectiveness of thought reform and "brainwashing." The process has also been called "coercive control" by Serum (1979).

Serum adds that many of these features, such as irrational guilt, low self-esteem, and fear of leaving have been used by some to support the idea that women in abusive relationships are either masochistic or suffer from a predisposing psychopathology that guides them toward victimization of this sort—a sad case of blaming the victims for their plight.

Schein and colleagues (1961), using the term "coercive persuasion," described the thought reform process, dividing it into three parts: unfreezing, changing, and refreezing. The unfreezing process is intended to disrupt the person's (prisoner's) psychological equilibrium and produce a form of psychological breakdown: "If the unfreezing experience had undermined or destroyed the prisoner's self-image and basic sense of identity, he found himself with a fundamental problem to solve . . . the re-establishment of a viable self. In other words, the unfreezing could precipitate an identity crisis" (p. 131).

The prisoner feels he or she must construct a self-image that is defined by the coercive controller as acceptable. Adolescent females trapped in pathologically dominating relationships find themselves struggling amidst similar forces and influences and may experience similar effects.

Schein and colleagues named five kinds of supports which contribute to a victim's resistance to this process. They, too, have striking parallels with the scenario of the dominating relationship. They are: (1) desire to resist, an initial attitude of noncooperation—as stated in the previous chapter, the young woman needs to assert herself in the early stages against unhealthy control; (2) physical strength and well-being—getting enough sleep, rest, proper nourishment, and good solid physical health are problem areas for many adolescent females; (3) emotional and cognitive support validating one's own beliefs, attitudes, and values—the progressive isolation of the pathologically dominated girl, the separation from family and friends often leaves her without this essential support. It also leaves her feeling she has no alternatives in her life to the relationship, no one else to go to; (4) a strong positive self-image; (5) basic personality integrity, including viable intrapsychic defense mechanisms and stable superego values.

Studies of brainwashing do not seriously question the effectiveness of these techniques, nor do they presume that the average individual should be able to withstand them. Quite the contrary—no suggestion of masochistic tendencies, predisposing psychopathology, or personal weakness is leveled or insinuated against its victims. According to the literature, no predisposition is necessary for one to succumb to brainwashing. Young women caught in controlling relationships are viewed differently due to cultural ideas of the nature of women and femininity, ignorance of the power and process of coercive control, and the belief that leaving should be easy and the need to do so obvious. However, for adolescents, bonded by love, prepared by adolescence itself for a heightened vulnerability, uncertain, confused, and lacking, in some cases, a belief in the presence of adequate alternatives, the snare may be a snug one. Their peers, often an important source of support, will be unable to help if they have been kept unaware of the worst aspects of their friend's relationship. Secrecy regarding physical abuse and extreme domination are common. Henton and colleagues (1983) found that 23 percent of abused teenaged girls told no one of their physical abuse. Those who did tell were, however, most likely to tell friends (66.6 percent). Not many told parents (mothers 16.6 percent; fathers 10.2 percent). Peers who are told may not encourage their friend to break up. They may urge her to work it out, to not give up, not throw away all the time they've put into their relationship. Finally, her dread of an anticipated cataclysm of unknown duration were she to break off the relationship may cause her to opt instead for the intermittent hardships of the present. She may be buoyed by her hope for change, her memories of how good it has been, and the wish and the belief that maybe, if she keeps trying, she will figure out how to make it work, how to help him. If she hangs in until they are older, out of school, out of their homes, in their own apartment, free of the nagging stresses of young life, they will break clear and be all right. She's never been to the future before, and she hasn't read the research that shows that over time and on into marriage, it tends to get worse.

There is a different sort of dynamic that may serve to hold a young woman in a developing dominating relationship. It is different from what has been described previously, wherein the female has been pulled in by attraction, passion, need, and finally love; then held despite mounting difficulty, domination, and perhaps abuse, with the aid of a combination of cognitive dynamics such as confusion, rationalization, denial, overanalyzing, intermittent reinforcement, and hope. She is struggling to sort out the paradox and inconsistency of pathological domination. She is trying very hard not to acknowledge what it means about him and what it means for her.

Instead, the young woman sees and acknowledges the problem. She understands that her love object is badly flawed, that he is obsessively controlling and jealous, that he often does not consider her needs, that he is angry, temperamental, and unfair. She may agree with much that is said about him by concerned friends and family. She may even accept, to some degree, that the relationship as it is may not be good for her or, at the very least, that it is not as a loving relationship should be. However, it is precisely that understanding which holds her. It is the error of her empathy. She remains *because* she understands him and his problems, *because* she is able to empathize with his insecurity, his neediness, his constant demands for proof that he has what he depends on and his incessant fear of losing it. She feels that, as the only one who does understand, she has a responsibility and even a moral obligation not to hurt him further. She must not be the instrument by which his worst expectations and fears are realized. She is, therefore, imprisoned by obligation, with guilt patrolling its walls, and she senses strongly the ominous potential for disaster should she abandon him. In this she is the purveyor and embodiment of a long tradition of womanly self-sacrifice and selfless care.

It may come as no great surprise that women have repeatedly been found to take the perspective of the other in intimate relationships more freely and frequently than men (Davis and Oathout 1987, Long and Andrews 1990, Stets 1993). Additionally, it has been suggested that men's greater difficulty with taking their love partner's perspective may contribute to their feeling less in touch, less secure, and, consequently, more apt to seek control as a way of dealing with it (Stets 1993). This capacity for perspective-taking opens her up to an understanding that may become a powerful compassion. Her abuser may then be viewed as a far more wretched and needy sufferer than she—and she may be right. Her error is only in sacrificing herself to no good end.

Resisting his demands, even his oppression, then becomes in her view an unconscionable denunciation of his needs, selfish and unfair. She cannot hurt him, even if it hurts her not to. She feels that she can take it and he can't. She judges herself in terms of her ability to care for others, for him, and considers very little where her needs fit in. Her needs have become lost, subordinated to the full-time job of caring for his and, she feels, this is as it should be . . . for now.

A guidance counselor came up to me at the high school where I worked one morning and told me that a double suicide might be underway. You hear a lot of things working in a high school, but he clearly took this one seriously and was visibly worried. He gave me the names of the two students in question and asked if I knew them. I knew the names but I didn't know either of them personally. He then told me what he knew.

A twelfth-grade boy and his tenth-grade girlfriend supposedly were planning to leave school together that day and kill themselves. A student who was a friend of the girl had come and told him this. She even knew the method:

carbon monoxide reinforced with alcohol, using the boy's truck.

Both students had come into school that morning. They had been marked present in their homerooms. The counselor had already checked their schedules and looked for them in their classes and around the building, but could not find them. The truck, a conspicuous red pickup, was no longer in the student parking lot.

Though neither of us had a relationship with either student, we found that we knew a good deal about both of them. The boy was a very well-known, even notorious, fifth-year senior trying to get it right this time. He was struggling against his weaker instincts, trying to do enough work and attend enough classes to graduate. His chances were marginal, the outcome still very much in doubt. He was a poor student, weak and lazy. He did not lack adequate intelligence, merely strength.

She was a quiet 15-year-old from a family well known at the school, whose older brother had been rather famous for his fistfights, general aggressiveness, and all-around sullen and menacing manner. Up to this point she, in comparison, had been his much more studious and well-behaved younger sister.

As a couple they were distinctive. They appeared inseparable, but were an odd match. Though he was much older and extensively popular, she seemed so much "better" than him. The physical contrast was striking and discordant, she being prim, neat, and bookish, while he was obese, sloppy, and unruly. He was garrulous, in motion, animated, arms gesticulating, his features broadly expressive as he held the center of a crowd around him. She would be still, silent, holding books to her chest, standing by his side. It was known that her family disapproved of the relationship and that her brother had threatened her boyfriend. Nonetheless, they had remained together.

We called and informed the parents of what we had been told, got the plate number of the truck, and called area police departments with the information. It was in their hands from that point. They never found them.

The next day I was told that the girl, but not the boy, was in school. I sent for her and she came. She had no idea who I was, so her manner toward me initially was bland and neutral. When I told her who I was and that I needed to talk with her about what had happened yesterday, her expression immediately fluttered with anxiety, then settled into coldness.

"I see. So you're the one who called the police about us," she said. I was afraid she would head for the door.

"Yes, that's true. I heard they didn't find you, though. But I'll tell you why we called and then I hope you'll tell me what you think of it." I told her exactly what we had been told, by whom, and what we had done, including having called their parents.

"Yes, well, that was great. They were quite thrilled with that." She sat stiffly on the edge of her chair, about as far away from me as it was possible to be in my fairly small office. She kept her books on her knees. I was struck by her precise, controlled, adultified manner and speech and its contrast with her mate and the recklessness of their behavior.

"How did they react?" I asked.

"They can't stand Bill. They thought I wasn't seeing him anymore. Now they hate him more. My brother is definitely going to kill him and I'm grounded until forever, so I can only see him in school. In addition, they now hover around me and watch me constantly, like I'm a mental patient or something."

"Well, no one would like that much. But on our end, we had no choice. We took it seriously. We realize that if people are determined to kill themselves we probably can't absolutely prevent it. But we do have to make it as difficult for them to succeed as possible. That's the way it works. Sorry if it's caused you a lot of added trouble, though."

"He would have done it, you know, if the stupid hose had been longer. It was too short. It wouldn't reach from the tailpipe into the window. I suppose it is a bit unfair to blame the hose, though." She had put her books down and I began to relax. It seemed she would stay.

"What do you mean '*He* would have done it?' Weren't you both intending to die?"

"Well, yes, but I was mostly doing it because he was. He needed me to do it too, though, so he could."

"Could you have done it? Gone to your death for someone else, or did you have strong reasons of your own?"

"I don't know." She had softened visibly. "I don't know." She began to look pained. "Probably not without being drunk. That's when we mainly think about it. He couldn't get any alcohol, though."

I asked her some other questions about her beliefs and feelings regarding death, the likely effects on significant survivors, and about things in life she might miss, and I grew convinced that she did not want to die at all. In fact, she appeared to have a great fear of it. Among other things she believed in Hell and considered it highly likely that she would end up there if she died now, especially if it were by suicide. She felt very guilty about the effect her death, particularly in this manner, would have had on her mother and grandmother. She wanted to play softball in the spring.

"What about Bill?" I asked. "How strongly does he want to die?" She paused, staring down into her hands.

"I don't know about him. He probably does. He says if he can't be with me, he would rather be dead. He has many problems. And we can never be together. It seems like we can only be together this way."

"You mean, in death, together in death?"

"Exactly," she said weakly.

"Do you two agree on that?" She looked up from her tangled fingers.

"I don't think I can just leave him alone. If he did it alone I would want to die for that, anyway. So if I'm going to die anyway, I might as well keep him company and go with him. I have to do what he does." She said this with more desperation than conviction. "And I won't miss the shit I'm going through over this and neither will he," she added.

"Yeah, well, the problem is, though, you don't seem to want to die," I said. She was silent, her head back down again. "Who do you talk to about this? Anyone?" I asked. She shook her head.

"Nobody anymore. Of course not my parents. My friends can't stand Bill and just tell me to break up with him. They don't want to hear about it anymore."

"Why can't your friends stand Bill?"

"They have a number of complaints. They say that he's changed me, that I never see them anymore. They think he has me on a leash and runs my life and I just put up with it. Like I've melted or turned into some kind of a slave or something. They don't know the whole story, though. They don't know how *I* treat *him*."

I asked her if she would be willing to talk to me again the next day. She said yes without resistance, almost eager. It had not been a physically abusive relationship, yet it had nearly caused two deaths.

So, in this dynamic, these girls are not so confused. Instead, they may be deluded. Usually, especially if the girl is young, she believes that his problems will not last. Most young people believe in the future as a better place for them. One question I always ask a teenager who is contemplating suicide is, "If you could be any age you would like, would you choose to be a different age than you are?

What age would you like to be?" In the vast majority of cases, teens in this circumstance will choose an age a few years older than their chronological age. They may say 18 or 21. Responses such as, "I wish I were 2, so that I could begin my sorry life all over again," or "Seventy-five, so that I'd be near the end," or "No age at all. I'd prefer nothingness to another day of this," may be cause for great concern. Fortunately, most young people do not want to die. Most fear the uncertainty and permanence of death, and in the end prefer to take their chances with life. They are young, and therefore with a little push they can be helped to see, to remember, that at their age change is certain. Most consider life to hold positive possibilities. Adolescence, for many, has not been the best years of their lives. With the end of adolescence, however, comes changes, opportunity, or simply the expectation of escape. You don't have to remain in school. You won't have to live at home or even in your present town. You will no longer be trapped within the sometimes oppressive confines of your current teen peer group. The realization of this is one reason why teen suicide rates, while they have grown in recent decades, are far lower than those of any other age group (except preteen) and why so few adolescent suicide attempts end in death (Curran 1987).

Hope for the future and faith in the healing power of her nurturance and love help to hold her within the relationship. Time and care may mend his wounded soul. It is a heady brew, and its power can be captivating. A girl may invest her whole appreciation of herself in it. She thereby establishes a coherent identity through her role as "she who ministers to him." Her self-esteem and self-image may come to entirely depend on it, thus subjecting herself to the crushing dual force of his treatment of her combined with self-blame for not effectively helping him to be more loving. Tragically, she may be pursuing a mirage down a wrong road, convinced that if she just keeps on a little farther she will arrive at where she wants to be, unaware that she is going in the wrong direction.

PHYSICAL ABUSE

Certainly, the most spectacular and concrete manifestation of abuse and the need for control is a direct physical assault. This form of behavior, when perpetrated by men against women, has become a matter of national and even international concern. A perusal of bookstore shelves, talk-show offerings, or the daily newspaper will confirm this. The O. J. Simpson trial has provided an exclamation point.

As was stated in the introduction, the vast majority of attention on this subject has been devoted to married adults, though it is evident that physical abuse is a common problem in adolescent dating relationships as well. It's just that it gets worse later on. Hotaling and Sugarman's (1986) review of the literature on dating violence, nearly all of which was derived from samples of college-aged or high-school students, reported percentages of dating couples who are violent of between 9 percent and 65 percent, with an average rate of 30 percent. The February 25, 1995, edition of *The Boston Globe* (Shea 1995) listed eleven murders of women by current or former male partners in Eastern Massachusetts since January 1st of that year. Of those eleven, five were girlfriends killed by present or former boyfriends. Four of the men then killed themselves. In a dramatic proof of the increased danger females face when attempting to escape an abusive relationship, Partoll (1995) reported that 75 percent of the female victims of spousal or couples homicide are killed *after* they leave their male partner.

Physical abuse in dating relationships becomes more likely after a relationship has become serious and sexual. Sexual jealousy and sexual conflict, along with issues regarding alcohol use, are the factors most strongly linked to the physical abuse of females by males, be they adolescent or adult, married or dating. In an associated finding, reported by many (Browne 1987, 1993, Gayford 1975, Gelles 1972, 1974, Okun 1986), pregnancy increases a woman's chance of being assaulted. The Partoll (1995) stated that one in six pregnant women experiences some form of physical abuse, with the incidence of violence higher as the pregnancy progressed. Reasons for this behavior include the stress and strain upon the individuals and the relationship due to the pregnancy. This would include the increased responsibilities placed upon both partners and the increasing need for both to attend more to the needs of the female. Ambivalence or actual opposition to the pregnancy and the coming child and the changes it represents is another reason. Finally, and perhaps most important, is male sexual frustration due to a decreased and decreasing frequency or desirability of sex. Conflict over sex or denial of sex has been cited by Browne (1987), Lane and Gwartney-Gibbs (1985), and Okun (1986) as among the leading causes of physical abuse of females by males.

Jealousy, a central issue in the dynamic of the pathologically dominating relationship, has been repeatedly found to be the number one precipitant to aggression between partners in serious relationships (Browne 1987, Makepeace 1981, 1983, Okun 1986, Roscoe and Benaske 1985), followed closely by sexual conflict. A precipitant can be different from a reason. The precipitant is the spark, the last straw or the superficial, overt event which triggered the action. A cause or a reason is the deeper force behind the act. Jealousy is a normal feeling. Sex is a common and natural area of conflict to some degree. These only become supercharged issues that get out of control when they represent issues or trigger feelings that are intensely problematic to the individual. For the dominating male the denial of sex, or an incident which provokes jealousy, carry as well the fear of loss, abandonment, the perception of rejection, a threat to self-image, self-esteem, or personal adequacy and the feelings associated with them. He then responds in fear and anger to reassert possession and control in order to save himself. She, on her part, is then forced to give herself up so that he can maintain his equilibrium. Jealousy has also been named as the number one cause of attacks of boyfriends upon girlfriends in 65 percent of dating relationships (Roscoe and Benaske 1985).

Henton and colleagues' (1983) work offers further insight into the perceptions and emotions that give rise to such behavior in some males. Teenage aggressors (predominately male, in this case) reported feelings of "hurt" (52 percent) emotionally, in association with their attack. Something within the interaction led to him feel diminished and demeaned. He responded with anger at this (33.8 percent) but also out of fear (16.9 percent).

It must be reemphasized that all relationships feature uncertainty, misunderstanding, slights to one another, fear of loss, as well as hurt and anger. One's ability to cope maturely with these feelings and conditions, rather than their mere presence, determines their significance. The dominator and abuser cannot bear them.

This study provides insight as well into why these attacks are often rationalized or interpreted as acts of love, and why in many cases they do not end the relationship. Often, couples have reported their relationship improved in the immediate aftermath. Henton and colleagues asked their teenaged couples how they felt and behaved after the attack. Sixty-nine percent of the aggressors reported feeling sorry. So did 34.2 percent of the victims. Many of the aggressors cried (25.4 percent); talked to their partner

(41.8 percent); apologized (68.7 percent); and tried to make up (53.7 percent). These may have been some of their most open, vulnerable, and intimate moments, times when he may have been at his very best, the kind of lover she would like him to be. The contrast, then, between the unreasonable and violent nature of his attack followed by his solicitous self-flagellation, only adds to her confusion. It further confirms her perception of him as a wretched and suffering soul in need of her care. She is inclined to accept his apologies, believe in them, feel renewed hope for their relationship and uplifted in her image of herself as healer and as one beloved. It has not come free, however. She may fail to notice that she has paid beyond its value for it.

Browne (1987), in her study of women who eventually killed their batterers, found that while even these severe abusers professed remorse (87 percent) in the earlier stages of their ill-fated relationship, the percentage expressing remorse dropped sharply as time went on and attacks continued. Increasingly, the victim was blamed even though the attacks became more severe.

ALCOHOL

Alcohol has been implicated, of course, in all problems of violent and destructive behavior. I have had police officers tell me that if alcohol, our society's approved drug of choice, were to magically disappear, you could immediately lay off half the policemen in the country. It often plays a role in violence between couples as well. Conflict fueled by alcohol or about alcohol use is often cited as the number two (or a leading) "cause," "reason," or "precipitant" for violent attacks (Browne 1987, Makepeace 1981, Murphy and O'Farrell 1994, Okun 1986, Roscoe and

Benaske 1985). Those men who drink in order to cope with negative emotional states seem to be especially prone to using violence (Fagan et al. 1988), as were binge drinkers. These men also had a higher rate verbal abuse, anti-social tendencies, and early-onset alcohol problems (Murphy and O'Farrell 1994). Any teenage male showing signs of alcohol abuse should be considered to be in the early onset category. Alcohol abuse is also often used as an excuse by both parties in the relationship. They both say it wouldn't have happened if he or she hadn't been drunk, as if it therefore doesn't count. The drinking self is separated out from the nondrinking "good" self.

Many of my young clients take undue solace in this idea. They are both confused and encouraged by the inconsistency. Some girls seem to be waiting for him to become bad literally all the time for them to be sure that it's no good. I say to them that it will never be bad "all the time" anymore than it will ever be good "all the time." The question should instead be, "Is it bad more than I can bear, or is good for me?" and "Is it as good as I need it to be?"

MUTUAL AGGRESSION

"Research shows that women are as aggressive (if not more) as men" (Stets 1992, p. 167). Indeed considerable research, beginning with Straus, Gelles, and Steinmetz's *Behind Closed Doors* (1980), has supported that statement (Riggs 1993, Stets 1990, Sugarman and Hotaling 1989). It is, however, a conclusion which requires further analysis to be fully understood.

Browne (1993), in a review of the literature on male violence against women, critiques this statement and finds it simplistic and misleading. She points out that such a conclusion has been drawn solely from participation rates:

a simple tallying of admissions by men and women that they have committed at least one aggressive act from a presented list (push, shove, slap, kick, hit, beat up, etc.) at least once during their relationship. She goes on to point out several oversights leading to their conclusions. First, the intent of the aggressor is usually not considered, nor are the consequences of the attack (injuries caused). Second, findings were largely based on only one respondent per couple, methodology which she says does not provide a clear test of mutuality. Male underreporting must be considered as well. Third, even with these "limited measures" men have been found to rank much higher than women in types of aggressive action, severity of attack, and frequency of assault (Fagan and Browne 1993). Finally, women are much more likely to be injured and even more likely to be seriously injured by an attack.

Many studies also ignored the psychological context of an attack by a more powerful male upon a female as compared to an attack by a female on a male. Viewed in this way and from the standpoint of the potential for harm and harm actually done, the two are not really comparable.

> The potential for severe bodily harm from being kicked, punched with a fist, "beat up," or raped by a typical unarmed man versus a typical unarmed woman cannot be simply equated. It is unlikely that many unarmed women, simply by physical menace, would put their mates in fear of severe bodily harm or death. Yet physical menace is a powerful dynamic in assaultive male and female interactions. A recognition of the potential for severe bodily harm deeply affects women's, but usually not men's, responses to actual or threatened physical assaults by an opposite sex partner. [Browne 1993, p. 1078]

Additionally, studies equating male and female violence often do not include sexual assault, confinement, abduction, or the power of threats perpetrated by males in their counts or considerations. The experience of having been attacked and completely overwhelmed by any overpowering force is an unforgettable and traumatic experience, whether it be from a stranger or a lover. It leaves behind a heavy residue of anticipatory fear and sometimes a hypervigilant attitude of extreme caution that can pervade all aspects of one's everyday life. When the attack has come from a loved one, a person with whom one spends a great deal of time alone, the effect may be even more profound. If the attacks are repeated and unpredictable, the terror, conscious and repressed, is constant. His physical power and will to use it become the overriding theme and context of the relationship. If a young woman remains in such a relationship, she will find herself living her life primarily to please him in order to keep herself safe. She will have two choices: live with the overwhelming and debilitating stress born of a realization of the pathology and danger in which she exists, or deny, minimize, reinterpret, or numb herself to the reality of her circumstances in order to function and maintain an idealized relationship. In choosing the latter perspective, she opts for a deeper intrapsychic strain and a perspective that will require constant effort to support.

Nonetheless, female violence against males in dating relationships does exist and, if the observations of veteran high school teachers and personnel are accurate, teenage girls, in general, have become increasingly violent. A study on the Status of Girls in Massachusetts prepared by the Massachusetts Governor's Alliance against Drugs and reported in *The Boston Globe* of August 26, 1995, stated that "the rate of violence is accelerating among girls even faster than among boys"(Scales 1995, p. 16). The study also reported that more girls were being battered by their boyfriends than in the past. Though their courtship violence against their partner may not cause him much physical harm, it is no less an unhealthy and dangerous form of expression and problem solving. Furthermore, as Henton and colleagues (1983) have shown, violence instigated by one partner tends to raise the incidence of violence perpetrated by the other. In attacking her boyfriend she may trigger a retaliatory response far more severe and then find herself hard-pressed not to take on some, if not all, of the blame for her own injuries. Females who, in some way, help precipitate a violent episode by their own physically aggressive behavior not only risk physical harm but become highly susceptible to feeling a guilt that may obscure a clear perception of her partner's contribution to the relationship's problem. It has been well established that adolescent females have a strong tendency to internalize problems, to overly self-scrutinize and self-blame. Their own aggression certainly will not help them in this. Lastly, aggression, whether perpetrated by the female or the male, is simply very poor problem-solving. Riggs and colleagues (1990) found that aggressive couples scored lower than nonaggressive couples on a measure of social problem solving. In a later study, Riggs (1993) found violent dating couples reporting a higher number of problems in their relationship, resulting perhaps from a tendency to view any disagreement as a problem or conflict.

Finally, however, it is usually the young man's internal state, charged by his own alert and skewed perceptions of threat, that is ultimately responsible for most of his assaultive behavior against a love partner, rather than anything she herself has said or done. It is his own peculiar sensibility that causes him to feel the need to defend his shaky and vulnerable sense of status and adequacy, and to maintain a hold, through the use of domination, on that which he cannot bear to lose. It is his intense self-centered neediness, his demanding sense of entitlement to her heart and mind, that brings him to the point of rage at the perception of her rejecting or denying him. It is his own pathological and obsessive jealousy, born of a weak faith in his own lovability, his own desirability, which sparks his attack. All of these insecurities are likely to be increased within him if he is physically abusive, because at some level, despite his likely blame of her for some share of responsibility for it, he knows he is dirtying his own waters. He knows he is fomenting discontent in his own kingdom, perhaps even revolution. Yet in a dismal cycle of desperation, increased control remains his only available response and remedy.

The dominating male, at this point in his love relationship, is well on his way to serious trouble. His appreciation of that fact will be more or less clear, depending on the style of his personality, his defenses, and the resistance being put up by his female partner. His manner of coping with the problem of his increasing dependency, and the struggle to establish and maintain a level of control and certainty that he hopes will give him peace of mind, will vary. In any case, he too is speeding down the wrong road, convinced that if he just keeps going he will achieve the unattainable in absolute form. He too is unaware that he is traveling in precisely the wrong, the opposite, direction.

At this stage, some controllers maintain an impenetrable certainty and insistence on the absolute rightness of their feelings, actions, and present conditions of the relationship, regardless of any restless discontent or overt complaints on the part of his partner. They externalize, deny, and minimize all problems, and dismiss or turn back all dissent. In doing so, they will try, consciously or unconsciously, to induce confusion, self-blame, and guilt in their female partner, leaving her more uncertain, weaker, and more frustrated than she felt before she expressed herself. Her assertions and needs will be discredited. He will have been seeking to isolate her from other relationships, other voices, opinions, and supports, so that she is less able to objectively observe the relationship, him, and his effect on her. She is also rendered more dependent by virtue of her declining alternatives. He will insist that his way is the right way and is what is best, not only for him but for her and the relationship. He may support this position with testimony recounting his many sacrifices for her, his constant thoughts of her and need for her, and wonder accusingly why she can't do the same. He may also become verbally and/or physically abusive, depending on the degree to which he feels threatened or at risk, his impulse control, substance abuse, and personal style. The overriding features of this type, however, are the sense of certainty and the unwavering perspective of denial and externalizing.

At another level we have the individual who admits he is jealous, possessive, and demanding. His excuse, however, is that it all derives from the zeal and abundance of his love and is, therefore, essentially good and so can create nothing but good in the end. He acknowledges his insecurity, his enormous need, and his dependence, citing how little he has and perhaps has had without her. He may rarely, if ever, resort to abusiveness to establish or maintain control. If he does, he may become intensely remorseful, apologetic, throwing himself to her mercy. She finds, eventually, that her mercy is mandatory. He binds her with responsibility and guilt mixed with a sense of power over his well-being. Yet it serves as a form of emotional blackmail if her view of herself as a good, loving, caring, and competent person becomes contingent upon his welfare, even his very life. This then becomes the hook. If she can only feel tolerably good about herself by serving his needs, even to the exclusion of her own, then he has her, in a velvet grip. Progressively though, the grip may turn to a more painful iron one if he is unable to achieve peace of mind by those more benign means. He will gradually grow more dissatisfied, feel less served, less cared about, more deprived and ill-used. This may lead to more jealousy, possessiveness, overt anger, abuse, and violence as his partner is increasingly perceived as withholding, selfish, inconstant, and untrustworthy.

A third group features the most violent and most behaviorally and emotionally disordered individuals. They may possess a past and present littered with visible problems, arrests, failure in work and school and relationships, a highly pathological family, substance abuse problems, and a whole panoply of blaring anti-social and character-disordered features and symptomatology. They are the ones whom everyone would have advised a girl to avoid from the start. They are the rebellious and deviant bad boys so many girls find so attractive. To gentle and tame such a wild creature and win his thorny love, as in *Beauty and the Beast*, holds an ancient and powerful allure. Their domination is likely to be more crude, less subtle. When he messes up, either with her or in other ways, he will turn his prodigious anger outward, blame others, rail against his world's treatment of him, complain bitterly of the pain it's caused him, even admit to how it's screwed him up. These are excuses rather than apologies. He, too, needs his external world to adapt and accommodate to him, to cease its unfair persecutory treatment of him. He may lump her in with these forces. Or he may, instead, castigate her for having set him off, for having precipitated whatever outburst or abuse he may have heaped upon her by not having read or handled his volatile nature better. She is given most of the responsibility for maintaining his emotional and behavioral control regarding her. If he mistreats her it is because she set him off in some way.

She should know what he's like and his ways and avoid doing or saying this or that. He will admit his regrettable wrongdoing, but put the ultimate responsibility for it outside of himself. He places her in the hopeless position of maintaining his equilibrium by unreasonable levels of patience, solicitude, blind support, and tolerance. It is she who must constantly strive to do better. His imperfections and transgressions become her failings. He will support and reinforce her guilt, and self-reproach.

Regardless of his particular and individual style, background, use of violence, verbal abuse, or the variety of rationalizations, excuses, apologies or hooks that he may employ, the overriding constant is his focus on his own needs and the denigration or ignorance of hers. He is seeking to make her an appendage of himself, a colony under his lordship. There is no mutual focus on what is happening to *her*, what's good for *her*, what *she* needs. The focus directed toward her consists of what more can she do, how she should do it, what is wrong with what she does, what's wrong with her. For it is difficult to colonize the strong, the well-organized and unified. Though he may cry out that he would die without her, be nothing without her, he will shed no tear that she is dying *with* him.

It is from this perspective and from these constructs that the pathologically dominating young man will draw his thoughts, feelings, and responses regarding his love relationship and its struggles at this serious stage. However, these "types" are largely artificial categories, which are not mutually exclusive. They are descriptions of styles and ways of relating that a dominator may move through and among depending on his internal state or the apparent requirements of the situation. He will use various coping styles for overt attack or as defensive fall-back positions if he senses that a temporary strategic retreat may be necessary. But internally, his attitude may not have changed a bit.

THERAPEUTIC IMPLICATIONS

Since the pathological dominator is unlikely to view any problems in his love relationship as his problems, he is unlikely to seek help in resolving them. If he is aware of, or distressed by, difficulties at all, he is far more apt to perceive and experience them as external to himself and, therefore, someone or something else's fault or problem rather than his own. These may bother and frustrate him to varying degrees, but his attitude toward those conditions may be to insist or wish that they would simply "cut it out." Not exactly optimal material for psychotherapy. Most of what I have to say about the treatment of this type of young man or boy will come later when the breakup of a relationship of this type is discussed. At that point, the fatal flaws in his way of loving within a dominating relationship will have come to get him and will have smacked him right in the forehead so that they cannot be so easily ignored.

In the meantime, the abusive, excessively controlling young fellow remains an individual who is doing himself, as well as another, very great harm. He is at risk in many ways: developmentally, in terms of his own internal psychological and maturational growth, regarding the development of his ability to relate and to love in a healthy manner as a prelude to marriage and parenthood; legally, if he is violent or might warrant restraining orders; physically, since he presents a very real and dangerous suicide risk. Suicide risk in cases such as these create homicide risks as well.

If a male client in therapy for other reasons makes the therapist aware that he is a pathological dominator, the therapist should seek at every opportunity to draw out material regarding this area of his life and functioning— all thoughts, perceptions, and feelings associated with it. Every statement he makes that conveys distress, anxiety, uncertainty, or confusion—especially if it suggests an awareness, no matter how dim, of the basic faults in this type of relationship—are gold, must be noted, preserved, and reflected back to the client at every opportunity. For instance, he may complain of his own miserable jealousy, of his temper or abuse of her, and of the threat these pose to their relationship. He may describe how he cannot bear to be apart from her and tell of his obsessive need to check on her constantly. He may report on how all of this looks to others, friends, family, teammates or teachers. He may feel diminished by how he looks to them. There can be little else in his life with the potential to cause him as much harm as his unhealthy way of loving. Provided he is honest, doesn't exclusively externalize, is not physically abusive, and truly wants to change, he can be worked with on this. Sadly, these qualities are scarce in a controller.

Some have recommended working to increase the dominating male's capacity for empathy or perspective taking in the hopes that a fuller appreciation of the effects he has on his female mate, as well as of her feelings and needs, might motivate him to change. This may help. Often, however, his capacity for empathy is severely and steadfastly limited. He cannot budge from his own distorted personalized perspective. It is as if there is a hole in that part of his psyche. It is truly amazing how persistent can be his inability to "get it."

There is an eighteen-year-old girl with whom I have worked on a number of issues, including her two year captivity in a dominating relationship. She broke up with him after several tries, once and for all, about a year ago. Her former boyfriend, who lives just up the street from her and occasionally pops out his front door like a jack-in-the-box when she walks by with her dog, still has no idea what went wrong. He proves this by his questions, his demands, and by the complaints he makes to mutual friends. In these encounters, which continue up to the present day, he always begins and ends the same way. He leaps down his front steps to the street in a stale burst of exuberant friendliness. As he attempts to be carefree with her, he will pat the dog (that does not like him), and make a joke, which never makes her laugh. He straightens up, now ignoring the impatient pup and immediately asks her either how so-and-so is, if he knows she's dating someone (he keeps close track), or whether she's seeing anyone, if he isn't sure. He will tell her she looks nice and comment more particularly about some change in her appearance or new clothing she's wearing, gently giving the impression that she looked better before, meaning when she was still with him. At this point, regardless of her responses, his strained joviality slips away. She knows what's coming, but doesn't have the heart to just walk away. "So can we go out sometime? You know, go to dinner. Just friends." He won't pause for long. He studies her intently for her reactions because she doesn't say much or get a chance to. Her hesitation causes him to press on more forcefully. His composure from here on in rapidly melts. "Christ, you can't even be friends." She'll cut him off: "Don't start, O.K? I don't even want to get into this. You can't handle being friends." She usually makes the mistake of sticking around to battle it out, as in a dream that keeps repeating itself.

"If you weren't such a bitch, we'd be fine. I'll walk with you and we'll talk. There's no problem."

"No. I don't want to walk with you or talk to you. What else is there to say?"

"So you don't care about me at all. Two years and you don't give a shit. I was the first boyfriend you ever had. I know you better than anybody does. So now you think you're some kinda freakin' queen and you can just walk away."

At this she finally does begin to walk away. Sometimes he'll grab her arm to stop her. In any case, the verbiage does not stop there. It will continue on right to her door: "I still love you. . . . We can try it again. . . . It'll be better this time. . . ." She must eventually close it right in his face. He will have ended up yelling, swearing, accusing her of all kinds of sexual depravity with other guys. He'll swing back and forth within seconds from plaintive beseeching insistence that he is much better now, succeeded in the next statement by abusive attacks that prove he hasn't changed, that he has no idea what was wrong before or what he's talking about when he says he'll change or he has changed. What has finally become obvious to her is that he is poking at her with different approaches trying to find one that will work, allow him access, give him a hook. And it is always the same. He has learned absolutely nothing about himself or about her. All he knows, literally it seems, is that he wants her to be his. It is remarkable, really, and if it weren't so vile it might even be funny. In short, he appears to have no capacity for empathy in a love relationship. *The Boston Globe* recently (July 4, 1995) printed a front page story of a 31-year-old man, considered by local court officials the worst batterer with whom they have ever dealt, a man with many victims and dozens of arrests and restraining orders. His comment after his latest outrage: "I've had bad luck with women, but I have a heart of gold" (Ferdinand 1995, p. 32). Here is a man who doesn't get it.

Other dominators may understand or could be led to understand the perspective of their dominated partner, but approve entirely of the effect upon her and her subsequent plight. If the relationship has made her weaker, diminished, isolated, dependent, lowered in self-esteem, totally submissive, and less sure of herself, good. He will be her life. He will grant her the allowable dosages of good feeling, deriving solely from him. This is the condition he wants and needs her to be in to maintain his own sense of security, self-esteem, and peace of mind. He may not be inclined to give up any of that.

The dominating male who is physically abusive may be in therapy willingly or find himself there due to a court order or compelled by his mate as a condition to maintaining their relationship. These cases are different. Though the prognosis is no better, the urgency is no less. One's focus and the handling of confidentiality and legal issues, however, are all changed.

Success rates reported by programs for adult male batterers are very low, 10–15%, though no true longitudinal outcome studies exist. The rate may be even lower. Very few physically abusive men come to counseling programs voluntarily—5–10 percent, according to Jones and Schechter (1992). Data from the EMERGE program in Boston shows that, of those in treatment (many of whom are court ordered), only about two-thirds finish the program.

Many abusive men come to counseling only because they believe it is necessary to keep the relationship or to regain it if it has been lost. According to David Adams of EMERGE, "Most of these clients have sought counseling only once it becomes clear that their relationship will not continue unless they attend. . . . For most of these men, the problem, as they see it, is that their wives have left them, not that they have been violent. Some drop out as soon as they reconcile with their wives" (Jones and Schechter 1992, p. 108).

Indeed, the strategy, which is often all it is, seems to work. Gondolf and Fisher (1988) found that while only 19 percent of abused women living in shelters returned to men who were not in counseling, of those women whose male partners had simply entered counseling 53 percent returned to them. Real consequences are usually the only forces which will move the pathologically dominating man to change. Regrettably, the change often is only skin deep. Once the pressure is relieved, he returns to his former shape, internally unchanged.

Nonetheless, for those males in therapy who are physically abusive, certain conditions must apply absolutely. First, the physical abuse must stop and remain absent. Easier said than done, but, as with substance abuse programs, users are out. Consequences for his actions must be clear and absolute. He is used to manipulation and would use counseling in the same way.

There should be available to the therapist an independent source of information as to the possible presence of continued or recurrent violence perpetrated by either partner. Unfortunately, one cannot rely on the veracity of the abuser. In my work with teenagers, I am able to hear from parents, school personnel, including the school nurse, friends of the couple or the victim. This is especially true at the high school where I work. It is more difficult to achieve in other settings, such as my private practice.

Most writers and counselors who specialize in this field urge great caution in choosing a couple's treatment modality. Many strongly insist it never be utilized. Joint sessions suggest a mutual problem and shared responsibility. They depend on trust that the truth can safely be told and that each can communicate openly without fear of repression or repercussions outside the office. It also implies that each of their welfare is best served and is obtainable through the relationship and through each other. Usually, none of this is true, nor should it be striven for. Couple's therapy can, therefore, be harmful and dangerous. Furthermore, it is of central importance that both the male and female establish, and learn to tolerate in comfort, greater independence and physical separateness from one another. There is no other way for either of them to exercise their psychological/emotional tolerance of loosened control; no other way to master the acceptance of uncertainty or to come to learn that they still have the other even when apart, that the other can leave and will return. They must learn to get some of their needs met elsewhere and to tolerate sometimes just being alone. Both need larger lives outside the relationship. The young woman or girl, especially, needs opportunities to express herself freely, to have her thoughts and feelings heard, clarified, validated. Therapy sessions, at least, must be places were he must give up his control and she must take it for herself. Separate therapy from separate therapists is, therefore, the necessary format in nearly all cases.

Couple's treatment should be considered only if there is no violence, the individuals appear truly motivated, and especially if it is the only condition under which they will agree to begin. From the start, however, the therapist should be planning and preparing them for the likelihood of eventual separation in their therapy.

The Massachusetts Guidelines and Standards for the Certification of Batterer Intervention Programs—Revised (1994) prohibits the use of models and techniques that have been found to jeopardize the safety of victims and may be counterproductive. These include couple's counseling, "fair-fighting" techniques, psychodynamic approaches, anger management and models that view violence as addictive. Violence is considered to be a choice rather than an impulse that cannot be controlled. Psychodynamic approaches that center causality in the past or upon others may encourage the client to view the antecedents to his behavior as excuses rather than merely possible reasons. Its relevance pales before the immediate necessity of the cessation of the symptom.

Chief Probation Officer Dr. Andrew Klein of the Quincy (MA) District Court, which is a widely recognized leader in its response to physical abuse in male/female relationships, is quoted in the *Massachusetts Psychological Association Quarterly*:

> Our experience over the past ten years with dozens of psychiatric, psychological and socialwork-oriented treatment programs and counselors for batterers has been uniformly disappointing to say the least. To put it bluntly, the typical batterer wraps these therapists around his finger, getting them to commiserate with him over his victimization by his wife/partner and concentrate on his depression, lack of self-esteem, anxiety, etc. The latter, of course, are often the result of his finally getting caught for his battering behavior, not the cause of it.   [Adams 1995, p. 15]

Again, as with alcoholics or drug addicts, therapy can be fruitless indulgence unless the target behavior has completely stopped.

CONFIDENTIALITY

The issue of confidentiality becomes one of great importance in cases such as these, particularly with adolescent clients. Regarding adolescents who are living at home or in the charge of some adult, be it parent, relative, foster parent or other, I would inform that caretaker of a physically abusive relationship involving their daughter if I judged that she was in likely danger of significant physical harm. The same would apply in the case of a boy who appeared to be in danger from a girlfriend. I did have a male client in real danger from an ex-girlfriend who had used her car as a weapon and had threatened the use of a gun, which she did have access to and under the right circumstances would possibly have used.

I have added several qualifiers in my statement such as "likely danger," and "significant physical harm." I want to maintain confidentiality. I do not wish to blow a person out of needed and productive therapy by an ill-advised breach of it. I do not wish to ruin a young person's ability to trust in therapy and confidentiality. I am cautious about giving information to persons, guardian or otherwise, who may, in some cases, be ill-equipped by virtue of their temperament, judgment, or the quality of their relationship with their son or daughter to handle the news I would be giving them. I consider, also, what options and resources are available to help the adolescent beyond just the immediate family, if the immediate family is inadequate or the client simply does not want them to know for some defensible reason. I consider the magnitude and immediacy of the physical damage only, not psychological danger. I would certainly deal with the rare shove differently than the frequent punch. I will allow time if the danger is not too great or imminent if the client is using therapy well and making steady progress toward changing or leaving the relationship. I am more willing to give time if I am convinced I know exactly what is going on and can verify it.

So there is no blanket statement that I can give regarding the limits of confidentiality as it applies to dominating and physically abusive relationships. I do not want to break it against the adolescent's wishes. On the other hand, where I judge that serious harm or, of course, death is an immediate danger, I must inform the client that I have no choice but to act to protect her. I cannot help her to remain in danger by remaining silent. I will ask for and may accept her advice as to whom to inform and how. I will do it in her presence, if she wishes. If the danger is life-threatening, I must inform all persons or officials in a position to protect the intended victim of the danger and prevent the perpetrator from acting. This includes the appropriate police department and campus police services.

Technically, it can be argued that confidentiality, even in the case of a minor, should not be broken unless the situation is one of life or death, or sexual or physical abuse. I do not reveal to parents knowledge of substance use or abuse, unsafe sexual activity, pregnancy (unless the girl is well into her second trimester, is not having an abortion, and is not receiving medical care), criminal behavior, or anything else I can think of except imminent risk of death by suicide. All of the other behaviors could result in serious harm or death; nonetheless, they are not matters that a therapist has the right to reveal. I feel, though, that a physically abusive relationship can be likened to the situation of physical or sexual abuse of a minor who is trapped and dominated by a more powerful adult. The adolescent female may be trapped as well by a similarly powerful boyfriend. The course of the phenomenon is so predictably damaging and dangerous, in some cases so strongly associated with the serious risk of sudden murder, that sometimes it will be necessary to set the needs of confidentiality aside. Finally, a girl attempting to break away from an abusive dominator will, in nearly all cases, need the help of others, particularly those she lives with, to keep him away from her and to protect her.

Males in treatment programs, court ordered or otherwise, are informed at the outset that confidentiality, in their case, will not apply to their physically abusive behavior. Their attendance may also be reported to significant others. These limitations on traditional client confidentiality are similar to policies adopted by sex-offender programs which recognize that public safety is a more compelling societal right than a client's right to privacy. Though the batterer might certainly feel safer if he were ensured greater privacy, there is no evidence that this leads to better outcomes. It is the position of the Mass. Standards that the word "treatment" not be used to describe the education of batterers. Their behavior is not viewed as a mental health problem. Most do not suffer from a diagnosable mental disorder. Instead, their aggression is focused on specifically as a criminal behavior. Therefore, confidentiality, relevant to "treatment," should not apply to that behavior.

Many young women will seek help with their relationships at this point. They may reveal the true nature of it to parents, friends, or school counselors. Some will enter therapy. The revelation of severe, dangerous physical abuse and the possibility of murder will, of course, change the intervention from one of therapy to one of crisis intervention involving many other persons. The details of handling that problem will be discussed in the chapter on leaving the relationship.

For those whose relationship does not involve physical abuse or significant physical danger, there is much work to be done. Certain rules apply. I do not speak ill of the boyfriend and I do not urge a break-up. To do so would jeopardize the production of important material by the client and seriously jeopardize ongoing treatment. Often the client will enact, in therapy, her most angry, discontented feelings about her mate and the relationship, speak bravely of breaking up and make impassioned pronouncements of her bold intentions, of what she will say and do. Stay calm. Support her feelings. Clarify and interpret her feelings. Repeat the value of her sentiment and intentions. Ask structuring questions regarding the what, how, and where of her plans. But don't fully expect her to actually do it. We must especially refrain from grabbing the banner and charging out ahead of her. We will often find ourselves alone if we do. These are usually nothing more than emotional and cognitive trial runs, exercises in mental imaging. She is trying to bolster herself, boost up her courage. It begins as wishful thinking and generally needs *many* imaginary and theatrical repetitions before it can begin to become enacted in real life. The real life enactments usually need several repetitions before they become real, as well. So we must be very patient and follow along but keep before her eyes the image she has created and presented us with so that she can remember how it is she should be trying to see, to feel, to think, and, finally, to act.

Our negative attitude toward the boyfriend or too zealous efforts to pull her toward a premature break will work against us because she will be deeply ambivalent regarding her mate and her relationship. If she didn't love him, wasn't deeply attached and dependent on him and the relationship or at least in fear of him, if she had well developed alternatives to go to, we wouldn't even know her. She'd have no need of therapy. She would simply walk away from him and get on with her life in some other way. Instead, powerful feelings and bonds will exist. When her more loving feelings toward her boyfriend resume, when he has been good to her, when she basks in the glow of what feels like good love, she will recall the negative attitude of her therapist toward it and him and consider the therapist discredited and a fool. Or she will feel ashamed at *her* weakness and *her* foolishness for falling back to him against the too obvious wishes and expectations of the therapist. She will feel she let him or her down. She may, therefore, withhold important information from therapy, tell the therapist only what he or she seems to want to hear or skip sessions altogether.

Therapists can avoid erring in these ways by keeping their expectations in check, acknowledging to themselves and their client how difficult the task is, remembering that the pathologically dominating male is a victim as well and does not get off free, and focusing as exclusively as possible on material, feelings, thoughts, experiences the client has offered and the harm or good in them that the client herself has been able, or helped to be able, to see. These personal observations and emotions are what are used to guide her, support her, or challenge her. I find that using research findings and the experience of others are near to worthless, as are most references to or warnings of the future, which, since it hasn't happened yet, isn't real. The past carries a lot more weight. That is where all the personal, real, and relevant material and evidence is. Sometimes, though, I must admit, I am moved to challenge a client with the question, "Do you think you will marry this person, and maybe have him be the father of your kids?" Often the girl's reaction is to shrink back in horror or sometimes even to laugh at such a preposterous suggestion:

"Of course not. He's my boyfriend, but he'd never make a *father* or a husband."

"So, that means you will break up someday, I guess," I then say, deadpan. That,too, has been unthinkable. Now she is expressionless or shoots me a knowing smirk.

I do urge one thing, and that is the keeping of a journal, as I have said before. It is the best way of helping the client to become an observer of herself. I don't want her feeling that I am observing her. I want her to keep an eye on herself and her life, to get her observing ego into it and have more of a say, rather than mine. Self-observation provides the emotional distance one needs to better evaluate oneself, others, and the situation. The emotional effects of fear and dependency may, thereby, be less powerful and less able to interfere with one's perceptions. This is an essential prerequisite to understanding and then deciding what one *should* do. Doing it remains another matter.

Included in this program of observation is the study and evaluation of her mate and the relationship. His statements and behavior toward her should be noted and written down. Inconsistencies and inaccuracies will emerge, as well as a truer conception of the overall nature of him and the relationship, the "big picture." One is, thereby, less likely to get lost in the details. His criticisms of her, as well as his statements regarding himself and their relationship, should be written down, pinned down, kept still and then scrutinized, ruminated on and held to the light of day. Is it true that she is selfish in wanting time away from him? Is she a slut for having male friends? Is he the only one she could ever have or love? Are her complaints really valid or is she a bitch? What comes out in her that is bad, yet comes to life nowhere but in their relationship? What does that mean? Does it mean she doesn't care about him if she cares about other things too? Is *he* selfish? Does he care far more for himself than for her? Is his jealousy and possessiveness fair? What does it cost her? What would I think and do if my parent or teacher or coach tried to control me as my boyfriend does? Can he *ever* take the blame? Does *he* ever try to change for *me* ? Do others agree with the bad things he says about me? How well does he *really* know me?

Emotions must be recorded and studied, as well. What are the primary positive and negative ones? What provoked them? What effect do they have on her perceptions, thoughts, behavior, and health? It may be found that the good feelings, provoked by intermittent, random, positive reinforcement are a very powerful hook. Love of this kind has been called "addictive love." It is a solid analogy and one I use a lot, since drug use and addiction (to cigarettes, for instance) are some things young people know a lot about. They, their friends, and their family may have had experience with problems in this area.

People do drugs, including alcohol, for very good reasons. They are fun, feel good, feel different, feel better, feel relaxed, at peace, exhilarated, brave, confident, uninhibited, open, just like love. They can also make you overly dependent, make you crazy, make you paranoid, make you angry, make you sick, and destroy you, just like unhealthy love. You stay with it for the good, though it's destroying you inside and out. You go back to it for the good and ignore, deny, or minimize the bad. People do break free, but it's real hard. You have to be brave, independent, and strong, and have something else to do. People know that you can get addicted to drugs and that drug addiction is bad. It can take some effort for them to see that some lovers are like an addictive drug and that some love is bad. Still, she is afraid nothing else can or will provide her with the good feelings this love has given her. If she believes that too completely, she may opt for the occasional good despite the corrosive bad, rather than never ever having any good at all.

Fear is at the bottom of all the negative emotions that create a hook and maintain a bond. These emotions must be closely studied, as well. They must be credited and respected for their power. They make sense given the subjective conceptual underpinnings that support them. The girl with low self-esteem and a negative self-image is not crazy to imagine that no one but her, albeit dominating, boyfriend could love her or accept her, tolerate her, and want to keep her. It has been easy for him to reinforce what she is already prepared to believe. So she is afraid that if she left him or pushed him enough, he might leave her (as perhaps he may often threaten to do) and she might end up permanently alone. She might feel that she cannot bear to be alone. She knows the feelings she gets, the state she gets into when that happens, and it overwhelms her. She may be afraid that she will die or literally become insane without him or fall into a deep nonfunctional depression. She is afraid he will find another, that she will be easily replaced. She is tormented by vivid images of him in the arms of another, having sex with another, and liking it. She reels away from the very thought of it, back to conformity to his demands.

In therapy, all of these negative emotions and fears, rather than fled from, must be held. The therapist must take her hand and follow them down. They must be pursued to their darkest conclusions, repeatedly. She must become habituated to them, desensitized to them so that they can be borne and studied as one should treat any debilitating fear.

This provides rehearsal for the real thing. It prepares the mind for it. At the same time the client is hopefully carving out for herself time apart within the relationship to get used to the feeling of separateness *in vivo* and preparing alternatives to go to for support and sustenance. She needs to develop other sources of peace and good feelings for herself instead of solely through him. She should be encouraged to exercise, read, write, paint, dance, whatever is within her talents, interests, and repertoire to do. She must learn not to run to him to ease every bad feeling she has, including those that derive from him.

From all of this, constellations of ideas will emerge. One or two will be representative of central issues with special and powerful appeal. I recommend that the client write these down in her own words, concisely, and to carry her with her always. Better still, for those with a more visual orientation, a pictorial symbol may be devised that holds within it a condensation of meaning that is immediate, powerful, and can be put on a key chain or drawn on book covers for contemplation. All religions make use of meaningful symbolic representations of their central ideas. Examples are the Christian cross, the Taoist yin and yang, the Hindu image of dancing Shiva, and the mandalas of every other cultural or tribal belief system.

Again, the individual will need to go over all the emotional and cognitive issues many times, in therapy and on her own, before she will be ready to change or leave. This is not a linear curriculum. It will not proceed in stepwise fashion, contrary to the constructs of brief therapy proponents and managed care dictates. However, with luck the client will come to a true and steady realization of what she has, what she is involved in, and what she needs. Only then, will she be ready to effectively act.

8

CHANGING THE RELATIONSHIP

The following is an entry from Caroline's journal, dated March 30, 1994, written during her senior year in high school. She tore it out and gave it to me to read the morning after she had written it. She was in particular distress at that point because John was going through one of his distant cycles, wherein he would ignore her and scare her with his neglect. Sometimes he would do this as a response to her efforts at independence, to scare her back into submission. Sometimes he was simply on a drinking or drug binge and didn't want to be bothered by her.

I am diffident and impetuous. I am extremely jealous and vindictive. I have zero self-esteem and zero self-confidence. I hate myself. I am never happy. I do not feel secure in my relationship. I do not trust *anyone*. I am dependent. I can only recieve [sic] self-satisfaction from my boyfriend. He makes me happy, sad, and angry. I do not understand why he is so unappreciative lately. He has changed into a totally different person. He used to be jealous and obsessed with me. Now he doesn't care what I do with who [sic]. I am very worried that he is falling out of love with me. I ~~never~~ hardly ever see him anymore and I miss him a lot. But he seems to be doing fine w/out me. The weekends are terrible. When he doesn't see me I get so upset and I feel worthless and neglected. I think I am crazy, well my father and boyfriend say I am, so I have come to believe it. I believe anything anyone says about me. After all if you hear it enough you start to believe it. John told me if he wasn't jealous than [sic] he didn't care or love me. He used to tell me that his jealousy showed that he loved me. Now what do I think because he isn't jealous anymore. But I still hide things from him. I feel neglected, unappreciated, and unloved by John. I can get so depressed and scared about my life w/out him, that I say I'm going to kill myself. I drive crazy when I am upset. I see my brother's temper tantrums in me lately: the screaming, crying, and breaking things. I am afraid of myself. I need help. I always tell myself no drugs, drinking, or dropping out of school. My parents are never proud of me no matter how well I do in school or athletics. I have come to the point that I am no longer proud of myself. I do not know what to do next year. Should I go run away with John because I do not think I can live w/out him? Should I go alone and distance myself, withdrawing from reality? I wish I was a baby. I wish I had no decisions to make. I wish I never fell in love. I wish I never ~~had~~ made love to John, it just got me deeper under his control and manipulation. I need help! I need lots of therapy. I wish I didn't have to wait every week. The weekends are my worst days. I totally relapse. I go against all my plans. I am a weak person. My family makes me sick and I fear that I will never become stable. I try to become stronger, but I have failed, like everything else. At my worst times I feel self destructive, but I don't think I could ever go through w/suicide, but I feel if I was dead or away everyone would be happier.

Young women involved in pathologically dominating relationships will deteriorate very significantly. This will become painfully obvious. They will come to realize why. It will have taken a terrific toll upon most aspects of their health and functioning, and still the situation and its effects will continue to worsen. The symptoms of stress will accumulate, and they will all be used against her. They will serve as evidence of her failings, craziness, her flawed and flayed self. To the degree that it causes distance between the woman and her dominating partner, he will feel compelled to increase his control and abuse in order to solidify what will seem to be a loosening bond.

She will have reached a very low point. Her perception of her personal faults will have proliferated and intensified. In fact, she will certainly have more of them by this time. For this she will be hammered inside and out, by herself as well as by him. She will have been condemned for being a female, a member of her own family, for her friends, her craziness, her moodiness, her weakness, and perhaps even for her religious, ethnic, or social background, while all aspects of his existence are elevated.

Anger and hostility may begin to emerge with greater frequency and virulence from her. She may find herself being critical, nagging, insulting, or negative and generally "bitchy" for reasons and to a degree that she may not understand, precipitated by trivial or seemingly benign events. She may grow increasingly jealous and possessive of him. As her self-image has become increasingly obliterated, she finds herself more dependent upon him but less secure in her belief that she holds a place in his mind. How can she if she is such a worthless, pitiable nothing? She may begin to swing from frantic jealous rage to desperate clinging remorse. She is behaving in ways she never has before. The sickness of her circumstances may have penetrated deeply enough to make her sick as well. Her body will have probably begun to protest and to express the rebellion that her mind may have yet to embrace.

This stress may manifest itself in nearly any of the body's systems. In the musculoskeletal system it may express as backaches, muscle spasms, tension headaches; in the digestive tract as ulcers, colitis, chronic indigestion, and various bowel disorders; in the cardiovascular system as elevated blood pressure, vascular headaches, and migraines. The body's immune system is highly reactive to stress, which often depresses its ability to fight off infection and illness. Skin conditions may flare or worsen, as may any number of allergic conditions. Additionally, sleep problems, in the form of too much or too little sleep, eating problems or disorders, and sexual dysfunction are common reactions. Finally, cognitive impairment of some form, affecting attention, concentration, and memory, would be expected as well as the vast array of emotional sequellae that would fall within the category of agitated or major depression. Given her own internal confusion and the relentless refusal of her mate to accept any responsibility, it will be difficult for her not to blame herself to some degree for her own deterioration. At least at first. At least for a while.

She can see that her mood is unpredictable, that she is no fun anymore. She may see herself as diminished and dysfunctional as a girlfriend, a friend to peers, a student, an athlete, a daughter. To the degree that she is unaware of the reasons for her condition, she will be more apt to castigate herself for them and have less control over them. She will have become an abhorrent stranger to herself.

Her condition, particularly any physical ailments, may serve an expressive function. Her illnesses may punish, frustrate, and present problems and difficulties for him as well. They may express her rage, her need to be cared for, attended to, and loved. Her condition may constitute her unconscious wish that her suffering, her demise, her distress, even her "craziness" might communicate to him the message that he is harming her and must stop. They may support her need for distance, form a barrier, and help her to avoid him. Sickness can serve as retribution, escape, or an effort to turn the tables on control.

However, it is a poor form of communication that will not be understood by her boyfriend. On the contrary, it is far more likely to worsen the domination and abuse. Therefore, the expressive function of her stress-related ailments cannot be gratifying healthy needs, only neurotic ones. They can only gratify her needs to bother him as he has bothered her and to control, enrage, frustrate, and avoid. In the end, they are corrosive, unproductive, and self-destructive. They are unlikely to elicit caring, are not strengthening of the individual, and will not produce mastery. They are, therefore, the opposite of healthy coping or problem solving.

The young woman who is entangled in the web of the dominating relationship has learned by this point that the love is a poisonous one, sickening most aspects of functioning. This will include sex. The couple's sexual relationship may become an expression of much that is wrong with the relationship as a whole. Anger, resentment, ambivalence, fear, anxiety, and all the many troubling feelings that may lie unattended and unexpressed will often stir with the stimulation of sexual expectation. Once awakened, they do not rest easily. They do not contribute to an atmosphere of mutuality, openness, giving, and a loss of self-consciousness without the loss of self-awareness. When there are serious doubts about a partner's love and of one's own adequacy, attractiveness, and desirability there will be a great deal of self-consciousness. When there are brimming reservoirs of anger, withholding may replace giving. Domination has replaced mutuality. And regardless of what is expected or intended, the body may not smoothly follow where the head may seek to bring it. Consequently, they will not be as one (if they ever were). It may become more and more difficult for her to "be there" at all. Conflict and the learned expectation of conflict will exacerbate the problem. Sexual criticisms, among the cruelest, piercing kind, will ensue and echo forming additional barriers, closing her off even further. And a vicious cycle is underway, or something even worse.

It has been established that sexual aggression becomes more common once relationships become serious. In terms of outright rape, women are far more at risk from husbands, boyfriends, and dating partners than from strangers. Women who are the victims of physical aggression from male partners are especially at risk (Browne 1993). Burke and colleagues (1988) reported that 20 to 50 percent of college-age women have been the victim of sexual coercion at least once while dating, while 15 to 25 percent of men have reported inflicting forceful attempts at intercourse. Gooding-Garrett and Senter (1987) reported that persons in relationships perceived as serious held more accepting attitudes toward sexual coercion. There is good reason to expect that the coercion, abuse, and control that characterize pathologically dominating relationships extend to the couple's sexual life as well, with devastating consequences.

Nonetheless, force or no force, it will be apparent to the always-sensitive, perpetually-on-the-alert, dominating male that things, sexually, are not the same and are not well. Jealous suspicions may rise as his insecurity and self-esteem are painfully piqued. Sex and jealousy are a volatile and dangerous mixture.

When sex becomes so strongly associated with conflict and abuse, verbal or physical, any form of intimacy or togetherness can provoke anxiety, avoidance, and withdrawal on the part of the victim. He cannot fail to notice her pulling away and the loss of the genuineness and enthusiasm that had been there. It is as if a light has gone out. He will resist engaging in a healthy critique of himself. He will only be aware that something in her has dimmed. He will blame and criticize. He will complain that he is doing all the work in the relationship, that he is the only one who cares. He may begin to withhold as well. He may play upon her own jealousy and fear of abandonment by threatening to leave such a "cold bitch" behind and replace her with another. He may taunt and torment her with the specifics of a new girl's superiority, emphasizing the "former" girlfriend's intellectual, physical, relational, and sexual deficiencies. Indeed, as her self, her spirit, her individuality are progressively eroded, as there is less of her there, she will become less able to satisfy his need for recognition. He will feel increasingly alone. She will feel increasingly at risk for abandonment. The character of their love is moving each of them further away from truly gratifying the other. Yet it is in the nature of their relationship to exacerbate this process as it is in the nature of it that they remain intensely dependent on each other.

Sex, unfortunately, can mask problems as well as illuminate them. For some, sex may be the best, the only, satisfying part of the relationship. He may seem very loving and caring. This can reinforce wishful thinking that what they have is love and that their love is good and can last, that she is lovable and will not be alone. The sheer physical pleasure can be a hook as well, bolstered by the delusion that it represents far more than it does, and the fear that, if lost, it will never be replaced.

However, most young women will have reached a point of acute suffering. She will feel increasingly sure that something, everything, must change and that she needs help. If her words cannot express this her body will. Shame, on the other hand, may inhibit her efforts. She may consider her weakness, her submission to be despicable. The mere thought of revealing to another the pathetic foolishness of her predicament, or to relate the many anecdotes that would characterize her plight, may be humiliating. No one likes to depict herself as the fool or describe herself as powerless, stupid, or crazy. She may feel ashamed for having excluded so many caring people from her life as the dual isolation of the relationship advances. She will rue the lies and secrecy of it all. She will be ashamed of her sexual victimization and the likely belief that she could be sexually perverse or dysfunctional. She may be ashamed that she is no longer a virgin and fear that now no one will want her.

She may also feel enormous guilt. Speaking to another of her relationship, of its secrets and intimacies, may seem like betrayal. She knows that separation or change may hurt him, seriously destabilize him, or worse. She may know, for certain, that he would not remain in school, that he may resume or intensify substance abuse, behave with reckless disregard for himself, or become overtly suicidal. For this she may feel responsible. He will be sure to keep that idea steady before her eyes. Finally, there will be great fear. She may seek simplicity but is moving toward chaos. She has been trying mightily to understand, to believe that she can manage. It is a frightful realization to admit that her situation is entirely beyond her control and comprehension. She fears irrevocable abandonment, perhaps even physical harm, should she attempt to venture forth from her lonely tower.

THERAPEUTIC IMPLICATIONS

It may seem obvious to a therapist that the relationship being described to them is an unhealthy one. It may seem clear that the thing for the young client to do is simply leave it. Certainly this should be explored. But what if she isn't prepared for that? She has presented herself in conscious and debilitating distress. She knows (or quickly learns) that her relationship with her boyfriend is central to her various presenting problems, yet she is not ready to believe that leaving it is in her best interests, that it would be the right thing to do. She may maintain strong hopes for his, her, and its improvement. She may consider the trauma of separation and the ensuing loneliness to be unacceptable at this time. She may lack the strength, resources, support, and alternatives that could make such a loss tolerable, survivable. She may fear the effects of such a break upon her and/or him.

In any case, she can't or won't leave it, nor can she stand how it is. It becomes quickly clear that the relationship must change and that she must be the one to try to change it. To do so means that she must change. Once that need is established, she will need specific, structured guidance as to how to proceed, preparation on what to expect, and steady, noncritical support regardless of her performance. If she has been seen in therapy with her boyfriend, as a couple, that must end at this point. At the same time, all of the feelings which inhibit her, motivate her, or are provoked by the process of challenge, conflict, and uncertainty, must be recognized, explored, and managed. In many respects, the therapist will provide for her the functions that her embattled and depleted ego often cannot.

First, however, she must feel convinced that she should try. Why should she try? Can she do it just for herself? To what degree does she care for herself in this? Why does she care? Does she have a self to care about? What, specifically, does she hope to regain, restore, ameliorate, assuage, or develop within and for herself by change in her relationship and in her life? In short, what is wrong and what must change for her, not in the relationship, but in her, in how she feels, functions, lives? What pain, pathology or dysfunction needs to ease, improve, or be eliminated? I emphasize specificity and concrete forms. They are more tangible, accessible, and immediately gratifying. If she says she needs to be less depressed or less moody I will ask, "How are you depressed? What does it look like on you? How do you behave? What do you do, not do? What does it feel like and when? How does your body react?" If she says she needs to sleep better, get her grades up, stop lying to her parents, I will want to know why she wants these things, which sounds like a stupid, even an annoying question, but I need to know, and so does she, that she wants these things for herself, for reasons that benefit her, not someone else. If she wants her grades to rise only to please her parents, then it may be a weak reason and a development that may not provide her with a stronger, prouder self; it may not affect her self-esteem or sense of adequacy at all. It may merely fend off or reduce one more agitant. If, on the other hand, she adds, "And I want to get into college, a good college, and have as many choices of schools as possible because I really want to go," then we have something of real personally strengthening value to hold before her as a goal and a guide.

Even sleep, which should be an end in itself, should be broken down into its instrumental functions. How will more sleep help? What is the difference in you when you are rested versus deprived? How does your improved functioning benefit you? Or is she only conscious of not wanting to be so irritable and boring to her boyfriend?

Often, it proves discouragingly difficult to find any reasons within her for changing herself or her relationship solely on behalf of herself. If reasons are elicited they may be weak, tenuous ones, almost vaporous and hard to hold. In any case, regardless of the presence and solidity of her consideration for herself, the effect and value of change for him must be added. We must accept that our client will continue to feel love and concern for her troubled and troubling mate and that she will desire for many reasons to minimize the harm done to him by challenge and change. The clear benefit to him must be shown. In describing the value and appropriateness of change for him, an opportunity is present to help her to see some of what is presently lacking in him and what must and should change, for her, for the relationship and for his own sake as well. It helps to clarify her conception of the pathology in the relationship and shifts focus off of herself and more onto him and keeps it there as his progress is observed along the lines prescribed. She may come to believe with greater firmness and confidence that challenging him, forcing him to adapt in reasonable ways, is a healthy and maturing exercise and one that is necessary and good for all. Finally, it serves as a test of his capacity to love and relate in a healthy and mature way, and leads her to a more solid decision on whether to stay or leave.

Therefore, I will raise the question of whether and how her submission, her self-negation, helps him. Does it help a person to always have his way? Does it help a person to be cruel, selfish, critical, abusive, and get away with it? Does it help a child to "spoil" it? I want to bolster her resolve to press for change, to corner her with the realization of its healthful necessity for her sake, his sake, or for both, and to establish solid commitment to the effort. I will start wherever I have to.

Change creates turbulence and, in this case, change is likely to meet some level of resistance, conflict, perhaps even their own form of war. In anticipation of this, a thorough assessment of the client's strengths, resources, available supports, her coping skills, her capacity to deal with counterattack, with fear, anxiety, depression, and suicidality, is needed, as the inevitable turbulence rocks and shakes the relationship on which she stands. What is her capacity to ride it out? What are her hobbies, talents, activities? Is she able to calm herself, by herself, without the external assistance of others? Does she have others to go to? Can she ride out the uncertainty and the distress? Is he her only source of relief? If so, others must be discovered.

Caroline had several strengths. She was intelligent. She could understand the abstract and the concrete issues regarding love, relationships, and her welfare, as well as the concepts regarding John's problems. She was extremely honest and insisted that her perceptions perform likewise. She fought hard to minimize the feeding of inaccurate and distorted information to herself about what was going on. In therapy, she held nothing back. She was convinced that change, if not absolute separation, was necessary. Furthermore, she consciously sought it on behalf of herself. She did not want to disappear or be driven crazy by too much stress and not enough love, as her mother had. She wanted to grow to be the "normal" one in her family and, despite her badly damaged self-esteem, she sensed she could be. She had ambition. She could imagine achieving a good life for herself and happiness through her own efforts.

Her coping skills needed broadening and shoring up. In the past, conflicts with John left her weak and depleted. Estrangement threw her into a panic that she could not ease by herself. She had no others to help her. She would try desperately, with the wild-eyed craving of an addict, to connect with him to get relief, which she would be granted, but only as a supplicant. Until then, she'd pace restlessly, frantically, talk to herself, scream at herself. In her house there was usually no one home but her, day or night, so there was no one to intervene in her frenzy. She would cry, call him incessantly, obsess on terrible thoughts. When she got a car, she would drive about madly in search of him, at any hour, under any circumstances. Eventually, she learned not to pursue him and to achieve some relief on her own. She wrote in her journal, she listened to music, or she simply rode it out. Exercise helped too; it took her mind off things and helped her feel stronger mentally as well as physically, as being able to make oneself do what is hard always will. It helped her feel more independent too, since individual exercise is such an absolutely solitary act. As she got to understand John better and came to believe in his enormous attachment and dependency on her, her tendency toward panic greatly lessened as did the challenge to her burgeoning coping skills.

Unfortunately, her supports were almost nonexistent. Her fragile and inconstant mother lived elsewhere and had profoundly and aggressively rejected her. Her father was rarely home. He lived a semi-secret life, attending to various murky business affairs and, to make matters worse, dated John's mother! She, in turn, doted on her son extravagantly, could see no wrong in him and, therefore, often clouded Caroline's father's view of the seriousness of his daughter's problem. He hurt her by not helping her, by being unavailable and ignorant rather than being rejecting or cruel.

She had no extended family. Her social isolation had become complete. Growth in that area was proceeding at a crawl. She lived, therefore, virtually alone and spoke to no one.

In school, which she attended every day no matter what, she existed ghostlike. She sat, listened, read, wrote, traveled invisibly from class to class, ate silently, alone in a crowd. She told me once that she purposely avoided conversation and to do so she even avoided eye contact with other kids, because she knew she couldn't share their lives and didn't want to have to explain why. Instead, she drifted through their world for four years as if enclosed within a transparent bubble, as all around her buzzed their talk of boyfriends, parties, intrigues, games, and the petty complaints about teachers, homework, and the injustice of parents. Earlier, it had been family trouble which had caused her to remain secretive and apart. Later, it was life with John.

In the fall of her senior year she entered therapy on the advice of a teacher. Later on, she added a car, a friendship, daily swimming, and a job as additional resources.

There are cases more dismal than this, those where the girl is unsafe at home, or literally has no home and her boyfriend is her only out. He is preferable to home, and it may be a point difficult, if not impossible, to argue against. If on top of that she lacks a self to consider, value, or care about, if she defines herself entirely through him, exists only within the relationship, would be as a deflated balloon without it, the situation is certainly bleak. We cannot speak of separation or breakup. We can only speak in terms of saving the relationship, translated for the therapist to mean saving her, by pointing out the danger in losing his respect should she shrink too small. Can he love her if he doesn't respect her? We can point out how her presenting complaints, be they emotional, behavioral, sexual, or physical, are related to difficulties in the relationship which consequently interfere with and threaten the relationship. Finally, we can draw attention to the benefits for him in recognizing her in a more mutual, adaptive, mature love relationship. Again, in finding the place to start we must sometimes back up a very long way.

In Chapter 6 I described the need for and value of setting limits with the would-be dominator early on in a relationship and discussed the necessity of maintaining a life outside the relationship. Additionally, closer observation and evaluation of the dominator's reactions to limit-setting was recommended.

In order to have reached the point described in this chapter, the couple must have either never tried or utterly failed to establish or maintain these important conditions. Here, it ceases to be a recommendation but becomes a necessity. The cost of failure may be extremely high.

Certain principles guide our work. They must be shared with the client as the basis from which all of her specific efforts will derive. She must embrace them and believe in them in order to be motivated by them. Though they are somewhat more abstract than the concrete, tangible features advised earlier, they should be made accessible and clearly relevant.

First, unwilling sex at his demand must stop completely. If she is unaware of her feelings about her sexual relations with her boyfriend, if she has numbed herself or feels she has no right in this area, this must be worked on and a greater, healthier understanding achieved. A sovereign person, like a sovereign state, needs secure boundaries that are recognized and respected. The habitual sexual penetration of these boundaries dissolves them entirely and allows for the usurpation of the self they were intended to protect.

This will be a difficult area to master if a habit has been set, yet there can be no meaningful progress without it. If he is able to accept this in comfort, a great leap forward will have taken place. She should point out to him that the lessening of sexual pressure may free her up to be a far better companion. It will also reveal to her whether he values her companionship, and free her to consider its meaning if he doesn't.

If he uses force, she must respond as strongly as possible. At the very least, she must deprive him of all contact with her for a significant period of time, until it has really cost him (physical abuse should be dealt with in the same way). She should, again, at the very least, threaten to inform others of his act, and she has to convince him that she means it. Finally, she should point out that their physical relationship has been set back a very long way, and she must follow through on these actions.

It may sound outrageous that a therapist not insist upon an outright and immediate break and the filing of criminal charges. Sometimes the therapist should. It is also outrageous, however, that the victim would not take that action on her own. Unfortunately, we know that the dominated female is likely to have a lot of trouble doing so. We know from experience that many young women involved in a pathologically dominating relationship will have a very hard time achieving even what I am recommending as the minimum response. In the long run, however, to have her boyfriend revealed as a rapist may prove to be the trigger that activates her.

Second, she must spend less time with him. She should begin to take in less of what poisons and weakens her. At the same time she must build independent strength, broaden her life and sources of sustenance, and increase her tolerance of separation. This step is essential both as a strategy for changing and improving the relationship and as being a preparation for leaving it. One is unlikely to leave such a relationship without having first established alternatives and built resources and strengths. His reactions to these efforts may also provide her with a greater feeling of certainty that he and the relationship are not what she needs. As reviewed in Chapter Six, prying the couple apart will be a progressive, step-by-step process that will probably meet some resistance every step of the way. Again, the client should start with what she can handle. She herself must be able to tolerate the separation so that she won't end up running back to him. She must also be able to handle the various pressures he will apply to make her give in. Mental imagery and anticipatory rehearsal might be utilized in helping her prepare for every imaginable eventuality. Meanwhile, there are several procedural points that must be emphasized in carrying these steps out: she must feel sure of the value and fairness of her action and her position; do not ask for permission; make a statement; speak in definitives, presented as facts, not as requests. Do not attack; do not defend. She should state her conditions calmly, firmly. I tell her, "If you intend, absolutely, to do what you say and if he cannot stop you, then there is nothing you need to fight about. Don't expect him to agree. You don't need him to agree."

In the movie *Annie Hall*, Woody Allen's character said something like, "Love is like a shark. If it stops moving, it dies." A relationship is a living thing. As such, it does not stand still. The dominating relationship will only get worse if it isn't getting better. Consequently, if she wants change, she will have to keep pushing for it, step by step. The moment she lets up and gives in, it will roll backwards on her. It will sink, and take her along with it.

Jealousy and fear of losing her will be the likely products of her rising independence and his associated loss of control. In the face of his exhibition of these feelings she must believe that he can never fully satiate his needs for absolute security and control by domination. He can only gain peace of mind and, perhaps, her love and commitment through faith that he has her even when he is not with her. To have any chance of getting what he needs, he will have to reverse direction. She can try to teach him this with words, but she must prove it with behavior.

As difficult as her attempt to assert herself will have been, coping with his response is likely to be even harder. The simplest and most common reaction is the use of force. He will try to overpower her by means of the methods that have worked on her in the past. He may scoff, insult, put down, ridicule, turn the tables, threaten, and/or simply insist that he will have his way regardless. She must avoid the pitfalls of a verbal wrestling match with him. Again, she should state her intention in the simplest terms and stick to it, regardless of where he tries to pull her, remembering that nothing will be won here with words.

His frustration often produces an increase in his pressures. This must be anticipated and calmly withstood. Parental involvement at this point can be extremely helpful, even decisive. She may need their help to limit his access to her. She will need someone to talk to, be with, support her, keep her mind right, almost constantly, as she struggles to withstand the storms that may have gathered around her. Her access to her therapist will probably be insufficient in and of itself to cope with the situation.

On the other hand, he may pull back from her. He may play jealousy games. He may make more or less overt references to other girls, specifically threaten to take up with someone, compare her to them unfavorably, even parade around in front of her with other girls. He may submit resentfully, failing to accept or embrace any of the value in it for either of them. He may expect unreasonable concessions on her part and expect payback of some kind now or later. He may appear to accept accommodation but stay crouched watchfully at the very edge of her tolerance, ever ready to creep back in.

He may profess contrition for his ways. He may even turn on himself in more or less sincere self-flagellation. "I'm a jerk. I ruin everything. You'll dump me now," tearfully castigating himself for his many faults and failings. He may hope, consciously or not, to disarm her assertiveness and shift her focus away from herself and back onto him. Perhaps she will ease his distress by giving up and giving in. She must resist the desire to fix him at the cost of herself.

Most threatened dominators will use a variety of approaches, shifting styles, looking for the soft spot that can best be penetrated and exploited. It can be very confusing if these maneuvers are taken at face value instead of viewed more simply as various manifestations of the same desire born of the same need—the desire for control based on dependency needs. In order to keep her balance and hold her ground, she will need help in translating his array of words and behaviors, a strong belief in his need of her and in her power, and confidence in the value of her efforts. She must keep in mind that the only promising response from him is an honest acknowledgment of her reasonable needs and a demonstrated desire to support them comfortably.

In attempting to achieve a greater degree of recognition and autonomy, many young women will seek to avoid all this by lying. This is what Caroline did at first. She joined a health club, went to therapy, swam, and went out with her friends, but hid it all from John. She needed to do more for herself but she couldn't withstand his reaction. She lied every day about her whereabouts when she wasn't with him. Her head was constantly filled with things she could not talk to him about, words on the tip of her tongue she could not say. Soon there was less and less to talk about. He noticed this and gave her a very hard time about it. The pressure was terrific.

Lying is of limited value, though, practically speaking, it will often be necessary to some degree. However, it increases stress and the work of maintaining a specious equilibrium. It focuses too much on his needs and his reactions. Most important, it avoids entirely the twin functions which limit-setting should offer: conscious accommodation on his part, and an overt manifestation of self and autonomy on hers. These provide a rewarding feeling of healthy power for her and, if things go well, may help him to respect her more and love her better. This open empowerment can yield increases in self-esteem, feelings of adequacy and competence, and elevated mood. If his is not a love that can appreciate her growing stronger, better, and healthier, then she should know that about his type of love.

Throughout this process, important information about the nature of the young man and the nature of the relationship he may be struggling to press upon her will be presented to her daily. She should be helped to wait, watch, evaluate, anticipate, imagine, rehearse, and cope with the feelings which will arise in her, bolstered by a simple belief in her course. For the heretofore pathologically dominating young man, this challenge to his control is an opportunity. It presents him with a chance to learn to love in a more satisfying and enjoyable way. It is an opportunity for the clenched intensity of possessiveness to become a more relaxed love, to slowly build a truer faith in the intangible bond between him and his loved one. By according her recognition and respect he may come to realize the boon he bestows upon himself, for in doing so he nurtures and develops that which sustains him, rather than reducing to nothingness that on which he depends.

It is a lot to learn, a revolution in his thinking. Leaps in maturity such as described above occur seldom and usually only by passage of the individual through a great and harrowing trial. Many fall back to where they began. Others are humbled by the experience, though, by learning its lessons well, they may ultimately rise to master the challenge. For the young men who are the subject of this book, how they respond here may prove to be a defining moment in their lives. As adolescents, some are still malleable enough to reshape this characterological structure. However, it cannot be done alone and will not be done willingly.

In the end, inevitably, the young woman will be left with a very difficult decision. It will be based in part on her perception of what has come before, in part on the state of the relationship in the present, but largely it will be based on her view of what is to come. This is often the weak spot in her judgment. The future offers no hard evidence, no facts. Nothing bad or harmful has occurred there—it is indefinite. Its image is susceptible to the influence of all one's hopes and wishes. It is easier to create a more positive picture of the future than of a fact-strewn past.

The future can also present an image of difficulty and danger great enough to paralyze. Many girls remain in a troubled relationship out of a firm dread of the cataclysm of a break-up. Nor are they far wrong in viewing it in those terms. They believe they can exercise *some* control over what happens if they remain in it. If they leave, they fear that things will get entirely out of control, emotionally and behaviorally. They hold desperately to the seemingly safer course between fight or flight.

The point in the relationship has been reached, however, where she knows her development and existence as a person is in danger. Her condition psychologically, perhaps physically, cannot tolerate the present situation. She is like a person in a burning room who is faced with the decision of whether to keep throwing water on the fire or to run through the flames to safety, leaving the room behind. She wants to stay and manage it, save what's there, conscious of its sentimental value and the slim possibility of mastery, and she dreads fleeing through the fire. Yet the need to act one way or the other presses on her with increasing urgency. Is the fire growing or diminishing? If she stays put will she be consumed? She cannot wait until it will be easy. She cannot wait until she is 100 percent sure or until the fire has reached its full fury. She cannot even wait until she is strong and brave. Caroline said to me once, "How will I get the self-esteem to leave him?" I answered, "How will you get it if you don't?"

Throughout the summer after her high-school graduation, Caroline continued her secretive workouts and therapy. Her relationship with John continued as it had. She had made some progress in taking control of her sex life. She had no stomach, however, for any other major confrontation with him. She had been accepted to a college in the far West, where John could not follow, and intended that to be her break from him.

He tried everything to keep her from going. Failing that, he pressed very hard to be the one to drive her to the airport. We did not trust that he would bring her there. She held out and had her father drive her, and she left.

That was not the end of it, however. Following are three letters she wrote to me from college (reprinted with her permission).

Dr. Curran,   10/24/94

. . . I went on a double date with my roommate, Chris, Mark, and me. It was perfect. We went out to dinner, a haunted house, bought and carved pumpkins, then for a 100% pure adrenelin rush on his motorcycle. Mark and his roommate took my roommate and me for a race. They drove 120 mph. I thought I was dead. But now I say, "Let me do it again." I had a perfect evening and I didn't have to pay for anything. I liked Mark, but he has a girlfriend. It's too long to get into on paper, but I can tell you that I am learning a lot out here (having to do with relationships). I am really depressed though because I keep remembering what John told me, "That I will never be able to find another guy who will like or love me." He is proving that statement right because so far everyone I like doesn't like me in that way. I feel that John is all I have. But don't worry, I like another guy Sal—he's very adventurous. Both Mark and Sal are 23 years old. I want to hold off on Sal because I don't want to get rejected again.

I am listening to a radio call-in show. I wanted to call because me and my roommate cannot sleep.

The weather here is great—shorts & T-shirts. How's it there? I had a snowball fight yesterday in the mountains, but it was warm.

Have a Happy Halloween.

Caroline

P.S. Oh, I saw your paragraph about "suicide" in my psychology book—congratulations.

When Caroline returned home on semester break in December she resumed her relationship with John. He returned to college with her.

Dr. Curran,   1/15/95

Sorry I haven't written sooner, but things have been chaotic. The bus ride to Utah was hell. I felt so gross and dirty. I was separated from John the first night. The bus was completely full. . . . I was almost in tears, and talk about uncomfortable I felt like a can of sardines. John changed seats with me after I began to bitch out loud. . . . Well I changed seats and now I sat with a woman and her baby (the baby kicked me all night). So still I was sleepless. I lived off Burger King and McDonald's—yuck, fake food. Oh, I don't recommend you take the bus out west because you'll kill your neighbor. It is so flat, ugly and drab. Every state looks the same. The ride sucks. The driver wakes you up 2x's in the middle of the night—so don't plan on getting a peaceful nights sleep. And make out a will prior to leaving because they drive all over the road—who knows where they got their license. I arrive (we) on New Year's Eve. My New Years was terrible.

O.K. now about manipulating John. He's been trying & somewhat succeeding in hurting me. Yup. He was clinging to me in the beginning, but now he's getting familiar with the area so he's back to the emotional abuse shit. Every few months he changes his methods. Now he says I don't want to be your lover just your friend. He tells me that since I know all these people that I owe him. I saw a counselor here last week because I wasn't going to class (Math) because John wanted to go to lunch and not alone. I am going to begin an assertiveness seminar (4 classes) this Tuesday. I have been trying to keep busy. I work two jobs. I am working right now. I have to work (12 hours today—8:45–noon then 4:45–midnight) at the front desk of my dormitory. I get to meet a lot of people. Then I baby-sit during the week for the Smiths.

Jim, my aerobics instructor last quarter called me. He left such a nice message on my machine. He wanted me to take his class again and he just wanted to know how I was doing. I left a message on his machine telling him I had a conflict in my schedule but that I would come by and see him or else I would see him next quarter.

My new roommate is nicer than Pam, she shares her stuff, and she's afraid of John. She heard John yelling at me and she wouldn't let her boyfriend leave. Nobody on my floor likes me with him, but then John yells at me for having friends that never leave us alone.

I need more confidence. I cannot let this same old bull continue. At least John studys—I am always at the library studying with him.

My brother doesn't live w/my dad anymore. Since my dad never heard from me that John was coming to school with me, he's very mad—he never calls. My queer mother said she's never talking to me. She thinks, she tells my dad, I came here to get married and pregnant. She thinks highly of her daughter. So my parents loathe me. I am working so I don't have to call for money. I am still putting up w/ emotional abuse from John. Doesn't sound too good. I never exercise, I cook & wash John's clothes—nothings for me. I didn't want him to come here and that was before I ever knew it would be like this.

It's snowing today, looks beautiful, but haven't had time to ski yet.

Sorry Dr. Curran that I write so sloppy, but I cannot keep up with what I'm thinking about writing (my hand doesn't write that fast).

Please keep in touch. Hope all's well with you. Happy New Year!

Caroline

Dr. Curran,   2/24/95

I read your letter and I see what your saying, but John has this control over me when he's in my presence. Whatever self-esteem I had last quarter is sadly lost. He's putting me down now and the abuse is both emotionally showing and physically (I'm ugly—eyes, ribs showing). And worse is that I have no support from my family. It hurts me so badly, I don't feel loved by anyone. I don't know what to do or where to go. I am so tired, I cannot sleep, I want to withdraw. I feel like my heart has shriveled up and completely disappeared. The self-esteem put-downs from him along with the constant negativism are giving me no confidence. I am so sad. My birthday's Thursday and I want it to suck because I feel like no one cares about me. I wish my family was there for me. I have lots on my mind, but all I seem to be doing is buying myself things. I am going through money like crazy. When I buy something for myself I for a brief second feel happy, then depressed again. I could write forever, I know I am leaving out a lot but these are the major highlights. I'm drained and I have a psychology test early in the morning.

Thanks for listening.

Caroline

P.S. Oh, if John comes on the floor he's arrested. I have nothing to say about it.

Dr. Curran, I am miserable. I cannot live here with him, functioning seems impossible. I want him to go back home. I told him I didn't want him to come here. I cannot sleep. Whenever I try, I hear John putting me down. It is totally different this time because I was going so well last October. I cannot handle this. Something is going to fail. I am already on academic probation and if I get on it again this quarter. . . . then I will lose financial aid for a year. What is going to happen to me? I want to come home.

9

BREAKING UP: DANGER AND OPPORTUNITY

The process of leaving a pathologically dominating relationship often resembles a caricature of the approach–avoidance behavior of the severe obsessive-compulsive struggling to pass through a doorway. The woman anxiously starts, stops, starts, stops, checks, rechecks, provoking feelings of contempt, ridicule, pity, and exasperation from waiting onlookers. A girl or young woman about to cross the threshold to leave her relationship behind will feel, and act, much the same way. Interested observers will find in themselves many of the unpleasant responses of the waiting onlookers. They cannot understand what the problem is. The need for the movement seems obvious. The effort should be so simple. The barrier is, for the most part, invisible and therefore seems insubstantial. It may, however, be the most dangerous thing a female can or will ever do.

THE DANGER AND DIFFICULTY
OF SEPARATION

Before any final crossing of that threshold can take place
the girl must deal once more with a drenching backwash
of all the questions and issues that the troubles in her
relationship have ever raised. She will experience an in-
tensification of self-scrutiny as all her perceptions, feelings, actions, transgressions, faults, and errors are reevalu-
ated. Her confidence to assert herself and to take action
grounded in belief in the rightness of her act and in her
capacity to survive is once more called into question. Her
competence and adequacy to venture forth alone and succeed will be intently appraised.

A bright, direct, lingering light, one that will accentu-
ate all blemishes and imperfections, will be turned on her
as she studies herself in its harsh glare.

Having finally confirmed the bad in the relationship
and resolved to leave it, she may linger on that threshold.
She will naturally recall the good. She will summon its
image and its feel, and review it, since it will soon be gone.
She will begin to miss it and grow afraid. Fear, anxiety,
and uncertainty halt her steps as she looks at the good and
tries to say goodbye to it, not knowing if it will ever come
to her again.

Questions of desirability, fears of future loneliness and
of unmet dependency and sexual needs, tended by a damaged self-image and depleted self-esteem, will remain open
to painful doubt. What her former mate says and does to
her at this point will turn up the heat on all her uncertainties, needs, and doubts. The misgivings she feels regarding
the leap she is about to take may slow her approach and
weaken her takeoff. Therapists will find themselves going
back over a lot of old ground, discussing issues thought
to be long since laid to rest.

Leaving will prove, therefore, to be an enormous challenge to the integrity and strength of her personality. It may be the hardest thing she will ever have to do, a kind of epic test of the sort described in heroic tales and quests. There will be unexpected, even mortal, dangers, self-doubt, vacillation, and self-propelled risk. There will be fear and loneliness. More than any other quality, courage will be needed to see her through. However, as with any quest or heroic ordeal, the experience can be transforming. I say this to clients—I openly acknowledge the immensity of the task and its many perils. I remind her of her reasons for undertaking the journey and hold before her its honor, its value, and its inevitability if she is ever to grow up.

The Chinese character for "danger" is sometimes the same one used to represent "opportunity." It hangs on my office wall, and I refer to it often in my work; its wisdom is compelling. I explain that because this separation will be so hard, she will find that having endured it, she will forever after be a stronger person. Every birth, every rebirth, involves a difficult and uncertain course. It is one of the riskiest journeys one can undertake, yet it is the only path by which one may enter life. Therefore, if one wishes to live, one has no other choice. For inspiration and a model I ask her to think of a favorite heroic tale, and we explore the parallels and search through it for lessons, value, and honor. Often they are tales first heard in childhood, allowing her to recall a pre-adolescent self which may have been more venturesome, less constrained, less beleaguered by self-doubt, a freer, surer, stronger self. Sometimes strengths and truths are to be found by looking backwards.

The dominating male will experience the rupture of his relationship like the rupture of a lifeline and will usually respond with a desperate scramble of activity, emotionally and behaviorally. It can be a literally life-threatening event. All this time he has been trying to make her attachment to him her only sustaining environment, her only source of oxygen, and now, ironically, he finds that she has been his.

The break offers him an opportunity as well. If it is a shattering event, it can also be a formative one. It presents an opportunity for him to improve his chances for happiness and peace of mind in future relationships by learning the nature of the fault line in his flawed way of love. I tell female clients that while breaking up with a young man of this type can precipitate untold commotion and distress in him, little else has the power and potential to jar him out of his way of being. Where he goes from there, however, must be his own responsibility. She is no longer the one to fix it for him or make him feel better.

As noted earlier, the young woman intending to leave a dominating and abusive (psychologically, perhaps physically) relationship must first overcome a number of very difficult psychological challenges. In most cases she must first be able to see and believe that there exist alternatives to the all-encompassing world of that relationship. At first this may be very hard for her to envision or value, much less move toward or create for herself.

Individuals held over a long period of time under conditions of overpowering domination will perceive the availability of alternatives as increasingly limited and escape to be increasingly dangerous. This is especially likely in dominating relationships in which physical abuse has been present. Experience with past attempts at separation may fortify these perceptions. Henton and colleagues (1983) suggested that the operative difference between teens who left abusive relationships and those who remained was their perception of the quality and number of alternatives. Many adolescents in dominating relationships see no adequate alternative. They may, in fact, have none. They may have entered the relationship having come from nothing and with nothing. For them, it is either togetherness through submission or loneliness. These were certainly Caroline's options during her high-school years. Nonetheless, alternatives or no alternatives, many eventually choose to make the break and cross the threshold, but, like water skiing or walking, it usually takes several attempts before any mastery is gained.

MULTIPLE SEPARATIONS AND
THE REASONS FOR RETURNING

Studies of battered adult women show that multiple separations are the norm. Even adults who have suffered physical abuse are rarely able to leave for good the first time. Promises are made and must be tested; hope has not been extinguished; vulnerability to self-blame is still high. Walker (1979) wrote that a woman will generally leave her abuser three to five times before quitting for good. Hilberman and Munson's (1978) group averaged four to five separations before leaving permanently.

Multiple separations, rather than a sign of weakness, are often used as a coping strategy, a progressively strengthening and instructive process in which the abusing partner and the quality of the relationship is tested and evaluated while the female exercises her competence and confidence at separation from him. Separation provides opportunities to build alternatives. She is, therefore, exerting pressure on her mate to improve while at the same time preparing the ground for a possible final leap. In my own work I see this as the common pattern and recommend separations for the reasons stated above. Furthermore, calling them separations rather than breaks eases some of the fear of irrevocable loss and allows her to make a move of a size that she may be more prepared to handle. They can be thought of as exercises, full dress rehearsals for the real thing, and, as such, often a healthy and productive process.

While successive departures can indeed serve as incremental advances, there remains, nonetheless, a powerful urge to return. The newly separated adolescent often rests precariously and uneasily on the knife edge between the unknown future and the familiar past. Her tolerance for that position is limited, and a fall back to the known may beckon with a promise of relief.

Again, drawing from the extensive literature on battered adult women, the most compelling reasons given for a woman's return have been consistently reported. Most apply to adolescent females as well.

Gayford (1975) lists as the most often cited reasons: (1) the man's promise to reform; (2) his threats of or actual physical violence; (3) her lack of alternatives; (4) concern for children at home; and (5) felt love or sorrow for the man. Roy (1977) also found "hope for reform," "no alternative," and "fear of reprisals" as the three most common reasons for return of dominated and abused women to their male mates. Pagelow (1981) reported virtually identical motivations from her sample. Okun (1986) feels that much of what sends the abused female back can be placed under the heading of fear: fear of danger, of increased harassment, of her own lonely and depleted condition, of the unknown, and fear for the condition and deterioration of her former mate.

The facts regarding the effects of a break-up on males, particularly excessively possessive, dependent, controlling males, strongly support her feelings. In this regard, many in the field consider the attempt to leave a dominating and abusive man to be, in the short run, the most dangerous thing a woman can do. As such, her difficulty in leaving and her tendency to return must be seen in a different light and not simply as "weakness."

THE IMPACT UPON THE MALE

It was stated in Chapter 7 that 75 percent of women murdered by their partners are killed after they have separated. Browne (1987) estimated that 50 percent of women who leave abusive mates "are followed and harassed or further attacked by them" (p. 110). Divorcing couples report a higher incidence of abuse. The condition of marital separation is associated with the most severe forms of couples violence and weapons incidents (Okun 1986).

Benjamin (1988) has written that "domination begins with the attempt to deny dependency" (p. 52). However, the breakup, with its experience of loss and abandonment, confronts the dominating male with the realization of a dependency so great and so complete that it is beyond his ill-prepared capacity to bear. Sometimes he will feel compelled to kill it, as if by erasing the needed but denied object he might also extinguish his overwhelming but frustrated need. He can also prevent the ultimate humiliation and rejection of being replaced by another. If her death is followed by his suicide, he may imagine a continuing togetherness in death.

Often, under the circumstance of this devastating loss, the pathologically dominating male will become suicidal instead of homicidal. Sixty-one percent of the severely abusive and dominating men in Browne's (1987) study had threatened suicide. Walker (1979) found that 10 percent of the men who had abused the female subjects of her study committed suicide after their mates left them.

Males, in general, have consistently been found to react more negatively to a breakup of a love relationship than do females. In the case of adult married men, Peplau (1983) reported that "divorce is associated with significantly greater increases in the rates of admission to mental hospitals, suicide, alcoholism, and mortality for men than for women" (p. 246). Bloom and colleagues (1979) concluded, similarly, that "the link between marital disruption and a variety of illness and disorders is stronger for men than for women" (p. 192). Though far less extensively studied, there is also evidence that in dating relationships, break-ups were more traumatic for males than for females (Rubin et al. 1981, Stets 1993). The literature on adolescent suicide repeatedly points to boyfriend/girlfriend loss specifically (Davidson et al. 1989, Hawton 1982, Jacobs 1971, Walker 1980) and interpersonal rejection, conflict, or loss in general as leading precipitants to suicidal acts (Brent et al. 1988a, Curran 1987, Kienhorst et al. 1995, Marttunen et al. 1993, 1994). However, adolescent males outnumber females approximately 4:1 in committed suicides (Curran 1987).

Given the extreme dependency of the dominating male, it is little wonder that he will seek to hang on to the relationship at all costs. It does feel like a life-or-death situation for him, and it may, in fact, be. His obsessive preoccupation with his girlfriend has left him with little else to fall back on. His low self-esteem cannot bear the rejection of a break-up. His aversion to introspection and objectivity, his denial of dependency, and his relentless externalization of all problems have left him completely unprepared for the separation, ill-equipped to cope with his emotional response to it or to make the necessary changes that could save him. His reactions run to extremes that he is hard-pressed to moderate or adjust. His self-esteem falls through the floor. His depression may be catastrophic, and he seeks relief only through her. He usually devotes all available energy to getting her back.

He may stalk, haunt, spy, intrude, plead, and bombard with gifts, love, and promises, in various forms and shifting combinations. His harassment is among other things an attempt to make sure, by material demonstrations and his physical presence, that he is still in her head. He lacks the confidence in himself to believe he continues to exist in her mind unless he is physically present. He attempts to maintain the assertion of power and control that have always worked in the past, and it is an expression of his great rage at having his demands denied, demands that, from his immature, egocentric perspective, he feels wholly entitled to. He may turn all his available intelligence, time, and effort to this end. He will think of nothing else. He feels he has nothing else and, therefore, nothing to lose. He may skip work or class and set aside all else to this end. Since his profound subjectivity keeps her feelings and needs unknown to him, the only feelings and needs he considers are his own. When a friend says to him, "Can't you see that she's furious, hurt, had it?" or, "Can't you see that your harassment of her is just driving her further away?" or, "Can't you see that it's over?" the answer is no, he cannot see. Speaking to him you have the sense that he is not there with you. His eyes are distant, restless, glazed. He does not seem to hear what you are saying. If he hears, it does not seem to be truly considered. It does not penetrate deeply. He is perseverating on a theme which will not be disrupted. All he can see is a mean, withholding, rejecting, unfair female whom he must have. If he must make admissions of fault and promises to change, they will be thin ones. His lack of understanding of himself due to his intolerance of mature critique reduces his concept of self-improvement to a superficial and rudimentary one. He will not identify or understand the scope and the fault in his possessiveness, domination, jealousy, or verbal abuse. His promises of change are likely to address only bits and pieces of the problem and will rarely grasp and hold the big picture. He may promise not to yell so much, not to hit, to allow her more time apart, or even to be less jealous or critical. But he will not know what these things mean and his *attitude* will remain the same. He may, for a time, bear her increased autonomy but he cannot value it or respect it. Finally, his often distorted perceptions will undermine whatever efforts he may genuinely be trying to make. His paranoia will erode his trust; his insecurity will weaken his tolerance; his anxiety will turn to anger. Control will press to reassert itself once again as the only way he knows of seeking peace of mind in a love relationship.

THE IMPACT UPON THE FEMALE

Regardless of the controlling boyfriend's reaction, the girl will be faced with a number of very difficult problems. While males, especially dominating males, are said to have a harder time dealing with break-ups than females, women don't get off easily either. Despite the efforts of feminism and women's liberation, culture and society continue to encourage women to derive a large part of their identity as a person on their involvement in a love relationship. By adolescence this connection between identity and attachment in the form of a heterosexual relationship has been firmly established and is wholly supported by the peer group culture. Orenstein's *School Girls* (1994) and Pipher's *Reviving Ophelia: Saving the Selves of Adolescent Girls* (1994) are recent testaments to this continuing reality. Adolescent females are particularly vulnerable to pressures to shore up their faltering teenage egos, uncertain identities, and depleted self-esteem by uniting themselves with a boyfriend. They have been taught to define and value themselves through their desirability to others, usually males.

Their self-image, self-esteem, and initiative come to be supported and directed by external rather than internal sources. Leaving even a bad relationship can be a wrenching experience for a girl, as anyone with any familiarity with adolescents or his or her own adolescence can attest. It will be even harder for those girls who have been weakened in all the critical areas of personality by a pathologically dominating relationship.

She, like her mate, will have lost the center of her world, and it is small consolation that the center of her world had been bad for her or that she has left it of her own free will. It is still gone and leaves only emptiness, pain, and turmoil in its place. (The addict is faced with the same problem.) Their substance of choice had been their one true love, the center of their world. They left it because it simply did them too much harm—it was leave or die. None of this means life without it will be anything but wretched for quite some time. Gone is the harmful substance or person or relationship, but gone too is the only way of having fun, the giddy exultant highs, rapture, bliss, utter peace, a full social life, all available means of feeling good and coping with problems and distress, a solution to loneliness and a palliative for problems of identity and adolescence.

She may have left with only a very limited repertoire of things that make her feel good. As an adolescent, her friends, if she still had any, might have all been friends of her boyfriend and therefore a continued link to him that may have to be avoided. I have known several young women who turned to drugs to cope with the loss of a relationship that had been like an addiction.

As the rejected male obsesses on how to get his girl back, the girl in question will be finding no rest from persistent thoughts and questions of her own. She will continue to struggle with her decision, calculating ceaselessly her reasons, searching for a "proof" that cannot be empirically derived. She will argue the issue of hope and change, wondering if she left too soon, if she tried hard enough, if in time he will change. Was he the one true love for her life? She will wrestle with projections of the future, asking questions which cannot be answered and, therefore, can be ceaselessly asked. Around these questions and possibilities she will construct a thousand imagined conversations. She will turn it to a hundred different views and angles, searching for one to lock onto that will hold her with its unwavering truth and let her mind finally rest. She will lose a lot of sleep, and she may have problems in school.

She will struggle with paradox, unprepared by her background or education to understand it. How could the good and bad exist in him together, at once? How could he love her and hurt her? Is she, therefore, lovable at all? How can he need her and have such contempt for her? What then is she? And, above all, why must she have to feel so much worse to get better? Why must she enter a world of trouble to leave a world of trouble behind? Always lurking just behind the struggle, the distress, the fear and pain, is the knowledge that she brought it on by leaving and she can grant herself immediate relief by simply going back. This is a reality and an inner conflict that the male does not have to wrestle with. It takes great strength to resist its tempting lure. It will often beckon with the support of others, friends who ask, "How can you let all that time together go to waste?", friends or family who say, "But he's so depressed," people who say, "Try to work it out." Of course, there are the pleas, promises, and love of the ex-boyfriend to consider. At last she may finally say, as one client of mine once said, "Why the hell don't I just go back to him and put an end to all this stupid misery?"

The adolescents' sense of time is an issue here. Their perspective is not the same as our adult one. While we complain that time passes all too quickly, they moan that it does not pass quickly enough. The future seems far away to them, unreal. It offers little consolation or hope since it feels so inaccessible. Distressed adolescents, having little or no experience with the healing properties of time or the length of time it takes, often feel lost and trapped, immobile in their suffering. They are unlikely to understand it as part of a known process along which they are moving steadily, if imperceptibly. Instead, they will feel stuck and afraid, not knowing where they are headed, how long it will take, or if it will work. That's the part of waiting which is intolerable, the worst sort of suffering. That's why at Disney World you tolerate the long lines—because they keep you moving.

Teenagers, young people, view time as if through a telescope held in reverse, expanding time to a fearful distance, and this reduces their tolerance. It is not that they are necessarily weaker than adults; rather, they lack experience. From their breakups they gain experience. They learn of the process of time and healing and gradually their faith in the process, time, and their ability to cope will grow along with their confidence and resources. As a consequence, several separations often must be experienced and processed before a young female can answer her doubts and questions sufficiently to keep herself apart. She must expose herself to the emotional effects several times before she is sufficiently inured to them to hold her ground. Finally, it will take time to discover, recover, and develop alternatives, to fill to some degree the empty center of her world. Again, like the addict, first-time cold-turkey withdrawals are rare.

THERAPEUTIC IMPLICATIONS

Therapeutic work with individuals, male or female, newly separated from a dominating and in some way abusive relationship, takes on an intensity and urgency similar to a suicidal crisis, but often lasts longer. It will probably include a suicidal crisis as well. The therapist must be available twenty-four hours a day, by phone and pager if not in person, during the initial stage. The ego of the young client, male or female, will be assaulted from all sides by powerful and, in their experience, perhaps unprecedented emotional forces. They may have few, if any, supports to hold and sustain them. They may have entered adolescence and the challenge of their break-up relatively unformed, undeveloped, and ill-equipped in terms of personal strength and maturation. Other chronic problems in their lives, if they have them, are unlikely to take time off to leave them free to turn all their attention and resources to the pressing problem of their break-up. Consequently, their judgment, perceptions, capacity for organization, reasoning, even memory are all subject to contamination and dysfunction at a time when it is critical that they keep their heads. It is only their clear-eyed understanding of what has happened, why, and what must happen next that can see them safely through this turbulent time. However, the ego functions on which they must rely are likely to be heavily stressed, if not overwhelmed. The therapist, along with all other available helpers, must provide the ego structure and support where it is lacking. While recognizing their feelings we must turn most of our attention to their thoughts and actions and be prepared to lead, guide, and direct them to the degree necessary. The time to help them see and understand the pain and distress they feel in their situation has passed for now. The exploration and bringing to consciousness of these emotions served their purpose earlier in developing the realizations that formed the motivation for the change. At this point, they must be wary of and, where necessary, stronger than their feelings. These feelings must be closely supervised, held to a tight rein and mastered. Each strong emotion carries a potential to become an open pathway back to the relationship.

Precipitants and Reasons

I am distrustful of precipitants to break-ups. There is often trouble in them. When a girl tells me she has finally broken up with her abusive, controlling boyfriend, I ask, "Why?"
"Why?! You know why! We've only been talking about the jerk and how stupid I am to be with him for about the last six months! You're asking why?" she responds incredulously.
"Oh, I'm not disagreeing with you. I just want to know, why now? Why on this particular day?" She will usually then tell me of the precipitant, which is different from a reason. A precipitant is a specific, usually behavioral, event. He hit her, he berated her, he humiliated her, he forced himself on her sexually, he had another jealous fit, he was drinking again, or he cheated on her. I am wary of the possibility that her reaction is tied exclusively to the specific, singular infraction and moment in time and ignores the larger issues and temporal quality. All too often this is the case, and when this is so it will be a weak case, unlikely to sustain her in her separation. A single event, if not held as a symptom of a more substantial whole, is easy to minimize, set aside, apologize for, and defend. Nearly any single act can, probably will, and perhaps even should be forgiven. It is only when a pattern of behavior is established, contained within an attitude and a mentality that support it, that one can feel confident in the perception and belief that the perpetrator must be avoided altogether. Only then can one project the future course of the person's behavior and attitude with reasonable assurance.
So I want to know why, and if what I hear is only a precipitant, I try to bring the client in touch with the rea-

sons, relying on her own past statements as much as possible. If the reasons have not been as yet recorded by her in writing in a readily available form I urge that it be done immediately. Otherwise, under the pressure of events to come they may be very hard to hold in consciousness.

The reasons should be large ideas composed of specifics. Caroline wrote in her letter of 2/24/95, "John has control over me when he's in my presence. Whatever self-esteem I had last quarter is sadly lost. He's putting me down now and the abuse is both emotionally showing and physically. I'm ugly, eyes, ribs showing. . . . The self-esteem put-downs from him along with the constant negativism are giving me no confidence. . . . I cannot live here with him. Functioning seems impossible. . . . I cannot sleep. Whenever I try I hear John putting me down." *These* are reasons—they are so much larger, more significant than any single act or precipitant. They are what must be kept in mind. In the end they will hold their ground far better.

The Management of Enemy Emotions

Earlier I spoke of emotions in the context of the individual trying to bear the separation, as if emotions were the enemy of this effort. In a way, they are. I will address these emotions (not in any particular hierarchical order) and their management specifically with the female in mind first, although much of what is said here will apply to the male as well. Later, I will focus on the male.

Fear

Fear is often the first emotion: fear of having made an irrevocable mistake; fear of retaliation, of serious physical harm, even of death; fear of harm to family members, friends, other loved ones; fear of harm to her ex-boyfriend, the "victim" of her act. Fear can take the form of persistent anticipation, of not knowing what to expect next or when. Another kind of fear is the fear of loneliness, of never having another love, of never again being or having a most special person.

Every one of these fears is either entirely reasonable or at least impossible to refute in any tangible way. All one can say is that while many dangers are possible, life within the relationship had proven to be a certain danger. Even death, while a possibility if she leaves, was a slow spiritual certainty if she stayed. This is an opportunity to reiterate the nature of the dilemma of the decision without good choices. The young have been brought up to believe that their choices were between good and bad, black and white, right and wrong. But when a girl gets pregnant or has to break up from a relationship like this there are only various degrees of messiness and you can take your choice. There is no good one to be found, so don't wait for one or bother to look for one. But they do—they wait and look. It is also a time to speak of honor in bravery, which is only born in fear, and to point to the danger/opportunity connection.

Since the fear cannot be dispelled, it can only be balanced. I want to add as much onto our side of the scale as possible. I will throw on the idea of marriage and children with this boy. Would you want him as the father of your children? Would you want to subject them to him and the way he treats you? I would explain that abuse escalates after marriage, and leaving, once married and with kids, becomes much more difficult. These are speeches, I know, but I hold off on them for as long as I can.

Finally, regarding the fears of physical harassment and assault, the therapist is most helpful when he or she can help plan the logistical strategies around safety, activating her in her own defense, and by enlisting the help of others to assist the young women in this area. These will be described in detail later on.

Guilt

The next emotion is guilt. If her dominating boyfriend has had any influence on her at all, she will feel plenty of guilt and possess a strong inclination for self-blame. She will continue to direct her attention to him and his condition and his needs while discrediting, denying, and doubting her own. He will be trying his best to maintain that particular effect after the separation. If her sense of identity is very uncertain it will be very difficult for her to defend herself against these influences and hold onto a belief in the rightness of her thoughts, feelings, and actions. It must be kept in mind that a break-up usually occurs when the female, who is nearly always the one to leave, is at a particularly low point rather than a relatively strong one. Breaking up, therefore, is the first step toward regaining or developing self-assurance, assertiveness, and self-esteem rather than the final expression of growing strength. Foremost among triggers for her guilt will likely be his wounded response to her departure. Without question, the loss of the relationship will be experienced as a tremendous blow to his narcissism and his fragile self-esteem. It is the loss of the center of his world. His dependency needs and fear of abandonment are probably much stronger than hers and here that perhaps hidden reality will be fully displayed. It will be very hard for her not to feel responsible for the pain, desperation, deterioration, or self-harm that seems so clearly to be the consequence of her act. All her anger, hurt, the full sum of her knowledge of the harm he and the relationship have caused her, may crumble in the face of the single question, "But how can I do this to him?"

The second source of guilt will flow from the self-evaluation that she will be undergoing. As she searches assiduously for her own faults, crimes, and misdemeanors in reviewing herself and the relationship, she is in danger of magnifying their number and their effect. She will be attracted to these notions not only by his and perhaps her life's cumulative influence, her self-critical attitude, and poor self-image, but also by a wish for efficacy. If it's her fault, then she might be able to change, save him, and relieve herself of this wretched and embattled estrangement, which is what she has probably been thinking and been led to believe throughout the relationship.

While it is important for her to acknowledge and understand her contributions to the relationship's problems, her behavioral or emotional problems, or her problems with close relationships, a firm distinction must be drawn between recognizing a problem and choosing where one should seek to work it out. In the case of a pathologically dominating relationship, all problems she may have must be worked on elsewhere. Regarding her responsibility for the pathology of the relationship and her wish to save it, she must be helped to understand that it was in the nature of this type of relationship that she could have no efficacy. This doesn't mean she is innocent; rather, it means simply that she could have no significant effect. She could neither create nor change the dominating personality. She may have dealt with it in a more or less healthy and mature way, but in the end, he was going to be whatever was his nature to be.

If she is concerned with the harm she feels she is doing him, I would ask her to consider the harm she does him by submitting to his style of relationship. Her participation in such an unhealthy arrangement supported his pathology and did not help *him* to grow and mature or to achieve anything near the pleasure, confidence, or peace of mind that healthy love should yield. I ask her to consider that she could not change that pattern while in the relationship, and remind her that leaving it may have a more productive effect. At the very least, she won't have to feel that she is helping him to continue to be the way he is.

Regarding her feelings about the difficulty he is having with the loss, I remind her that she is having difficulty too. She has done something very hard and is (hopefully) trying to deal with it, get on top of it, in a strong and healthy way. She is not going to him for relief, though she feels the urge to; she is reaching out to others instead. She is busying herself with other things. It is hard for her to be going through this in this way to help herself; he will have to do the same.

As for suicidal threats and behavior, I tell her to expect them. I will bring it up if she hasn't—I don't want her to be taken by surprise and knocked off balance by them. She must be prepared for whatever he is likely to say or do to get her back, and he is likely to say or do something of a suicidal nature. First, she must learn that it is a potential danger for her to go to him if he presents as being in a suicidal crisis. She may end up as half of a murder–suicide. Second, breaking up means that you have given up responsibility for each other. It means you have quit that. She can no longer allow herself to be his way of feeling better, nor can she allow his life to depend on her. She must tell him, and especially tell others to tell him, to seek help from others. She must turn his care over to others. He must learn in the most profound way possible that he cannot expect or demand anything further from her.

I will ask her to consider that breaking up, being dumped, and experiencing loss and pain are normal, necessary experiences in growing up. Normally people will learn and grow from these experiences. They teach us to cope, recover, improve, and whom to marry. They prepare us to raise our children and then tolerate their increasing separation and individuation from us. They help us to someday be a good parent to a teenager. So she should not feel guilty for putting him in a position where he will feel pain. If it doesn't help him, that is his responsibility.

Hope

Hope has been reported to be a major reason why women remain in abusive relationships and why they return after having left. The intermittent, random, positive reinforcement that has characterized her experience in the relationship creates an extremely persistent expectation of reward. This is experienced as hope, and is very difficult to give up. Her hope derives in part from her wish to believe that she can make it right. Therefore, her view of herself is involved as well. Making the therapist's job harder and the client's vulnerability greater is the fact that the future cannot be disproven.

I simply ask her to weigh the risk of finding out by returning to him. Can she afford the risk of more harm? Our collective memory of past events contains the measure of the degree of risk. If one is contemplating a wade through an alligator pit, one cannot prove or disprove in advance whether an attack will occur. Instead, one simply considers the risks based on what is known and accept that if one declines it will never be known for sure how the wade would have turned out.

Love

This is the word that may have started all the trouble in the first place. It must be blown up and reassembled. I try to explain that it is a huge word, encompassing many things, not all of which are good or good for you, some of which are very bad, if not downright deadly. Abused children love their abusive parents and are desperate for that love to be returned. Hostages often come to love their captors. The abusive and dominating, even murderous, man will steadfastly proclaim his love for his female partner. A lot of mayhem is produced in the name of love. So the word love alone is not worth much. A relationship must be examined to determine the type and quality of its love. Is the love about power or need or addiction? Does it corrode while offering only temporary pleasures? Does it offer respect, build confidence, strengthen the person, helping him or her to become bigger and better? Does it feel mostly good? Can it be trusted? Is it fair? Does it at least *want* to be this way and honestly *try* to be? "Love" alone is a cheap word, easily tossed around and, therefore, far from being enough merely by its invocation.

Relief

I alluded earlier to the great desire on the part of the young woman who has left to want relief from "this stupid misery" and to perceive a return as the only (or at least the quickest) way of getting it. First, there is value in *not* getting immediate relief. Delay allows an opportunity for exercising a greater tolerance and a reduced fear of distress. Second, she must be helped to use and develop other ways of gaining it. People are different in what they can or will find effective. Usually, various forms of activity work best. The hardest times are those when the opportunity for distracting activity is unavailable and one is alone. Bedtime and quiet class time are among the most difficult. Social activity, work, and sports are among the most effective forms of obtaining relief. Solitary activities, such as exercise, reading, writing (journal, letters, stories, poetry, songs), arts, crafts, meditation, yoga, playing music are all helpful at times and may be called upon when group activity is not available. Solitary coping, if it is successful, provides an enormous payback, fostering individual strength, confidence, and independence.

Loneliness

The next emotion I will discuss is loneliness, which few humans can tolerate for long and which adolescents find especially painful. Identity is formed during adolescence largely through one's relationships with and recognition by others, peers and non-parental adults. Attachment to individuals, friends, lovers, and groups is energetically sought and tenaciously clung to. Loneliness is equated with personal inadequacy. It is felt as a kind of death, and sometimes leads to that end literally. It has been suggested that the higher rate of male versus female suicide is due, in part, to the male's reluctance to open up and share his feelings with others. As a result, he leaves himself in greater isolation and loneliness. In adolescence, the disparity between male and female committed suicide has been found to be even greater than among adult populations.

Loneliness will be associated with the fear of never having another true love. The urge to relieve this loneliness by returning to "the one who knows you best" will be strong.

Again, the positive value of bearing the anxiety of independence and of easing it and mastering it through solitary means, if not through her relationships with friends and family, must be stressed.

The Outward Bound programs often include, as a centerpiece within a classic three- to four-week personal development ordeal, a three-day solo experience. Some adolescent drug treatment programs have adopted an Outward Bound model, including the outdoor solo experience, as part of the rehabilitation environment. Many young people consider the solo, where you are given adequate food and water (or the ability to obtain them from one's surroundings) for three days in an isolated wilderness location and prohibited from seeking contact with other widely-spaced participants, as the most difficult part of the physically and emotionally challenging experience.

Our modern society no longer offers rites of passage to our young as a means of strengthening and tempering their characters. Many tribal rites included such a solitary ordeal. Individuals were helped and motivated to withstand it by knowing that it was something that all must go through to advance themselves or else suffer extreme censure from the rest of the community.

Our young have no set traditional way that is clearly shared by and valued by all. Their loneliness and anxiety is, therefore, more complete and fearful, their will to endure it less steadfast. Yet the value of enduring and ultimately mastering the loneliness of the loss of an all-encompassing relationship through self-reliance is no less important for the young person today than for the young of long ago or far away. It holds the same opportunities for positive identity formation, personal growth, bolstered confidence, and increased independence. It fosters maturity by forcing a person to bear an unwanted but temporary and necessary state and by increasing one's ability to make oneself do what one didn't want to do. For these reasons, it is best if a girl (or boy) doesn't plunge immediately into another relationship, but instead, takes some time by herself.

Jealousy

Finally, there is jealousy. Though it is usually the male who exposes the dark power of jealousy in its most spectacular and devastating forms, the female can be possessed by it as well. Stachan and Dutton (1992) found that sexual jealousy provoked stronger anger responses from undergraduate females than undergraduate males. Females reported highest levels of anger when perceiving themselves to have little or no control over the situation. Buss and colleagues (1992) reported that females feel greater distress in their jealousy than males when they perceived their partner to have an emotional attachment and a sexual relationship with another woman. For the males in the study, their partners' sexual relations with a rival were most distressing. Paul and Galloway (1994) even found females, in their sample, giving a more positive endorsement to a violent response to partner infidelity than the males. These studies support and elaborate on the findings of earlier research that has established that both males and females possess a capacity for jealousy that is subjectively very strong and very distressing (Buss 1989). Sam Cooke, the singer, and Lyman Bostock, the all-star baseball player, were both murdered by jealous girlfriends. I have certainly encountered many females who were driven to frenzy at the thought of their partner's exclusively sexual infidelity without also needing the additional presence of an emotional attachment. I find in numerous circumstances that a female's primary reason for returning to an unhealthy relationship is to prevent or to put a stop to (control) her partner's involvement with a rival. They are compelled by jealousy to return. They cannot live with the intrusive thought and visual image of their partner having sex with another. They cannot bear the thought of being replaced and the associated suggestion that they are no good, easily discarded, out of mind, and perhaps, worst of all, never cared about at all. Some are driven to the type of physical aggression, destruction of property, stalking, and harassment that have distinguished the desperate jealous behavior of some men. A conscious strategy of some men is to use jealousy as the lure to draw back a lost girlfriend. Certainly, many men seek a new relationship immediately in order to ease the pain of rejection and loneliness and to save face. A woman must expect and be prepared to hear of, and probably see, her former partner with another. This is especially likely in adolescence, where couples usually live in the same community, perhaps even the same neighborhood, share the same bus, school, friends, and activities. She may have to watch her ex-boyfriend in the hall, in class, and at lunch cavorting with a new girl. She may not be able to separate herself from this enormously provocative situation. In this regard, as in some others, adolescent break-ups can be more difficult than those between adults. With their greater mobility and independence, adults are far less likely to be stuck together after separating.

Consequently, jealousy is one more constellation of emotions that the young woman must bear. She must be helped to withstand the powerful urge to reinvolve herself with her ex-boyfriend as her way of coping. If she can't bear to see him, she must be helped to find ways to avoid him. She should consider changing her job, her activities, bus route, locker location, even her class schedule and school if it is possible and won't cause more harm than good to do so.

Above all, she must be cautioned against allowing herself to be drawn into a reinvolvement that is propelled by anger or by a desire for control and prevention of his relationships with others. These are jealousy-driven and are entirely negative and unhealthy motivations that should be discouraged. If she feels a response is necessary, she must be helped to understand that no response is the strongest of all. Rather than envy his new girl, or nurture painful thoughts and feelings regarding his new relationship such as, "He treats her better than he ever treated me," "He loves and cares about her," "She's probably better than I am sexually," or allow her perception of the relationship to discredit her in other ways, she should consider pitying the new girl instead. She needs to be reminded that his love is deeply flawed and that his proven inflexibility makes it highly unlikely he will be much different in another serious relationship at this point in his life. She needs to be reminded that to fight with him or to engage him in any way on this matter is to reintroduce herself into a relationship with him. Furthermore, in breaking up with him she gave up all rights to having a say regarding his behavior with others. She can't have it both ways—she can't have her independence and seek to control him as well. Hopefully, earlier therapeutic work will have adequately prepared her to deal with this critically difficult eventuality.

The Problem of Maintaining Contact

Returning for a moment to the idea, the wish, "to have it both ways," I would like to mention two other manifestations of this frequently observed desire. The first is the desire to maintain a friendship; the second is the urge to keep up a verbal relationship, to keep talking to each other. As for the first, it is impossible. It would require a godlike quality of maturity and good will to move immediately from lovers to mere friends. As a rule, one should not attempt it. The results are invariably disappointing and upsetting. Nonetheless, many young couples who have broken up find the notion appealing. It seems a good way to soften the blow of parting and ease the transition toward independence. It has the look of benevolence and high-mindedness. It assuages the guilt of the one who left and offers hope to the one left behind. On the whole it appears to be a very civilized way of going about things.

It is a particularly bad idea in the case of the pathologically dominating relationship. It opens a door that must be kept firmly shut. Entering in the guise of friendship, the dominating male will inevitably seek to reassert his control, forcing the young woman either to submit or carry out another difficult and dangerous separation. He cannot limit himself to friendship. It lacks far too much. Would-be lovers who are constrained to friendship are overwhelmingly conscious of what is missing. It is frustrating; hope has been stirred and then thwarted, and anger is a likely byproduct.

The maintenance of a talking relationship need not involve an effort at friendship per se. It may consist of ongoing verbal battles or mutual crisis intervention. It should be a sad but firm truth that breaking up means there is nothing more to say, nothing more to fight about, nothing more to give. However, in real life, the death throes of a broken relationship often extend beyond what would seem to be the final separation. As a therapist, I do offer certain warnings and instructions regarding further communication. Paramount among them is the need for the female to exercise a control as close to complete as possible over those communications. They should not take place in person and absolutely not alone and in isolation. She should decide ahead of time exactly what she intends to say, keeping it as brief, simple, and repetitive (if necessary) as possible. She should not expect to obtain his agreement or even his understanding and she should beware if he seems to quickly grant it. She should have her say, ask her questions, and get out. If it becomes a verbal battle she will probably be at a disadvantage. If she uses the phone she must be prepared to hang up when she chooses to. She must say she *won't* speak with him any further rather than she *can't*, and not make up an excuse as to why she must get off the phone.

If she feels the need to express her feelings to him one more time, without conflict or confusion, disorganization, interruption, or a weakening of her resolve, she can write to him. This may offer her the satisfaction of having had her say and provide some needed closure.

Crisis communications constitute renewals of the relationship. If they continue to use each other to cope and for relief, or to accept and provide for those needs in the other, they have not broken up. Hopes and expectations are stirred and provoked that, should they be later dismissed, may precipitate unpleasant consequences. Again, the couple place themselves in the position of enduring repeated break-ups. As stated earlier, regardless of the type or magnitude of the crisis, the care of the other must be turned over to someone else.

One reason why adolescents find breakups so distressing is that they raise so many questions about their identity, self-image, and sense of personal and sexual adequacy. There is always so much they yearn to know and to understand about themselves that they feel the failed relationship can explain. They will often continue to press for this knowledge, maintaining an unhealthy and dangerous connection longer than they should. It is very hard for them to accept that they must, in the end, sometimes walk away without fully understanding it, him, her, or what it means about themselves.

Obviously, any client may terminate any therapy at any point, and they often do. Adolescents, in particular, are said to be noted for this. Regarding our present discussion, clients often leave therapy when they feel that they have gone against the wishes and expectations of the therapist. This is more apt to be the case when the therapist has, as I have rather strongly advised, offered specific directive instructions, advice, and opinions. Nonetheless, at times, in treating this problem with young people, I do not believe that the therapist can responsibly do otherwise. It falls, therefore, to the relating style, warmth, and clear positive regard that the therapist imparts to the client to fortify their bond. He or she must project an attitude that accepts with kindness, patience, and continued care and confidence the unsteady and erratic pace of the young client's growth. Therapists must acknowledge the great difficulties that challenge their clients and assure them that many failures, mistakes, and fallbacks are the norm. They do not make you angry, impatient, or uninterested (hopefully). You do not expect them to do exactly as you say. You cannot prove that you are right. You are only one of many influences in their lives and they must consider them all. Therefore, you do not take their contrary actions as disagreement, disrespect, or disobedience.

I bring this up here because the female's return to a dominating partner often means her disengagement from therapy as well. She may feel a fool in her therapists eyes, weak, recalcitrant, a waste of time. If the therapist has been perceived as having a strong dislike of and negative attitude toward the boyfriend, her renewed attachment to him may set her at odds with therapy. It is important to address this issue early on in the work, repeated occasionally and discussed again when a break-up seems imminent or is underway.

The therapist should find a relevant opportunity to anticipate the client's future periods of ambivalence, divided loyalties, or doubt about therapy and the premature terminations or interruptions that may ensue. The therapist must openly acknowledge these normal processes and encourage the client to always feel free to bring these feelings openly into the sessions. Despite the best of therapeutic efforts, a client may leave anyway, with or without explanation—usually without—often well before they are out of the woods and well before their need and danger have expired. All one can do in anticipation of this development is offer them an open door to return and an assurance of no hard feelings. When a client does leave prematurely the therapist should initially reach out, give them more time, if necessary, then reach out again to see how things are going, and reassert your openness to their return and your good will.

Safety and the Logistics of Separation

When a woman of any age leaves a pathologically dominating relationship a presumption of danger and harassment should be maintained. Relationships which have been physically abusive, of course, hold a greater potential for physical danger since the male has already demonstrated a willingness and capacity for violence as a means of expression and control. A woman who leaves must also be wary of previously nonviolent dominators. The loss of the relationship will expose them to a level of panic, anger, frustration, and desperation that may be far beyond what they have ever had to cope with before. Add the likely provocation of powerful jealously and the possibility of suicidal ideation and a dangerous stew may be brewing. Research, experience, and statistics strongly support this level of concern. Even vague threats of harm or worse should be taken literally until proven otherwise. The female should keep in mind that, regardless of how he has treated her or how she views herself, her former boyfriend has been absolutely dependent upon her for his tolerably positive view of himself and his identity. He has organized his personality and way of life around her in a fashion more complete and profound than is normal, healthy, or safe. His desperation to maintain his lifeline and his existence may, therefore, be quite extreme—he will need her. Her denial of what he needs may heighten that need and his effort to obtain it. He will focus only on that drive and be mindless of her perspective and what he may have done to push her away in the first place. In many cases the dominating individual, after separation, will think, feel, and behave like an addict in a state of intense craving. He cannot, therefore, be trusted or considered safe.

The most routine aspects of living must immediately become a matter of purposeful thought and planning for the young woman in the immediate aftermath of a breakup from this type of relationship. Nearly everything she does may need to become a conscious act. It is a tiresome, difficult way to live but will be necessary for a while. I tell a client in these circumstances that she must think like a Secret Service agent assigned to guard the president. It can be a bit of a struggle getting her to take herself that seriously or as that important.

Certain rules apply. She will need the help of those with whom she lives. They must deny his access to the girl within her own home. For this they need the cooperation and assistance of everyone living there. They can screen phone calls, answer the door, and set firm limits on attempts by the ex-boyfriend to contact the girl. Doors and windows may need to be secured. An answering machine can take and record incoming calls.

She should avoid, as much as possible, going anywhere alone. Simply walking from her house or job to her car can be an exceedingly vulnerable moment and is a common opportunity for abductions. I once had a man crouch in the bushes outside my building waiting to pounce on a girl leaving my office. If she drives, she should keep her doors locked and definitely not go for any rides with him. If she is in her car and finds he is following her and feels unsafe she can, of course, drive home if someone else will be there or drive to the nearest police station. When she goes out, she should tell someone where she's going and when she will be back and try to stick to it.

Her school may need to be informed that a potentially dangerous situation exists. If the male is a student there as well, a counselor should speak to him. If he does not attend her school, administrators should take precautions against trespassing and harassment. This is a growing problem in high schools. Outsiders create problems for schools not only by coming in to sell drugs or engage in gang activities; assaults, abductions, and other forms of harassment between former lovers are also carried out. When the school day is done, she should not leave school alone or travel without security. Her most vulnerable moments will be those involving locations and behavior patterns that are predictable and where he has open access to her. High schools must sometimes hold an at-risk student after school hours until a stalking ex-boyfriend has been forced to leave the area and a secure ride has been obtained.

College students and young women living independently in apartments face more difficult security problems since they are unprotected by family, may have more difficulty securing their dwellings, and, in the case of apartment dwellers, may spend more time alone. The basic rules, however, will still apply. Different environments simply require different logistical arrangements.

I don't want my client to be paranoid—almost paranoid will do. I hope she will be able to establish and maintain an attitude of sensible and vigilant caution: refuse to be alone with him, seek to control, absolutely, her former boyfriend's access to her, and enlist the help of others. Even these cannot guarantee her safety, but they will eventually discourage most unwanted intrusions.

Restraining Orders

The imposition of a restraining order issued against a former lover is a big and unpleasant step to take. Many fear it will intensify the level of acrimony and exacerbate the danger. It may raise the level of ill feelings with unpredictable results. The court can issue an order prohibiting contact between individuals within certain parameters, but it cannot prevent that contact before the fact. It cannot, for instance, incarcerate or limit the freedom of a person because of what he *might* do. It can only respond, after the fact, to what he has already done. Even that level of response is an imperfect one, because even if a person is arrested for stalking, harassment, threatening, or assault, they will, in the vast majority of cases, have bail set, pay it, and be free in a matter of hours or days, pending a trial that will most likely be many weeks away.

Nonetheless, despite the risks and imperfections, a restraining order is increasingly recommended, requested, and granted in cases such as these. It is recommended in cases where private, conventional limits have not worked, where a danger and/or unwanted intrusiveness exists, and where a stronger voice carrying the power of law is needed. The issue of increasing the danger is met with the observation that danger already exists. The court's limited control is set up against the very limited and perhaps failed control that had existed using only one's own resources.

A secondary value of the use of a restraining order is the feeling of support and empowerment it can provide. It is a powerful statement of a person's needs and demands, an assertive voice that amplifies one's own with the full and official backing of a judge and the public in the form of the institution of the court. It can provide a sense of validation and act as a catalyst for the emergence of much-needed family and peer support. It can precipitate a new coming together of an adolescent with her family in particular. Together with them she may find it possible to face her formerly dominating boyfriend in court with a greater feeling of strength and certainty than she ever had before.

Still, going to court, having to confront a former lover face to face, especially one who once held such power and control, in an atmosphere of open conflict, in public before family and officials, is not a pleasant or easy task. One final value of using a restraining order, however, is its role in beginning to build a court record regarding the offending party. It introduces the offending individual to the court and permits it to take note of his behavior. Generally, a court responds more forcefully the more repeated are a defendant's infractions, so the sooner his record is added to or begins to be built the better. Courts will vary from county to county and state to state in their procedural and attitudinal style, but all will have some provision for restraining orders and many make advocates available to complainants. Advocates provide information and counseling regarding the court experience, legal issues, available social services, and psychological and safety issues.

Persons seeking restraining orders or court action of some kind should gather and provide as much corroborating evidence pertinent to the case as possible. These might include dated photographs of injuries, tape recordings of threatening or harassing phone calls or conversations, medical records, police reports, and affidavits from witnesses. These lend added credibility to the overall picture being presented and to other uncorroborated material. Before going to court or deciding on the use of a restraining order, a battered woman's hot line may be called for information and advice. Local police departments can also be helpful in letting one know how the local courts operate and how to prepare.

Once a restraining order is issued, the complainant should, of course, adhere to it as well and initiate no contact. Failure to do so can damage her credibility and weaken the court's resolve to respond firmly to subsequent complaints. The complainant should carry a copy of the restraining order on her person so that she can immediately demonstrate that further transgressions are in defiance of a standing court order and part of a continuing problem. It will save a great deal of verbal and emotional effort to let it do most of the talking.

TREATING THE DOMINATING MALE

The type of young man under discussion here is unlikely to enter therapy by means of self-referral. He may be coerced by order of a court, he may do so at the urging of others, or he may be in therapy already for another problem. If he does seek help it is very unlikely that he will do so with a goal of substantial personal change in mind. Rather, it will most likely be to gain relief from his symptoms of acute distress, depression, and anxiety as soon as possible.

Engaging in a therapeutic relationship is often difficult for males, especially adolescent males. The relationship may be strongly associated with the type of mother/child dependency that he consciously avoids. The openness to emotional material and the acknowledgment of weakness and vulnerability therapy entails may be viewed as abhorrently feminine and thus emasculating. It has been a longstanding truth that males underutilize psychotherapeutic services. In my own practice females have consistently made up 60–65 percent of my client population, year after year. Saunders and colleagues' (1994) survey of over 17,000 high-school students found males to be significantly less likely to feel they had a serious emotional problem or to believe they needed professional help. Consequently engaging this type of young man can be particularly challenging.

The pathologically dominating male, post-separation, will be struggling with many of the same issues as his former partner and, therefore, much of what has been discussed regarding her will pertain to him as well.

Both will have experienced painful losses within the context of a high level of dependency. He too will have lost the center of his world. He will be struggling to cope with an overwhelming blow to his self-esteem, identity, and sense of adequacy. He may feel helpless in the face of unfamiliar and overpowering feelings, with no experience and perhaps little hope of mastery. He may be unused to having bad feelings persist, since his defense mechanisms of denial, projection, and avoidance (perhaps fortified by substance abuse) and his effectively demanding style have tended to either extinguish unwanted feelings or simply minimize them by getting his needs quickly met. His tolerance for emotional pain may be severely limited, as will be his understanding of the forces at work upon him.

Often he will experience his condition as anger or as major depression. Typically he will focus narrowly on the loss of the relationship as the sole source of his problems, and view himself as a misunderstood, uncared for, and ill-used victim. He may find it all incomprehensible. Regaining her is often his only desire and a relentless expectation. All of this lacks depth; it maintains a perception that the problem is largely, if not exclusively, external. It suggests little understanding of the need for change on his part, and places responsibility for his rejuvenation on others. In short, the dominating male will simply continue to be himself. Like the notorious woman-batterer quoted in the newspaper after his umpteenth arrest, "I've had bad luck with women, but I have a heart of gold," they often just don't get it. Their firmly set characterological structure allows them little flexibility in their capacity to perceive, understand, and respond, even to so significant an event.

Suicide risk management may be the first level of intervention. When present, the potential for homicidal behavior needs to be ascertained as well. When we have gotten beyond these issues and gained an understanding of the client's condition and perspective, I make several strong suggestions.

First and foremost among them is the insistence that he stay away from his former partner, with or without the presence of a restraining order. I tell him that it is both the best way of getting her back and the only way to start getting over her. Staying away is the single best thing he can do for himself. It keeps him out of trouble, and it is a much-needed exercise in self-denial, patience, frustration tolerance. It begins to help him tolerate and accept her independence and respect her as a separate individual who must be considered, accommodated, and recognized. Conceivably, this lesson, if learned, will carry over to his next relationship. The problem of staying away allows access to the issue of his dependency, which might then be explored and (to some degree) dealt with. Furthermore, staying away, being strong in that sense, can be associated with a healthy masculinity, a much-desired identity in any young man. To be "a man" he will have to leave her alone rather than grasp at her. He must take care of himself for a time, by himself or, at least, without her help. He must be helped to embrace the honor and value in this. I encourage male clients of this type to seek the company of other males, knowing that their influence is likely to support my effort to keep him away from his former girlfriend.

He also needs to keep busy. He, just like his former girlfriend, must learn to bear the anxiety of independence and find new supports, new activities, new healthy ways to feel good. He must cut himself loose, adrift, in order to move on, even though he won't know where he's headed. He will need to hear the word "bravery" too. If we are lucky, we may be able to get him to look at the level of care and attention he's been demanding and have him see it for the babyishness that it was and reject it. He will never obtain that level of solicitude again and the harm to him if he does, or even tries to, can be explained. His most recent debacle can be offered as exhibit number one.

It takes hope to persist, however. Hope is based on at least a minimal expectation of success, which is based on a degree of confidence and self-esteem. We have seen that dominating and abusive men tend to be very weak in these latter qualities. It will be difficult, therefore, for him to bear the hard and uncertain road to relief when a more immediate cure seems so available. Working at things, in general, may be hard for him if not impossible. Individuals such as this are often impatient with the effort, frustrate and give up easily, blaming the task for the failure. It may strain his tolerance enormously to have to muddle around with trial-and-error coping until new confidence develops.

From these challenges, however, come new opportunities for growth. As it is for the young woman, so it is for the young man. Adolescence is an opportunity to choose new paths, to learn new ways. It is probably the last best chance for major characterological change. If he is willing to try to recoup and recover without mere repetition of old ways, he may begin to break free of an otherwise ill-fated course.

In reviewing the nature and cause of his relationship with him, tracing and observing the origin and strength of his jealousy and possessiveness, looking at the intensity and unpleasantness of emotion that love has unleashed within him, one must put the questions, "Have you enjoyed love? Have you benefited from it? Are you *ready* for love?" I would urge my male client to study these questions in light of what has happened and how it has felt, and consider seriously whether love has been good for him. Love, I think, should be seen as too powerful and dangerous for him at this point in his life. Rather than something he should desperately pursue and seek to rely upon, it may be viewed as perhaps not at all in his best interest for now.

Throughout therapy (and if all fails, as it very well may), the therapist must have an ear for danger to the client's former lover and be prepared to inform her and everyone else in a position to care for her if a significant and imminent danger to her appears to exist. This was discussed in Chapter 6, but it bears repeating here.

This is also a good place to mention the possibility of danger to the therapist. As I said in an earlier chapter, the only time I have ever felt in any physical danger relating to my work has been in the treatment of the male or female in cases such as this. The breaking of confidentiality and the act of depicting him to the police and significant others, especially the girl in question, as a potentially dangerous character whom one should either flee from or restrain, may certainly place a therapist in jeopardy if the client is violent and views the "betrayal" as having caused him serious harm.

Therapists working to extricate a female from a dominating and abusive relationship may be labeled a noxious meddling interference, the sole cause of the loss of the girlfriend, and thus a personal enemy. Male therapists may become part of the young man's jealousy fantasies and may be perceived as trying to pull her away from him in order to have her for himself. Fearing and blaming the influence of others upon the girlfriend is a common control feature of the pathologically dominating man's perspective and a major reason for his need to increase her social isolation.

Needless to say, these circumstances can place a therapist at significant risk. I am surprised, actually, that I never hear of one assaulted for these reasons, though I suppose they sometimes are. Nonetheless, a therapist should sometimes take the precautions they advise their endangered clients to take.

Caroline and John III

I heard very little from Caroline after her letter of 2/24/95. The last letter I received was in March. I called her dorm room once and was told by her roommate that she was with John all the time and rarely used or slept in the dorm. In this case it appeared to me that no news was bad news. It seemed that she had fallen back to him entirely. Everything about her situation appeared dismal, including her academic status (and thus her financial aid status), which had never significantly suffered before. Still, I looked forward to her return from the West in mid-June.

Mid-June passed and I still hadn't heard from her. I wondered what this meant. I worried, but did not call. I had been presuming she was fully reinvolved with John and I must admit I was not eager to hear that. I didn't think I would be able to keep the deep disappointment out of my voice. At the same time I imagined that she was avoiding me for the same reason. I cannot honestly claim that I held back primarily to save her the indignity of having to report her condition. I felt discouraged, and that was pretty much it. However, I also believed that if she felt she needed something from me she would let me know.

By late June I was growing more restless. I had her name written in my schedule book on June 29, reminding me to call her, but I procrastinated further. I didn't want to make the first move, I didn't want to be pushy or intrusive, I didn't want to hear of her demise, an image of which I had fully formed in my mind.

Near midnight on July 3, a Monday night, my phone rang. I have two phone numbers for my house. One is the regular family number, the other is for professional emergencies. It has a different ring pattern which indicates that it is a call for me. Still, I never recognize it for what it is when I get a call after I've been asleep—I think it's the alarm clock instead. I've nearly missed more than one call this way. Now I have a pager, too, in order to broaden the confusion just a bit more.

It was Caroline. She has a remarkable ability to present the most devastating conditions and occurrences with a most composed demeanor. The only indication of the turbulence of her contained emotions are a more rapid than usual rate of speech, repeatedly saying "I don't know, I just don't know," and too much laughter. Sometimes she'll flush with hives as well. This night the tone of her distress was undisguised and unmistakable. After a profusion of apologies for having called me so late, she breathlessly told me she had just returned from the police station with her father to get a restraining order against John. When the police heard his name they recalled that there was an outstanding warrant against him for assault and battery perpetrated on a man last fall (which Caroline had never known about). When they heard her complaint, her description of his threats and harassment, and heard her answering-machine tape on which he spoke of "slitting her throat" and killing her and one of her girlfriends, they urged her to press charges, which she did. They arrested him an hour later. Bail was denied. He would have to remain in the county jail until his court appearance three days hence. It all took a long time, that was why she had called so late. More apologies.

But now she was scared. She imagined his rage building steadily as he lay in jail ruminating over her, blaming her, focusing on revenge. She felt guilt, too. She spoke now in a rapid-fire monotone.

"He's not tough. He'll be terrified. That will make him madder, but he won't show it there. He can't stand to wear the same clothes for even a whole day, much less for three days. He likes to wash several times a day. At home he complains all the time about everything. He's such a baby. He can only stand things a certain way. Everything has to be a certain way. It has to be quiet and clean. He can only sleep in his own bed. It has to be totally dark, not one blink of light. He even has extra-dark shades and curtains to block out all light. He'll go nuts in there."

At the same time she was clearly relieved not to have to worry about him being able to get to her for a while. It gave her time to think and plan, and she was very conscious of the value of that.

I found that I had been quite wrong in my suppositions about Caroline's state of mind and involvement with John since she had returned home from school. She had reached the end of the line with him by the end of the academic year. She found herself increasingly angry at him, incessantly discontent and combative when she was with him. She began to finally and fully understand his way with her. Most of all she could understand his intentions and clearly identify them through his varied screens of ploys, shifts, and manipulations. She knew he intended, as he always had, to break her down and control her. Furthermore, she had come to the point of being able to hang onto these accurate perceptions even in the face of stress. She was even able to predict his actions and thereby prepare for them. This allowed her to take a more objective view of him, as if observing him from a distance. She was able to maintain the viewpoint that he was an interference to her life rather than essential for her existence. The dramatic difference in her outlook, functioning, health, and mood from the first semester, spent without

him, to the second, spent virtually living with him, provided her with the final proof she needed.

Still, she avoided breaking up with him at school while
still so enmeshed. Instead, she intended to do it when she
got home and could separate more fully and with less
effort. It helped enormously that her father had recently
ended his relationship with John's mother and had grown
more supportive and understanding of Caroline. She
would be returning to a home environment in which she
could be stronger than she had ever been before, more
separated from John's life, more fully secured against him,
and at the same time less lonely.

As it turned out, she didn't have to do a thing. He broke
up with her before they even left school. He said she was
being too "independent" and had taken on a "conceited
attitude," so he was "punishing" her by "taking a break
from her for awhile." He couldn't say when or if he'd let
her see him, topping it off with, "Maybe I need to try somebody new."

She saw it all coming through like a pitch guessed
right, like a soft lob, like the questions on a test that just
happened to be the only ones you had really prepared for.
She just lay back on it and smiled inside. She could feel
the irony of it even then. The cataclysm she had anticipated had, instead, simply rolled out before her like a red
carpet. She could just walk.

In the past, these "break-ups" had worked for him
every time. It would snap her right back in line, like bark-
ing "heel" at a well trained dog. She wrote in her letter of
1/15/95 of his effective use of this manipulation upon her.
But it was too late for that now—she knew too much. She
knew that people liked her. She had come to believe that
she could be attracted to and probably love another. She
knew for certain that she could do well in many things if

she was free of him. So when he broke up with her she took the first big leap to freedom, simply by standing still.

Of course, with relationships such as this, the end dies hard. They had been back home in Massachusetts for only a week when he began calling her again. She avoided answering, letting the answering machine do the work. Finally, however, she let down her guard and he caught her on the phone. He reminded her that their anniversary was that week and he thought they ought to go out that night. He spoke to her as if they were together again and no separation had ever occurred. In his mind, of course, none had. She stopped him, though, by saying she had plans that night with a girlfriend (the one he also threatened to murder in one of his later recorded phone calls) and wouldn't be seeing him that night. "In fact, " she said, "I won't be seeing you at all anymore. You said it's over and this time it is. Not because you said so but because I say so, too." She didn't get much else out. He flooded her with screaming threats and insults until she hung up the phone, soaked in sweat but in command. She never spoke to him again. The phone calls that led to the restraining order and his arrest followed immediately after.

As I write this, it is six-and-a-half weeks after her midnight call and John's first night in jail and all has gone surprisingly well. For her part, she has stood her ground with her father's help and attended the restraining order hearing and a pretrial hearing regarding the charges of criminal harassment. She has reentered therapy in order, she said, "to keep me thinking the way I should." This has been very easy for me because she has not wavered. Instead, she has established a busy social life with new and old friends, worked, swam, made plans to enter some competitive meets for the first time in five years in preparation for trying out for the college swim team in the fall.

John has lain low. He apparently fears the police and jail more than he fears losing Caroline, or so it seems. He has not called or stalked her, as far as she knows. I hope she is continuing to take precautions and to be very wary. She says she is, but I wonder. At heart she is an adventurer and is feeling rather bold of late.

It may be that Caroline has survived and escaped. Her circumstances have in some ways been fortunate. Long term, mostly free therapy was available to her during her senior year in high school and later through her parent's insurance coverage. Therapy services such as her school provided are rarely available to high school students. Many families are without adequate medical coverage. She had a parent willing and able to help and a home she could safely live in. She had the ability to make and keep friends and she had talent.

Most important, she was able to leave. I would not have wanted to bet a great deal of money that she could have made and maintained the break despite all she had going for her, had she not been able to move two thousand miles away. Complete separation is the one essential condition.

For the young person who must continue to sit across the aisle from her boyfriend in class, must travel the same hallways and the same streets, and must share the same friends, separation will prove to be far more difficult.

Later though, it may be harder still. Those women who must share a home, children, and all available money and resources with a dominating man might look back upon their younger days as the last best chance to have saved their spirits and themselves.

REFERENCES

Adams, D. (1995). Coerced treatment: Contradiction in terms? *Massachusetts Psychological Association Quarterly* 38(4):9, 15.

Alexander, R., and Noonan, K. (1979). Concealment of ovulation, parental care, and human social evolution. In *Evolutionary Biology and Human Social Behavior,* ed. N. Chagnon and W. Irons, pp. 436–453. North Scituate, MA: Duxbury.

American Association of University Women (1990). *Shortchanging Girls, Shortchanging America: Full Data Report.* Washington, DC: American Association of University Women.

——— (1991a). *Shortchanging Girls, Shortchanging America: A Call to Action.* Washington, DC: American Association of University Women.

——— (1991b). *Shortchanging Girls, Shortchanging America: Executive Summary.* Washington, DC: American Association of University Women.

——— (1992). *The AAUW Report: How Schools Shortchange Girls*. Washington, DC: American Association of University Women.

Bandura, A. (1973). *Aggression—A Social Learning Analysis.* Englewood Cliffs, NJ: Prentice-Hall.

Benjamin, J. (1988). *The Bonds of Love: Psychoanalysis, Feminism, and the Problem of Domination.* New York: Pantheon.

Berman, L. (1992). Dating violence among high school students. *Social Work* 37(1):21–25.

Bernard, M., and Bernard, J. (1981). Paper presented at the annual meeting of the Tennessee/Kentucky Psychological Association, Louisville, KY.

——— (1983). Violent intimacy: the family as a model for love relationships. *Family Relations* 32:283–286.

Bernard, M., Bernard, J., and Bernard, S. (1985). Courtship violence and sex-typing. *Family Relations* 34:573–576.

Bertram, B. (1975). Social factors influencing reproduction in wild lions. *Journal of Zoology* 177:463–482.

Bettelheim, B. (1980). *Surviving and Other Essays.* New York: Vintage.

Billingham, R. (1987) . Courtship violence: the patterns of conflict resolution strategies across seven levels of emotional commitment. *Family Relations* 36:283–289.

Bloom, B., White, S., and Asher, S. (1979). Marital disruption as a stressful life event. In *Divorce and Separation,* ed. G. Levinger and O. Moles, pp. 276–291. New York: Basic Books.

Bowker, L. (1983). *Beating Wife-Beating.* Lexington, MA: Lexington Books.

Brent, D., Perper, J., and Goldstein, C. (1988). Risk factors for adolescent suicide: a comparison of adolescent suicide victims with suicidal inpatients. *Archives of General Psychiatry* 45:581–588.

Bronowski, J. (1973). *The Ascent of Man.* Boston, MA: Little, Brown.

Browne, A. (1987). *When Battered Women Kill.* New York: Free Press.

——— (1993). Violence against women by male partners: prevalence, outcomes, and policy implications. *American Psychologist* 48(10):1077–1087.

Browne, A., and Williams, K. (1989). Exploring the effect of resource availability and the likelihood of female-perpetrated homicides. *Law & Society Review* 23:75–94.

Burke, P., Stets, J., and Pirog-Good, M. (1985). Gender identity, self-esteem, and physical and sexual abuse in dating relationships. *Social Psychology Quarterly* 51(3):272–285.

Buss, D. (1989). Conflict between the sexes: strategic interference and the evocation of anger and upset. *Journal of Personality and Social Psychology* 56:735–747.

Buss, D., Larsen, R., Westen, D., and Semmelroth, J. (1992). Sex differences in jealousy: evolution, physiology and psychology. *Psychological Science* 3(4):251–261.

Campbell, J. (1949). *The Hero with a Thousand Faces*. Princeton, NJ: Princeton University Press.

Carlson, B. (1984). Battered women and their assailants. *Social Work* 22(6):455–460.

Carroll, J. (1977). The intergenerational transmission of family violence: the long-term effects of aggressive behavior. *Aggressive Behavior* 3:289–299.

Cate, R., Henton, J., Kaval, J., et al. (1982). Premarital abuse: a social psychological perspective. *Journal of Family Issues* 3:79–91.

Coles, R., and Stokes, G. (1985). *Sex and the American Teenager*. New York: Harper Colophon.

Curran, D. (1987). *Adolescent Suicidal Behavior*. Washington, DC: Hemisphere/Harper & Row.

Daly, M., and Wilson, M. (1988a). Evolutionary social psychology and family violence. *Science* 242:519–524.

——— (1988b). *Homicide*. Hawthorn, NY: Aldine.

Davidson, L., Rosenberg, M., Mercy, J., et al. (1989). An epidemiologic study of risk factors in two teenage suicide clusters. *Journal of the American Medical Association* 262:2687–2692.

Davidson, T. (1978). *Conjugal Crime*. New York: Hawthorne.

Davis, M., and Oathout, H. (1987). Maintenance of satisfaction in romantic relationships: empathy and relational competence. *Journal of Personality and Social Psychology* 53:397–410.

Deal, J., and Wampler, K. (1986). Dating violence: the primacy of previous experience. *Journal of Social and Personal Relationships* 3:457–476.

Deutsch, H. (1944). *The Psychology of Women*, vol. 1 and 2. New York: Grune & Stratton.

Diagnostic and Statistical Manual of Mental Disorders (1994). 4th Ed. Washington, DC: American Psychiatric Association.

Dobash, R. E., and Dobash, R. (1979). *Violence Against Wives*. New York: Free Press.

Dubow, E., Louko, K., and Krause, D. (1990). Demographic differences in adolescents' health concerns and perceptions of helping agents. *Journal of Clinical Child Psychology* 19:44–54.

Eisenberg, S., and Micklow, P. (1977). The assaulted wife: *Catch-22* revisited. *Women's Rights Law Reporter*, Spring/Summer.

Erickson, C., and Zenone, P. (1976). Courtship differences in male ring doves: Avoidance of cuckoldry? *Science* 192:1353 –1354.

Fagan, J., and Browne, A. (1993). Violence between spouses and intimates: physical aggression between men and women in intimate relationships. In *Understanding and Preventing Violence: Vol. 3, Social and Psychological Perspectives of Violence*, ed. A. Reiss and J. Roth, pp. 117–151. Washington, DC: National Academy Press.

Fagan, J., Stewart, D., and Hanson, K. (1983). Violent men or violent husbands? In *The Dark Side of Families: Current Family Violence Research*, ed. D. Finkelhur, R. Gelles, G. Hotaling, and M. Straus, pp. 310–320. Beverly Hills, CA: Sage.

Fagan, R., Barnett, O., and Palton, J. (1988). Reasons for alcohol use in maritally violent men. *American Journal of Drug and Alcohol Abuse* 14:371–392.

Ferninand, P. (1995). Repeat batterer is seen as "walking time bomb." *Boston Globe*, July 4, pp. 1, 32.

Flynn, J. (1974). Recent findings related to wife abuse. *Social Casework* 58(1):13.

Forward, S. (1986). *Men Who Hate Women and the Women Who Love Them*. New York: Bantam.

Freud, S. (1925). Some psychical consequences of the anatomical distinctions between the sexes. *Standard Edition* 19:243–258.

——— (1933). Femininity. *Standard Edition* 22:3–182.

Gayford, J. (1975). Wife battering: a preliminary survey of 100 cases. *British Medical Journal* 1:194–197.

Gelles, R. (1972). *The Violent Home*. Beverly Hills, CA: Sage.

——— (1974). Child abuse as psychopathology: a sociological critique and reformulation. In *Violence in the Family*, ed. S. Steinmetz and M. Straus, pp. 201–222. New York: Harper & Row.

Goldstein, D., and Rosenbaum, A. (1985). An evaluation of the self esteem of maritally violent men. *Family Relations* 34:425–428.

Gondolf, E., and Fisher, E. (1988). *Battered Women as Survivors: An Alternative to Treating Learned Helplessness*. Lexington, MA: Lexington Books.

Goode, W. (1971). Force and violence in the family. *Journal of Marriage and the Family* 33:624–636.

Gooding-Garrett, J., and Senter, R. (1987). Attitudes and acts of sexual aggression on a university campus. *Sociological Inquiry* 57:348–371.

Gwartney-Gibbs, P., Stockard, J., and Bohmer, S. (1987). Learning courtship aggression: the influence of parent, peers and personal experience. *Family Relations* 36:276–282.

Harter, S. (1990). Self and identity development. In *At the Threshold: The Developing Adolescent*, ed. S. Feldman and G. Elliot, pp. 352–387. Cambridge, MA: Harvard University Press.

Hawton, K. (1982). Annotation: attempted suicide in children and adolescents. *Journal of Child Psychology and Psychiatry* 23(4):497–503.

Henton, J., Cate, R., Kaval, J., et al. (1983). Romance and violence in dating relationships. *Journal of Family Issues* 4:467–482.

Hilberman, E., and Munson, K. (1978). Sixty battered women. *Victimology* 2(3–4):460–471.

Hofeller, K. (1980). *Social psychological and situational factors in wife abuse.* Unpublished doctoral dissertation, Claremont Graduate School, Claremont, CA.

Horney, K. (1933). The problem of feminine masochism. In *Feminine Psychology*, pp. 54–70. New York: Norton, 1967.

Hotaling, G., and Sugarman, D. (1986). An analysis of risk markers in husband to wife violence: the current state of knowledge. *Violence and Victims* 1(2):101–124.

Hrdy, S. (1979). Infanticide among animals: a review, classification, and examination of the implications for the reproductive strategies of females. *Ethology and Sociobiology* 1:14–40.

Jacobs, F. (1971). *Adolescent Suicide.* New York: Wiley Interscience.

Jaffee, L., and Manzer, R. (1993). Girls' perspectives: physical activity and self-esteem. *Melpomene Journal* 11(3):14–23.

Jaffee, P., Wilson, S., and Wolfe, D. (1989). Specific assessment and intervention strategies for children exposed to wife battering: preliminary empirical investigation. *Canadian Journal of Community Mental Health* 7:157–163.

JeJeune, C., and Follette, V. (1994). Taking responsibility: sex differences in reporting dating violence. *Journal of Interpersonal Violence* 9(1):133–140.

Johnston, M. (1984). *Correlates of early violence experience among men who are abusive toward female mates.* Paper presented at the Second National Conference for Family Violence Researchers, University of New Hampshire, Durham, NH.

Jones, A., and Schechter, S. (1992). *When Love Goes Wrong: Strategies for Women with Controlling Partners.* New York: Harper Perennial.

Kalmuss, D. (1984). The intergenerational transmission of marital aggression. *Journal of Marriage and the Family* 46(1):11–19.

Kalmuss, D., and Seltzer, J. (1984). *The effect of family structure on family violence: the case of remarriage.* Paper presented at the Second National Conference for Family Violence Researchers, University of New Hampshire, Durham, NH.

Kalmuss, D., and Straus, M. (1982). Wife's marital dependency and wife abuse. *Journal of Marriage and the Family* 44:277–286.

Kanin, E. (1967). Reference groups and sex conduct norms. *Sociological Quarterly* 8:495–504.

Kanin, E., and Parcell, S. (1977). Sexual aggression: a second look at the offended female. *Archives of Sexual Behavior* 6:67–76.

Kashani, J., Anasseril, O., Dandoy, A., and Holcomb, W. (1992). Family violence: impact on children. *Journal of the American Academy of Child and Adolescent Psychiatry* 31(2):181–189.

Kashani, J., Orvaschel, H., Rosenberg, T., and Reid, J. (1989). Psychopathology in a community sample of children and adolescents: a developmental perspective. *Journal of the American Academy of Child and Adolescent Psychiatry* 28(5):701–706.

Kienhorst, I., DeWilde, E., Diekstra, R., and Wolter, W. (1994). Adolescents' image of their suicide attempt. *Journal of the American Academy of Child and Adolescent Psychiatry* 34(5):623–628.

Kohut, H. (1971). *The Analysis of the Self.* New York: International Universities Press.

Komarovsky, M. (1962). *Blue Collar Marriage.* New York: Random House.

Korman, S., and Leslie, G. (1982). The relationship of feminist ideology and date expense sharing to perceptions of sexual aggression in dating. *Journal of Sex Research* 18:114–129.

Koss, M., and Oros, C. (1982). Sexual experiences survey: a research instrument investigating sexual aggression and victimization. *Journal of Consulting and Clinical Psychology* 50:455–457.

Lane, K., and Gwartney-Gibbs, P. (1985). Violence in the context of dating and sex. *Journal of Family Issues* 6(1):45–59.

Laner, M., and Thompson, J. (1982). Abuse and aggression in courting couples. *Deviant Behavior* 3:229–244.

Larson, D., ed. (1990). *Mayo Clinic Family Health Book*. New York: William Morrow.

Levinger, G. (1983). Sources of marital dissatisfaction among applicants for divorce. *American Journal of Orthopsychiatry* 26:803–807.

Levy, B., ed. (1991). *Dating Violence: Young Women in Danger*. Seattle, WA: Seal.

———— (1993). *In Love and In Danger: A Teen's Guide to Breaking Free of Abusive Relationships*. Seattle, WA: Seal.

Lifton, R. (1961). *Thought Reform and the Psychology of Totalism*. New York: Norton.

Long, E., and Andrews, D. (1990). Perspective taking as a predictor of marital adjustment. *Journal of Personality and Social Psychology* 59:126–131.

Maccoby, E., and Jacklin, C. (1974). *The Psychology of Sex Differences*. Stanford, CA: Stanford University Press.

Mack, J. (1976). *A Prince of Our Disorder: The Life of T.E. Lawrence*. Boston, MA: Little, Brown.

Mahler, M., Pine, F., and Bergmann, A. (1975). *The Psychological Birth of the Human Infant*. New York: Basic Books.

Makepeace, J. (1981). Courtship violence among college students. *Family Relations* 30:97–102.

———— (1983). Life events stress and courtship violence. *Family Relations* 32:101–109.

Martin, D. (1976). *Battered Wives*. San Francisco: Glide Publications.

Marttunen, M., Aro, H., Henriksson, M., and Lonnquist, J. (1994). Psychosocial stressors more common in adolescent suicides with alcohol abuse compared with depressive adolescent suicides. *Journal of the American Academy of Child and Adolescent Psychiatry* 33(4):490–497.

Marttunen, M., Aro, H., and Lonnquist, J. (1993). Precipitant stressors in adolescent suicide. *Journal of the American Academy of Child and Adolescent Psychiatry* 32(6):1178–1183.

Mayall, A., and Gold, S. (1995). Definitional issues and mediating variables in the sexual revictimization of women sexually abused as children. *Journal of Interpersonal Violence* 10(1):26–42.

McGee, R., Feehan, M., Williams, S., and Anderson, J. (1992). DSM-III disorders from age 11 to age 15 years. *Journal of the American Academy of Child and Adolescent Psychiatry* 31(1):50–59.

McGee, R., Feehan, M., Williams, S., et al. (1990). *DSM-III* disorders in a large sample of adolescents. *Journal of the American Academy of Child and Adolescent Psychiatry* 29(4):611–619.

Mowrer, E., and Mowrer, H. (1928). *Domestic Discord.* Chicago: University of Chicago Press.

Murphy, C., and O'Farrell, T. (1994). Factors associated with marital aggression in male alcoholics. *Journal of Family Psychology* 8(3):321–335.

NiCarthy, G., and Davidson, S. (1989). *You Can Be Free: An Easy-To-Read Handbook for Abused Women.* Seattle, WA: Seal.

O'Brien, J. (1971). Violence in divorce-prone families. *Journal of Marriage and the Family* 33:692–698.

Offer, D., and Schonert-Reichl, K. (1992). Debunking the myths of adolescence: findings from recent research. *Journal of the American Academy of Child and Adolescent Psychiatry* 31(6):1003–1014.

Okun, L. (1986). *Woman Abuse: Facts Replacing Myths.* Albany, NY: State University of New York Press.

Orenstein, P. (1994). *School Girls.* New York: Doubleday.

Orr, D., Wilbrandt, C., Brack, C., et al. (1989). Reported sexual behaviors and self-esteem among young adolescents. *American Journal of Diseases of Children* 143:86–90.

Ostrov, E., Offer, D., and Howard, K. (1989). Gender differences in adolescent symptomatology: a normative study. *Journal of the American Academy of Child and Adolescent Psychiatry* 28(3):394–398.

Owens, D., and Straus, M. (1984). Social structure of violence in childhood and approval of violence by adults. *Aggressive Behavior* 1(3):193–211.

Pagelow, M. (1981). *Women Battering: Victims and their Experiences*. Beverly Hills, CA: Sage.

—— (1984). *Family Violence*. New York: Praeger.

Partoll, S. (1995). Domestic violence: the alarm rings softly. *Massachusetts Psychological Association Quarterly* 38(4): 1–7.

Paul, L., and Galloway, J. (1994). Sexual jealousy: gender differences in response to partner and rival. *Aggressive Behavior* 20(3):203–211.

Peplau, L. (1983). Roles and gender. In *Close Relationships*, ed. H. H. Kelley et al., pp. 240–253. New York: W.H. Freeman.

Peplau, L., Rubin, Z., and Hill, C. (1977). Sexual intimacy in dating relationships. *Journal of Social Issues* 33(2):86–109.

Pipher, M. (1994). *Reviving Ophelia: Saving the Selves of Adolescent Girls*. New York: Ballantine.

Pirog-Good, M., and Stets, J., eds. (1989). *Violence in Dating Relationships: Emerging Social Issues*. New York: Praeger.

Power, H. (1975). Mountain bluebirds: experimental evidence against altruism. *Science* 189:142–143.

Prescott, S., and Letko, C. (1977). Battered women: a social psychological perspective. In *Battered Women*, ed. M. Roy, pp. 419–436. New York: Van Nostrand Reinhold.

Rapaport, K., and Burkhart, B. (1984). Personality and attitudinal characteristics of sexually coercive college males. *Journal of Abnormal Psychology* 93:216–221.

Riggs, D. (1993). Relationship problems and dating aggression: a potential treatment target. *Journal of Interpersonal Violence* 8(1):18–25.

Riggs, D., O'Leary, K., and Breslin, F. (1990). Multiple predictors of physical aggression in dating couples. *Journal of Interpersonal Violence* 5:61–72.

Roscoe, B., and Benaske, N. (1985). Courtship violence experienced by abused wives: similarities in patterns of abuse. *Family Relations* 34:419–424.

Rosenbaum, A., and O'Leary, K. (1981). Marital violence: characteristics of abusive couples. *Journal of Consulting and Clinical Psychology* 49:63–71.

Rosenberg, M. (1989). *Society and the Adolescent Self-Image.* Middletown, CT: Wesleyan University Press.

Rouse, L. (1984a). *Conflict tactics used by men in marital disputes.* Paper presented at the Second National Conference for Family Violence Researchers, University of New Hampshire, Durham, NH.

―――― (1984b). Models, self-esteem, and locus of control as factors contributing to spouse abuse. *Victimology* 9(1):130–144.

Roy, M., ed. (1977). *Battered Women.* New York: Van Nostrand Reinhold.

Rubin, Z., Peplau, L., and Hill, C. (1981). Loving and leaving: sex differences in romantic attachments. *Sex Roles* 7:821–835.

Russell, D. (1982). *Rape in Marriage.* New York: MacMillan.

―――― (1986). *The Secret Trauma: Incest in the Lives of Girls and Women.* New York: Basic Books.

Sadker, D., and Sadker, M. (1985). Sexism in the schoolroom of the '80s. *Psychology Today,* March, p. 54.

Saunders, S., Resnick, M., Huberman, H., and Blum, R. (1994). Formal help-seeking behavior of adolescents identifying themselves as having mental health problems. *Journal of the American Academy of Child and Adolescent Psychiatry* 33:718.

Scales, A. (1995). Study finds lack of support programs for troubled girls. *Boston Globe,* Aug. 26, p. 2.

Schein, E., Schnierer, I., and Barker, C. (1961). *Coercive Persuasion.* New York: Norton.

Schultz, L. (1959). The wife assaulter: one type observed and treated in a probation agency. *Journal of Social Therapy* 6:103–111.

Serum, C. (1979). *The effects of violent victimization in the family.* Paper presented to the Michigan Coalition Against Domestic Violence, 12/3/79. In *Woman Abuse: Facts Replacing Myths,* ed. L. Okun, pp. 79–89. Albany, NY: State University of New York Press, 1986.

―――― (1980). *Violent conjugal relationships: new psychological perspectives and treatment of the violent man.* Paper presented at the 1981 Spring-Summer Symposium, Continuing Education Program in the Human Services, University of Michigan School of Social Work. In *Woman Abuse: Facts Replacing Myths*, ed. L. Okun, p. 87. Albany, NY: State University of New York Press, 1986.

Shea, L. (1995). Another family grieves another domestic death. *Boston Globe*, Feb. 25, p. 6.

Smith, J., and Williams, J. (1992). From abusive household to dating violence. *Journal of Family Violence* 7(2):153–160.

Snell, J., Rosenwald, R., and Robey, A. (1964). The wife-beater's wife. *Archives of General Psychiatry* 11:107–112.

Sonkin, D., and Dunphy, M. (1985). *Learning to Live Without Violence: A Handbook for Men*. San Francisco, CA: Volcano.

Spence, J., Helmreich, W., and Stapp, J. (1972). The attitudes toward women scale. *Catalogue of Selected Documents in Psychology* 2(66), ms. no. 153.

Star, B. (1978). Comparing battered and non-battered women. *Victimology* 3(1–2):32–44.

Star, B., Clark, C., Goetz, K., and O'Malia, L. (1979). Psychosocial aspects of wife-battering. *Social Casework* 9:479–487.

Steinmetz, S., and Straus, M., eds. (1974). *Violence in the Family*. New York: Harper & Row.

Stets, J. (1992). Interactive processes in dating aggression: a natural study. *Journal of Marriage and the Family* 54:165–177.

——— (1993). Control in dating relationships. *Journal of Marriage and the Family* 55:673–685.

Stets, J., and Pirog-Good, M. (1987). Violence in dating relationships. *Social Psychology Quarterly* 50:237–246.

——— (1990). Interpersonal control and courtship aggression. *Journal of Social and Personal Relationships* 7:371–394.

Stets, J., and Straus, M. (1989). The marriage license as a hitting license: a comparison of assaults in dating cohabiting and married couples. In *Violence in Dating Relationships: Emerging Social Issues*, ed. M. Pirog-Good and J. Stets, pp. 33–53. New York: Praeger.

Storr, M. (1979). Sex role identity and its relationship to sex role attributes and sex role stereotypes. *Journal of Personality and Social Psychology* 37:1779–1789.

Strachan, C., and Dutton, D. (1992). The role of power and gender in anger responses to sexual jealousy. *Journal of Applied Social Psychology* 22(22):1721–1729.

Straus, M. (1974). Cultural and social organizational influence on violence between family members. In *Configurations: Biological and Cultural Factors in Sexuality and Family Life*, ed. R. Price, pp. 56–71. Lexington, MA: Lexington Books.

Straus, M., and Gelles, R. (1990). *Physical Violence in American Families: Risk Factors and Adaptations to Violence in 8,145 Families*. New Brunswick, NJ: Transaction.

Straus, M., Gelles, R., and Steinmetz, S. (1980). *Behind Closed Doors: Violence in the American Family*. Garden City, NY: Anchor/Doubleday.

Sugarman, D., and Hotaling, G. (1989). Dating violence: prevalence, context and risk markers. In *Violence in Dating Relationships: Emerging Social Issues*, ed. M. Pirog-Good and J. Stets, pp. 3–32. New York: Praeger.

——— (1991). Dating violence: a review of contextual and risk factors. In *Dating Violence: Young Women in Danger*, ed. B. Levy, pp. 27–41. Seattle, WA: Seal.

Telch, C., and Lindquist, C. (1984). Violent versus non-violent couples: a comparison of patterns. *Psychotherapy* 21(2):242–248.

Thornhill, R., and Alcock, J. (1983). *The Evolution of Insect Mating Systems*. Cambridge, MA: Harvard University Press.

Tolman, D., and Debold, E. (1994). Conflicts of body and image: female adolescents, desire and the no-body body. In *Feminist Perspectives on Eating Disorders*, ed. P. Fallon, M. Katzman, and S. Wooley, pp. 149–161. New York: Guilford.

Walker, L. (1979). *The Battered Woman*. New York: Harper Colophon.

Walker, W. (1980). Intentional self-injury in school age children. *Journal of Adolescence* 3:217–228.

Whitehurst, R. (1975). Violently jealous husbands. In *Sexual Issues in Marriage*, ed. L. Gross, pp. 67–81. New York: Spectrum.

Williams, S., and McGee, R. (1990). Risk factors for behavioral and emotional disorder in preadolescent children. *Journal of the American Academy of Child and Adolescent Psychiatry* 29:413–419.

Wilson, K., Faison, R., and Britton, G. (1983). Cultural aspects of male sex aggression. *Deviant Behavior* 4:241–255.

Winnicott, D. W. (1964). *The Child, the Family and the Outside World*. Harmondsworth, UK: Penguin.

Women's Sports Foundation (1988). *The Wilson Report: Moms, Dads, Daughters, and Sports*. New York: Wilson Sporting Goods Co. and Women's Sports Foundation.

Wyatt, G., Guthrie, D., and Notgrass, C. M. (1992). Differential effects of women's child sexual abuse and subsequent sexual revictimization. *Journal of Consulting and Clinical Psychology* 60:167–173.

CREDITS

INDEX

Abuse (non-physical). *See also* Domestic violence
  methodology of study, 3–4
  research on, 80–81
Adams, D., 220
Adolescence
  dominated female, 123–136. *See also* Dominated female
  dominating male, 75. *See also* Dominating male
  domination pathology and, 6–7
  sex differences and, 131
  sexuality and, 165–166
  sociocultural factors and, 14–18
  suicide and, 264
Age, dominating male and, 97–101

Aggression
  dating and, 163–164
  mutual forms of, 205–212
  women and, 82–83, 205–212
Alcock, J., 151
Alcohol, violence and, 204–205
Alexander, R., 151
Allen, W., 247
American Association of University Women, 124, 126, 128, 129, 131, 132, 133
Amos, T., 123
Andrews, D., 195
Athletics
  female adolescence, 134
  male identity and, 33–34

Bandura, A., 86
Battered wives. *See* Domestic violence

Benaske, N., 85, 99, 148, 202, 203, 204, 205
Benjamin, J., 39, 40–41, 43, 44, 51, 55, 190, 263
Berman, L., 99
Bernard, J., 61, 84–85
Bernard, M., 61, 63, 84–85, 119, 121
Bertram, B., 150
Bettelheim, B., 191
Bloom, B., 264
Body image, female adolescence, 131–132
Bowker, L., 118
Brainwashing, dominating relationship and, 192–193
Brent, D., 264
Bronowski, J., 48, 49
Browne, A., 82, 84, 159, 163, 168, 190, 202, 204, 205, 206, 236, 263
Bryant, B., 46–47
Burke, P., 99, 103, 236
Burkhart, B., 99
Buss, D., 150, 151, 281

Campbell, J., 46, 51
Carlson, B., 62
Carroll, J., 82
Case illustrations, 19–28, 67–73, 171–175, 299–304
Cate, R., 94, 163, 164, 167, 168
Change. See Therapy
Child abuse
    dominated female, family background, 115
    dominating male, family background, 87–89
    results of, 171
Cohen, L., 39
Coles, R., 130, 165

Confidentiality, guidelines on, 220–229
Control
    dating and, 108–109, 163–164
    jealousy and, 152
    sexuality and, 166
    uncertainty and, 51
Curran, D., 129, 200, 264

Daly, M., 149
Dating
    control and, 108–109
    control and aggression in, 163–164
    female violence in, 207
    rape and, 99–100
    violence and, 85–86, 98–99, 167–168, 201–202
Davidson, L., 264
Davidson, S., 13, 99
Davidson, T., 34
Davis, M., 195
Deal, J., 103, 162, 164
Debold, E., 132
Demographics, dominating male and, 89–90
Dependency, suicide and, 264
Depression, dominated female and, 129
Deutsch, H., 116, 117
Developmental factors
    dominating male, family background, 81–89
    domination pathology and, 7–8
    intersubjectivity, 40–41, 44
    separation-individuation, 38–40, 43
    sociocultural factors and, 14–18

Diagnostic and Statistical Manual of Mental Disorders, 132
Diderot, D., 126
Divorce, males and, 263–264
Dobash, R. E., 118
Domestic violence. *See also* Abuse (non-physical); Child abuse; Dominated female; Dominating male; Violence
  children and, 81–82
  jealousy and, 149
  onset of, 162–163
  perspectives on, 2
  relationships and, 8–9
  research on, 61–62, 77–80
Dominated female, 113–136. *See also* Dominating relationship
  adolescence and, 123–136
  female perceptions of, 185–190, 194–201
  overview of, 113–123
  therapy, change and, 231–256
Dominating male, 75–111. *See also* Dominating relationship
  age and, 97–101
  breaking up, 263–266
  demographics and, 89–90
  family background, 81–89
  female perceptions of, 185–190, 194–201
  overview of, 75–81
  personality characteristics, 101–111
  race and, 90–91
  religion and, 91
  socioeconomic factors, 91–97
  therapy and, 213–220, 248–249, 292–297

Dominating relationship
  breaking of, 257–297
    danger in, 258–261
    female impact, 266–269
    maintaining contact, therapeutic implications, 283–287
    male impact, 263–266
    multiple separations, 261–263
    restraining orders, 290–292
    safety and, 287–289
    therapeutic implications, 269–292
  case illustrations, 19–28, 67–73, 171–175, 299–304
  confidentiality and, 220–229
  early warning signs of, 137–159. *See also* Early warning signs
  female perceptions of, 185–190, 194–201
  onset of domination, 161–162, 170
  reinforcements and, 190–193
  sexuality and, 164–165
  therapeutic implications of, 175–183
Domination
  methodology of study, 3–4
  origin of, love, 40–47
  relationships and, 5–6
  submission and, 44
  uncertainty and, 47–55
  women and, 4–5
Domination pathology
  adolescence and, 6–7
  developmental factors and, 7–8
Dubow, E., 128, 131

Dunphy, M., 82, 87
Dutton, D., 281

Early warning signs, 137–159
  jealousy, 148–156
  neediness, 139–142
  overview of, 137–139, 156–159
  possessiveness, 142–148
Eisenberg, S., 62
Erickson, C., 151

Fagan, J., 82, 84, 205, 206
Family background, dominating
  male, 81–89
FBI Uniform Crime Reports, 78
Fear, therapeutic management
  of, 272–274
Female identity
  dominated female, 113–136.
    See also Dominated
    female
  male identity and, 60–61
Feminism, female violence and,
  82–83
Flynn, J., 83, 92
Follette, V., 93–94
Forward, S., 120
Freud, S., 36, 44, 116, 117

Galloway, J., 281
Gayford, J., 62, 83, 98, 202, 262
Gelles, R., 61, 62, 79, 82, 91, 94,
  95, 96, 98, 202, 205
Gold, S., 115
Goldstein, D., 103, 104
Goode, W., 92
Gooding-Garrett, J., 236
Guilt, therapeutic management
  of, 274–277
Gwartney-Gibbs, P., 93, 94, 98,
  166, 202

Harter, S., 130
Hawton, K., 264
Heisenberg, W., 48–49
Henton, J., 93, 94, 99, 163, 164,
  167, 168, 188, 193, 203,
  208, 260
Hilberman, E., 62, 261
Hinduism, 46
Hofeller, K., 82
Homicide, jealousy and, 281
Hope, therapeutic management
  of, 277
Horney, K., 117
Hotaling, G., 82, 83, 84, 92, 94,
  99, 119, 134, 201, 205
Hrdy, S., 151

Intersubjectivity
  developmental factors, 40–41,
    44
  sex role and, 44–45

Jacklin, C., 79
Jacobs, F., 264
Jaffee, L., 86, 134
Jealousy
  early warning signs, 148–
    156
  homicide and, 281
  therapeutic management of,
    280–283
  violence and, 202–203
JeJeune, C., 93–94
Johnston, M., 82

Kalmuss, D., 82, 84, 104
Kanin, E., 99
Kashani, J., 82, 127, 131
Kienhorst, I., 264
Kohut, H., 41
Komarovsky, M., 78, 92

Korman, S., 99
Koss, M., 99

Lane, K., 93, 94, 98, 166, 202
Laner, M., 85, 99, 163
Larson, D., 16
Lawrence, T. E., 116
Leslie, G., 99
Letko, C., 62
Levinger, G., 92
Levy, B., 13, 164
Lifton, J. R., 191
Lindquist, C., 82
Loneliness, therapeutic
    management of, 279–280
Long, E., 195
Love
    domination origin and, 40–47
    feelings of, 168–169
    male identity and, 29–40
    resistance and, 169
    sexuality and, 166–167
    suicide and, 1–2
    therapeutic management of,
        277–278

Maccoby, E., 79
Mack, J., 116
Mahler, M., 38
Makepeace, J., 80, 98, 148, 166,
    167, 202, 204
Male identity. *See also* Men; Sex
    role
    dominating male, 75–111. *See
        also* Dominating male
    female identity and, 60–61
    love and, 29–40
    sociocultural factors and, 56–
        61
    violence and, 61–66
Manzer, R., 134

Martin, D., 78
Marttunen, M., 264
Masochism, dominated female,
    115–118
Mayall, A., 115
McGee, R., 127, 129, 131, 181
Men. *See also* Male identity; Sex
    role
    domestic violence and, 9–10
    dominating male, 75–111. *See
        also* Dominating male
    domination and, 5–6
    therapy and, 11, 13–14
Micklow, P., 62
Mowrer, E., 78
Mowrer, H., 78
Munson, K., 62, 261
Murphy, C., 97, 204, 205

Neediness, early warning signs,
    139–142
NiCarthy, G., 13, 99
Noonan, K., 151

Oathout, H., 195
O'Brien, J., 62, 94, 95, 96
Occupation, male identity and,
    56–59
O'Farrell, T., 97, 204, 205
Offer, D., 128, 131, 132
Okun, L., 77, 81, 92, 93, 94,
    97, 98, 114, 118, 167,
    190, 191, 202, 204, 262,
    263
O'Leary, K., 84, 118, 119
Orenstein, P., 128, 131, 132,
    133, 166, 266
Oros, C., 99
Orr, D., 126
Ostrov, E., 131, 175
Owens, D., 92

Pagelow, M., 83, 86, 98, 118, 262
Parcell, S., 99
Parental involvement, in therapy, 181–183
Partoll, S., 201, 202
Paul, L., 281
Peplau, L., 164, 167, 168, 264
Personality characteristics, dominating male, 101–111
Pipher, M., 125, 266
Pirog-Good, M., 82, 92, 103, 104, 129, 162, 163, 164
Possessiveness
  early warning signs, 142–148
  jealousy and, 150
Power, H., 151
Pregnancy, violence and, 202
Prescott, S., 62

Race
  dominating male and, 90–91
  female adolescence and, 129, 132
Rapaport, K., 99
Rape
  dating and, 99–100
  incidence of, 236
Reinforcements, dominating relationship and, 190–193
Relationships
  domestic violence and, 8–9
  dominating, early warning signs of, 137–159. See also Early warning signs
  domination and, 5–6. See also Dominating relationship
Relief, therapeutic management of, 278–279
Religion, dominating male and, 91
Resistance, love and, 169

Restraining orders, 290–292
Riggs, D., 208, 205
Roscoe, B., 85, 99, 148, 202, 203, 204, 205
Rosenbaum, A., 84, 103, 104, 118, 119
Rosenberg, M., 130
Rouse, L., 82
Roy, M., 262
Rubin, Z., 167, 264
Russell, D., 115, 164

Sadker, D., 134
Sadker, M., 134
Safety, therapy and, 287–289
Saunders, S., 292
Scales, A., 207
Schein, E., 191, 192
Schonert-Reichl, K., 128, 131, 132
Schultz, L., 78, 116
Seltzer, J., 84
Senter, R., 236
Separation-individuation, developmental factors, 38–40, 43
Serum, C., 190
Sex role. See also Male identity; Men
  intersubjectivity and, 44–45
  sociocultural factors, 37–38, 53–55
Sexual infidelity, jealousy and, 151
Sexuality
  adolescence and, 165–166
  control and, 166
  dominating relationship and, 164–165
  jealousy and, 202–203
  love and, 166–167
  pregnancy and, 202

rape and, 236
therapy and, 237–238
Shea, L., 201
Smith, J., 82, 85
Snell, J., 78, 79
Sociocultural factors
    developmental factors and,
        14–18
    heroes and, 53–55
    male identity and, 56–61
    sex role and, 37–38
Socioeconomic factors,
    dominating male, 91–97
Sonkin, D., 82, 87
Spence, J., 61
Star, B., 62, 98, 118
Steinmetz, S., 82, 92, 95, 205
Stets, J., 82, 92, 103, 104, 108,
    129, 162, 163, 164, 167,
    195, 205, 264
Stokes, G., 130, 165
Storr, M., 116
Strachan, C., 281
Straus, M., 62, 80, 82, 83, 90,
    91, 92, 94, 95, 98, 104, 205
Submission, domination and,
    44
Sugarman, D., 82, 83, 84, 92, 94,
    99, 119, 134, 201, 205
Suicide
    breaking up, 263, 264
    dominated female and, 129
    love and, 1–2
    therapeutic management, 294

Telch, C., 82
Therapy
    case illustrations, 19–28, 67–
        73, 171–175, 299–304
    change and, 231–256
    dominating male, 213–220,
        292–297

dominating relationship, 175–
    183
    breaking of, 269–292
jealousy and, 153
men and, 11, 13–14
requirements of, 12–13
safety and, 287–289
Thompson, J., 85, 99, 163
Thornhill, R., 151
Tolman, D., 132
Treatment. See Therapy

Uncertainty, domination and,
    47–55
Uniform Crime Reports (FBI),
    78

Violence. See also Child abuse;
    Domestic violence
    alcohol and, 204–205
    breaking up and, 264–266
    confidentiality and, 220–229
    dating and, 85–86, 167–168,
        201–202
    jealousy and, 148–149, 202–
        203
    male identity and, 61–66
    perceptions of, 203–204
    pregnancy and, 202
    therapeutic implications,
        182–183
    women and, 82–83, 205–
        212

Walker, L., 92, 191, 261, 263
Walker, W., 264
Wampler, K., 103, 162, 164
Whitehurst, R., 92
Wife beating. See Domestic
    violence
Williams, J., 82, 85
Williams, K., 159

Williams, S., 131
Wilson, K., 99
Wilson, M., 149
Winnicott, D. W., 41
Women
  domestic violence and, 8–9
  dominated female, 113–136.
    See also Dominated
    female
  domination and, 4–5

female violence and, 82–83,
  205–212
separation-individuation,
  40
therapy and, 12–13
Women's Sports Foundation,
  134
Wyatt, G., 115

Zenone, P., 151